AUDACIOUS HOPE

Praise for *Audacious Hope*

'A highly readable testimonial directing our attention to the colourful cannonballs of democratic protests taking an aim at the Modi-era. This book is an excellent commentary on democracy and how its custodians remain the subalterns whose objective becomes nation-building.' —**Suraj Yengde, WEB Du Bois Fellow, Harvard University**

'Indrajit Roy's *Audacious Hope* is a luminous work of engaged scholarship. It acknowledges the ravages to India's democracy—the crumbling of institutions, the cult of the strongman, widening inequalities and the politics of hate—and the dangers each of these pose to the future of the Indian people. And yet Roy locates hope—iridescent, realist hope—in the non-violent struggles of people resisting oppression and autocracy. You meet in the pages of his book people who rose up against the violence of caste, who fought anti-farmer statutes and the changes in citizenship laws that discriminated against Indian Muslims. You meet activists, poets, writers, film-makers, stand-up comedians, students, workers, farmers and lawyers, each of whom wage brave battles to defend secular democracy. The book is ultimately a meditation on what makes up the soul of a democracy, and this is a people who are willing to stake everything for what is humane and just, a people committed to fighting righteous battles. Hopelessness, Roy concludes stirringly, is a luxury no Indian who cares about the future of their democracy can afford.' —**Harsh Mander, chairperson, Centre for Equity Studies and founder, Karwan-e Mohabbat**

'Indrajit Roy masterfully sifts through contemporary history to illuminate the collective power of people who risk defeat and annihilation to stand up to authoritarian, divisive forces. This book fulfills an urgent need. Hope is an essential strategy. Backed by experience, knowledge and data, hope is the energy that powers rebellion and change. By documenting stories of popular resistance, Indrajit Roy has written the most essential antidote for the age of democratic erosion.' —**Natasha Badhwar, writer and film-maker**

'A powerful book that serves as a reminder that ultimately democracy is about people. Divisive, polarising rhetoric, populist leadership and authoritarianism can help propel parties to power, even in functioning democracies. But the everyday practice of democracy remains its most powerful corrective. Ordinary Indians have always protected and nurtured India's democracy, and in times of crisis, it is they who will save it. A lesson not just for India but for the globe; a must read. It brings hope in these times of despair.' —**Yamini Aiyar, president and CEO, Centre for Policy Research**

'A chronicle of resistance in times of despair. Indrajit Roy's *Audacious Hope* is a valuable record of India's contemporary history, especially at a time when memory is being effaced through deliberate distortions and gaslighting. A book everyone must read and have, for record-keeping.' —**Ghazala Wahab, editor, *FORCE* magazine and author of *Born a Muslim: Some Truths about Islam in India***

AUDACIOUS HOPE

AN ARCHIVE OF HOW

DEMOCRACY

IS BEING SAVED

IN INDIA

INDRAJIT ROY

First published by Westland Non-Fiction, an imprint of Westland Books, a division of Nasadiya Technologies Private Limited, in 2024

No. 269/2B, First Floor, 'Irai Arul', Vimalraj Street, Nethaji Nagar, Alapakkam Main Road, Maduravoyal, Chennai 600095

Westland, the Westland logo, Westland Non-Fiction and the Westland Non-Fiction logo are the trademarks of Nasadiya Technologies Private Limited, or its affiliates.

ISBN: 9789360455477

10 9 8 7 6 5 4 3 2 1

Typeset by SÜRYA, New Delhi
Printed at Parksons Graphics Pvt. Ltd

Contents

Hope for Democracy

The turn of the second millennium had appeared promising for democracy. More people than ever before were living under governments that had committed to involving them in running the affairs of their country. Elections, freedom of association, freedom of expression and the rule of law were guaranteed, at least on paper, by such governments, indicating that they understood the importance of recognising the political rights of their populations. Governments that were authoritarian or autocratic—China, Saudi Arabia, Belarus—appeared to be anomalies: anachronistic regimes whose time was up. As at least one influential commentator proclaimed, 'the end of history'[1] appeared to be upon us. All other forms of government stood discredited. Democracy was here to stay.

And yet, today, two decades into the second millennium, democracies everywhere are mired in crisis. In some cases, democratic gains made at the close of the twentieth century face outright reversal: consider Russia and Venezuela. In others, countries transitioning from authoritarianism don't quite seem to make it to democracy and are stuck in what one political analyst called a 'grey zone'[2]—Central Asian successor states to the Soviet Union fall under this category. Another reason for the crisis in democracies is their inability to deliver basic services: countries in South Asia and Sub-Saharan Africa have long been in this category. Yet another reason is the inability of a democracy to resolve the fundamental unbalance that is characteristically ingrained in capitalism: while the world is richer than ever before, even fewer people share in its income and wealth. Of course, democracies do not cause economic challenges but they appear unable to fix them when they occur, fomenting public discontent.

Then there is something far more insidious: countries that have retained the shell of democracy after having scraped all the substance out of it. This is not about entities such as the self-styled Democratic People's Republic of Korea whose authoritarian character is plain to any reasonable observer. Rather, consider the countries where rituals associated with democracy are routinely performed, but the substantive practice of democracy is barely respected. Examples that spring to mind include Turkey, Hungary, Brazil, the Philippines, South Africa, the USA and India where elections are routinely conducted and their verdicts respected. Politicians seek power in the name of the people, which legitimises their authority. However, electoral mandates are interpreted as enabling those in control to do as they please, all in the name of the people. Once in power, politicians treat rivals as enemies. The press is muzzled. Dissent is stifled. Courts are co-opted. Bureaucracies are bent to the whims of those in charge. Leftists often find themselves on the receiving end of attacks by politicians while immigrants make for easy scapegoats. Any condemnation of the government is regarded as an attack on the nation and, worse, as a criticism of the people in whose name the politicians rule.

Further, in a subset of these countries, the idea of 'the people' can assume exclusive forms. A supremacist ethic is nurtured.

Members of specific social groups are constructed as core to the nation while others are identified as peripheral to it. Such marginalised groups are regarded as alien to the nation and even dangerous to it. The basis of this distinction varies. It could be racial as, for example, in the USA under Donald Trump when its white population was identified as core to the country's nationhood. Alternatively, it could be religious as in Turkey, Brazil and India where Recep Erdogan, Jair Bolsonaro and Narendra Modi have respectively upheld their countries' Muslim, Christian and Hindu religious identities while excluding others. Critics of the government in such countries find themselves branded not only as enemies of the people but as enemies of the majority religion professed by their countrymen.

But doesn't democracy mean the 'rule of the people'? The term *demos* does after all connote 'people' in Greek. Could the politicians not be considered the most robust upholders of democracy today? After all, men like Trump, Erdogan, Bolsonaro and Modi, as well as Hungary's Viktor Orban, the Philippines' Rodrigo Duterte and South Africa's Jacob Zuma did not seize power through military coups. They were voted into office through elections that were recognised globally as free and fair.

But democracy does not merely mean conducting routine elections. If that was the case, then we would not perhaps worry about it being threatened. Or if it meant imposing the will of the majority, then we could say that it is indeed in able hands under the Trumps, Erdogans and Modis of the world. Rather, it is a social process in which people can assert their equality before one another and before the law. It is about treating people, even political adversaries, with respect. It is about affording dignity to people, irrespective of their social backgrounds and political opinions. Democracy welcomes, rather than stifles, dissent.

These are not qualities we associate with the aforementioned men and their style of governing. In the USA, President Trump repeatedly attacked his political rivals and labelled racial justice movements as toxic and antithetical to American values and, upon being voted out of power, went as far as to accuse his opponents of trying to 'steal' the 2020 elections when the results revealed he had lost. Halfway across the world, Turkish Prime Minister Erdogan strengthened his authority when the country elected to switch to a system within which he became the president. He has expelled dissidents from his own party who have been reluctant to support his views, suppressed opposition and decreed the conversion of the iconic Hagia Sofia museum into a mosque. Despite supposedly governing in the name of the people, both men demonstrated they have little patience for democratic niceties.

Democracy in India since 2014

India has always been an unlikely democracy. For decades, it defied the conventional wisdom that development is a prerequisite for democracy. When India became independent in 1947, few people expected the impoverished country to survive. Nevertheless, Indians introduced universal adult suffrage soon after obtaining independence and adopted a republican constitution in 1950, a full fifteen years before economic superpowers such as the USA lifted literacy and tax qualifications for voting.

Throughout the first few decades of its existence as an independent republic, international observers remained sceptical of India surviving as a democracy, given its high levels of poverty and illiteracy. Yet, India not only survived but also emerged— warts and all—as one of the world's most thriving democracies.

The country presented a very moving story of the ways in which some of the poorest people on the planet have sought to construct and sustain a fair political system against enormous odds. Free and fair elections were held as scheduled. Dissent was not only permitted but also celebrated. India's states, many of which are larger than several European countries, were asserting their voice in national politics and steering it in the direction of a truly inclusive polity. The Parliament and provincial legislative assemblies were becoming more and more representative of the country's diverse population.

Since 2014, many of those achievements have been threatened and are close to being undone. In May that year, Narendra Modi won a landslide victory in the elections to India's Parliament, the Lok Sabha, the assembly of the people. The Bharatiya Janata Party (BJP), of which Modi has been a member since 1985, won 282 of the 543 seats in Parliament, far more than any analyst had predicted. For the party, the results culminated a meteoric growth since its inception in 1980: in the 1984 elections, it had won a mere two seats. Its aggressive advocacy of Hindutva, a political ideology that considers India's majority Hindu community as India's core national identity, had made it suspect in the eyes of many. Now that it enjoyed an absolute majority in the Lok Sabha, Indians faced the very real prospect of an exclusive Hindu nationalism supplanting an inclusive Indian nationalism.

For Modi, the verdict signalled the crowning glory of his own career: from a vendor of chai at a railway station in small-town India to the highest office in the country's parliamentary democracy. Now, as he entered the Lok Sabha for the first time, kneeling at its entrance and touching his forehead to the steps that led inside as a show of respect, Indian democracy was faced with a major test. A person who had been outside the charmed circle of national politics was about to take control. That should have been a matter of celebration. Unfortunately, the person in question was not known for being particularly democratic—he had previously faced accusations of engineering violence against the Muslim minority population as chief minister of Gujarat and had unapologetically proclaimed himself a 'Hindu nationalist'. Such a profile filled many Indians with dread.[3]

While in power, the BJP has done little to inspire confidence among critics. The party has repeatedly whipped up war hysteria with neighbouring Pakistan. It has shied away from reining in vigilantes who have taken it upon themselves to protect cows, an animal sacred to many Hindus. Such vigilantism has resulted in the lynchings, beatings and killings of individuals suspected of slaughtering cows and eating beef. Labour laws have been diluted. In 2016, the government demonetised high-denomination currency notes, rendering worthless over 85 per cent of all cash circulating in the economy. Since its re-election in 2019, the BJP, led once again by Modi, has rammed contentious legislations through the Lok Sabha, the most significant of which was the introduction of a religious filter to India's citizenship laws specifically targeting Muslims.

Democracy has always been India's strongest brand. The country has justly been celebrated as the world's largest democracy for decades. But this brand is now under threat. Noting 'a multiyear pattern in which the Hindu nationalist government and its allies have presided over rising violence and discriminatory policies affecting the Muslim population and pursued a crackdown on expressions of dissent by the media, academics, civil society groups, and protesters', global thinktank Freedom House downgraded India's status as a democracy from 'free' to 'partly free' in March 2021.[4] Within a few weeks, the internationally respected Varieties of Democracy Research Institute noted India's shift from the world's largest democracy to an electoral autocracy.[5]

Democratic Crises in Historical Perspective

There was a time when we associated a crisis in democracy solely with a spectacular show of circumstances. Men in jackboots parading across public squares, armed folks storming homes or offices of politicians and arresting them, abrupt halts of normal broadcasts, declarations of the suspension of government affairs are images that would come to mind when we heard about a democracy being dismantled. Often, it was the military that overthrew elected politicians due to incompetence, corruption or some ideological deviance. Or politicians themselves suspended democracy, citing internal disturbances or foreign aggression. Such events are what defined democratic breakdown.

Take, for instance, Chile. On 11 September 1973, Chile's capital, Santiago, witnessed the country's armed forces staging a coup. They were aided by Hawker hunter jets bombing the palace of President Salvadore Allende. Earlier that morning, Allende had made an impassioned plea over national radio, hoping that his many supporters would defend their country's democracy on the streets if necessary. His pleas went unheard. By the time night fell, Allende and Chilean democracy were both dead.[6]

Or consider Pakistan. In the wee hours of 5 July 1977, Prime Minister Zulfiqar Ali Bhutto found himself under arrest. The Pakistani army, under General Zia ul-Haq, was taking over the country. General Zia promised to hold elections within three months. He even released Bhutto so he could campaign, although he changed his mind upon seeing Bhutto's popularity, leading to the latter being arrested for a second time. Elections were postponed. Legal charges were brought against the former prime minister. An elaborate trial lasting almost eighteen months was staged. Bhutto was found guilty and hanged. Pakistan's democracy had been strangled to death.[7]

Military generals are not the only ones who have annihilated democracy. Elected representatives have been equally capable, citing a combination of internal disturbances, social unrest, economic crisis and political uncertainty as viable reasons to suspend democratic principles and practices. On 23 March 1933, Adolf Hitler persuaded fellow parliamentarians in Germany's Reichstag to pass the Enabling Act. His party had emerged as the single largest party in the elections held earlier that month but fallen short of a majority. Although appointed chancellor, Hitler's Nazi party found itself hamstrung by coalition partners and a variety of opposition parties. The Enabling Act freed Hitler from these constraints as it gave him the right to pass laws without the Reichstag's approval for the next four years, effectively destroying all institutional opposition to his rule. The Reichstag barely met for the remainder of Hitler's rule.[8]

Closer to home, a few minutes before the clock struck midnight on 26 June 1975, a state of Emergency was proclaimed across India. Unlike Hitler, Indira Gandhi had decisively won a national election three years prior on the back of a crushing military victory against Pakistan. That did not prevent her from suspending India's Parliament. Opposition leaders were jailed. Elections were cancelled. Civil rights were suspended. State legislatures were dissolved. Gandhi held absolute authority and ruled by decree, advised by a coterie that included her younger son. Throughout the nineteen months of the Emergency, democracy in India struggled for breath.[9]

Breakdowns like these may also be triggered by the disenfranchisement of certain sections of the national population. Such disenfranchisement could be initiated by military rulers—Myanmar's 1982 Citizenship Act, which effectively stripped the country's Rohingya minority of their status as citizens, comes to mind.[10] Once again, elected representatives have been known to leverage such tactics as well, possibly with even more devastating efficiency. The Herenigde Nasionale Party's (HNP) rise to power in South Africa during the winter of 1948 signalled a turning point in the country's history. Elected on the promise of sustaining white domination in that country, HNP lawmakers introduced Apartheid policies of racial segregation that cemented social separation between members of different racial groups—for instance, interracial marriages or sexual relations were prohibited and the population was classified into four racial groups with each being assigned a separate homeland. A series of legislative manoeuvres was introduced to ensure that the majority Black population remained politically unrepresented. Democracy in South Africa was only for its white minority until the Apartheid ended in 1994.[11]

The spirit of South Africa's Apartheid legislations was mirrored in the Jim Crow laws that segregated racial groups in the USA. These laws were introduced by elected officials across the southern states of the USA in the aftermath of the American Civil War. On 18 May 1896, the country's Supreme Court upheld the segregation of public services through the now-infamous 'separate but equal' doctrine. The court ruled that racial segregation was not inconsistent with the USA's constitution. As a result, the federal government could not intervene if states introduced policies to entrench racial segregation in public life and disenfranchise their Black population. Several states (in the south but also in the north) continued to pursue policies of racial segregation through most of the twentieth century. Despite its proclamations of freedom, the USA was a democracy only in name till the civil rights movement compelled the dismantling of segregation laws after 1965.[12]

Hope Amid Democratic Crisis

Episodes of democratic crises hardly appear to be germane to hope. The repression unleashed during such times is rightly associated with fear. Dissent is crushed. Discipline is celebrated. Divisions are fomented. Suspicion bordering on hatred becomes the order of the day. Under such conditions, hope seems to be nothing more than a wasted emotion.

And yet, it is powerful. By wielding it, democratic erosion is constantly challenged. Often, such challenges are mounted by ordinary people who appear weak, meek and powerless in the first instance. Their resistance may not always be successful. The regime might remain unchanged. But nevertheless, their actions reflect the value of sustained dissent. Hope expresses itself through ordinary people's resistance in the face of brutal, unrelenting repression.

General Augusto Pinochet discovered this soon after assuming power in Chile. The wave of executions, torture and 'disappearances' his regime unleashed did not go unopposed. Even as protests were officially banned, women began sewing secret messages of rebellion into quilts that were then sold in domestic and international markets. These narrative quilts, or arpilleras, conveyed powerful messages of hope for a future in which they would enjoy economic and political freedoms. One arpillero showed women holding up signs demanding 'bread, work and liberty'.[13] Another showed women in a neighbourhood pooling their money together to buy staples to share. Other signs declared 'We women demand our rights', 'No more jails' and 'If women are not here, democracy does not go anywhere'. The arpilleras showed the world not only the horrors faced by people under Pinochet's brutal regime but also the hope for a return of democracy harboured by some of Chile's poorest citizens.

In Pakistan, General Zia ul-Haq discovered something similar. His regime limited political activity in the country and introduced a slew of legislations that curtailed human rights in the name of Islamising the country. But hope could not be crushed. The couplet *Hum Dekhenge* (We Shall See) composed by poet Faiz Ahmed Faiz gave voice to the regime's opponents and the people at large:

> Inevitably, we shall also see the day
> that was promised to us, decreed
> on the tablet of eternity.
>
> When dark peaks of torment and tyranny
> will be blown away like cotton fluff;
>
> When the earth's beating heart
> will pulsate beneath our broken feet;
>
> When crackling, crashing lightning
> will smite the heads of our tormentors.[14]

The couplet became a collective expression of courage, faith and optimism for a generation of Pakistanis confronted with the deadly cocktail of military rule and the infusion of religion in politics. It became a rallying cry for the thousands of ordinary folks across the country to challenge the authoritarian tactics of their dictator through myriad overt and covert ways, not least through poetry, drama and works of art.

Likewise, Nazi Germany's totalitarian regime also found it impossible to completely snuff out hope. One must remember the White Rose resistance group founded by a group of university students in Munich: the siblings Sophie and Hans Scholl, Christoph Probst, Willi Graf, Kurt Huber and Alexander Schmorell. The group secretly printed leaflets and painted graffiti that urged Germans to support 'freedom of speech, freedom of religion and protection of the individual citizen from the arbitrary action of criminal dictator-states'. Although Sophie and Hans Scholl as well as Christoph Probst were eventually arrested and guillotined, their efforts were an exemplary display of courage and persistence in the most desperate of times.[15]

India's nineteen-month Emergency was also not unchallenged. Street mobilisations, cultural activities and individual acts of sabotage continued despite numerous arrests. Many among those imprisoned refused to give up. The letters exchanged regularly between Pramila and Madhu Dandavate, a socialist couple who were jailed, bear testimony to their faith. Married for over twenty-three years, they found themselves housed in prisons separated by over 400 kilometres. Their weekly letters commented on society and politics around them and also served as a reminder, as a reason to persist. When either showed signs of despair, the other sought to lift their spirits:

> Your last letter had a shadow of sadness over it. You said that our home and life together would be completely destroyed by the time we get out of here. And you don't know if you have the strength and persistence to do it all, all over again. Your comment felt exceedingly hopeless to me. We have always carried our life together on our backs. As long as our spine is in place, who can possibly touch our life together?[16]

Similarly, people in Apartheid-infested South Africa continued to believe in the possibility of a return to democracy despite the viciousness of the regime. One among several instances of such faith was expressed by school students in the township of Soweto, Johannesburg, during 1976. Under the leadership of Teboho Tsietsi McDonald Mashinini, they protested the imposition of Afrikaans, the language of the Dutch-speaking white population, upon the rest of the country. The Soweto Uprising (as the protest came to be called) lasted three days and saw up to 20,000 students from high schools streaming through the streets. The state's response was swift and brutal: almost 700 children were killed in police firings. Although the uprising was eventually quelled by sheer government repression, it marked the beginning of the end of the Apartheid regime.[17]

Hope similarly fused with resistance against the segregationist policies of the United States. In an essay poignantly titled 'A Testament of Hope', civil rights advocate Martin Luther King tells us why he remains an optimist despite the brutality of segregation enforced by the state:

> Millions of people have fought thousands of battles to enlarge my freedom; restricted as it still is, progress has been made. This is why I remain an optimist, though I am a realist, about the barriers before us.[18]

In a well-known interview with *Playboy*, King recounts this conversation over the telephone he has with his brother:

> My brother described the terror in the streets as N*****s, furious at the bombings, fought whites. Then, behind his voice, I heard a rising chorus of beautiful singing: 'We shall overcome.' Tears came into my eyes that at such a tragic moment, my race could sing its hope and faith.[19]

These examples are far from comprehensive. But they illustrate the larger point about the importance of belief in democracy against all odds. Ruthless repression, divisive machinations and autocratic practices are rejected. Resistance stems from a spirit of stubborn hopefulness—an ability to persevere despite the entrenchment of despair. Far from a wasted emotion, hope motivates action against injustice, allowing one to imagine an alternative world that is fairer and more just than the existing one. And from such audacious hope spring the ideas that allow people to confront, subvert and undermine democratic decline.

The next chapter outlines the crisis that confronts India's democracy. While India was never the perfect model of a democracy, during the last few years, the country has witnessed a reversal of its democratic achievements. The chapter thus offers a glimpse into the recent erosion of India's democracy, setting the stage for discussions in subsequent chapters of how Indians have faced these challenges.

The Erosion of India's Democracy

Narendra Modi's rise to power in 2014 was fuelled by the anticipation harboured by millions of Indians for a better future. During his election campaign, he promised achche din or 'good days' for Indians. He styled himself as vikas purush to signal his purush or 'personification' of the ideal India's vikas or 'development'. Above all, Modi's meteoric rise from humble origins as a vendor of chai in a small-town Indian railway station to a prime ministerial candidate of the world's largest democracy resonated with members of classes struggling to better their social standing.

India in 2014

As 2014 dawned, Indians were an anxious people. The two-digit rates of economic growth they had enjoyed in the previous decade had slowed down. Jobs were difficult to come by. The federal government led by the centrist Congress Party was mired in corruption. The ageing Prime Minister Manmohan Singh appeared to have lost control over his own colleagues. The government seemed paralysed and decision-making had all but ground to a halt.

It was a chilly Sunday morning early in January. Ram Kumar, the local scrap dealer, cycled through the street, announcing his arrival. Kumar was essential to our neighbourhood in South Delhi: he bought old newspapers, metal or plastic utensils that families no longer used and sundry household items to sell them to scrapyards in the city. Kumar stopped when he saw me and asked how I was (he hadn't seen me for a while, he added). His next question stumped me: 'Who are you going to vote for?' After I'd hemmed and hawed and tried to sound vague, he advised me, 'It's a very important election. Do choose wisely.' He then added, his sparkling eyes a sharp foil to Delhi's cold January fog, 'I am voting for Modi. The man knows what is good for the country.'

Kumar went on to list all of Modi's achievements as the chief minister of the western state of Gujarat. According to him, Modi had transformed the state, improved its economy and made life better for everyone. 'Even Muslims,' he added, pre-empting any question about the chief minister's actions during the violence of 2002. Kumar's excitement for Modi knew no bounds. It was a stark contrast to his view of the government then in power; 'Have you seen their faces? They are so tired. So old, like this,' he pointed to his own grey stubble. 'They were good when they came to power. I voted for them—my family and I, we have always voted for them, forever. But now, they have lost their way. They have messed up the economy. There are no jobs.'

I had known Kumar since I was a child. Over the decades, he had expanded his business and was no longer the ragpicker he used to be. You could still hear our neighbours snigger about his origins as a member of the 'untouchable' caste and his childhood as a scavenger. But you could also sense a jealousy about the two cars he owned, the fact that he sent his two sons to a private school and that he celebrated their birthdays with cake bought from the posh neighbourhood bakery.

Kumar and other entrepreneurs like him rode on the wave of economic growth India enjoyed since the turn of the millennium. Even as the global financial crisis ravaged the West, Indians appeared relatively unaffected. The government's gradual liberalisation of the economy allowed entrepreneurs to take risks that had been unimaginable. Affirmative actions in universities and public services enabled members of historically oppressed communities like Kumar's to pursue higher education and even apply for public sector jobs. A plethora of social welfare schemes pulled 27.1 crore people out of poverty. But as economic growth eventually slowed (not reversed, just slowed down) around 2010, newly minted members of the middle class such as Kumar grew anxious. A Carnegie Endowment study found that economic growth was the foremost issue that worried voters.[1]

Narendra Modi emerged as a solution to voters' worries. Unlike the Congress Party which harped on poverty reduction, the BJP led by Modi offered the prospects of inclusive development—*sabka saath, sabka vikas*, Modi thundered in Hindi, emphasising his commitment to sustain economic growth, increase jobs and ensure that everyone benefitted. For people like Kumar, the Congress promise of reducing poverty sounded hackneyed, a throwback to the slogans coined by former Prime Minister Indira Gandhi in the 1970s that may have lured Kumar's father and grandfather, but not him. By contrast, Modi's promise of inclusive development offered hope, and a vision for the future.

Kumar identified with Modi. They both shared a similar social origin in that they were both members of communities categorised as 'low' in India's complex caste hierarchy. Kumar had helped his parents pick through garbage piled on the streets to take away anything that might be valuable to resell. Modi grew up helping his father sell chai at a railway station in small-town India. As the Kumar household's economic position improved, he invested in a bicycle and rode through a cluster of neighbourhoods in south Delhi to establish his scrap dealership. Modi joined the Rashtriya Swayamsevak Sangh (RSS), a network of organisations committed to eventually establishing Hindu Raj in India. While Kumar did not immediately or at least overtly sympathise with that specific goal, he identified with the way in which both he and Modi rose up the ranks as it were—he in business and Modi in politics. That mattered, didn't it?

The ruling Congress Party was led by Rahul Gandhi, who seemed the opposite of everything Modi embodied. If Modi had risen from humble origins to lead the BJP, Gandhi had been groomed for his position in the Congress almost from the day he was born. His was an old and powerful political lineage. His mother, Sonia Gandhi, had held power within the Congress for over a decade. His father, Rajiv Gandhi, had been the prime minister between 1984 and 1989. His grandmother, Indira Gandhi, had been the prime minister between 1966 and 1977 and again between 1980 and 1984. His great-grandfather, Jawaharlal Nehru, had been the prime minister between 1947 and 1964. His great-great-grandfather, Motilal Nehru, had been a leading light in the Congress Party, and had drafted the Nehru Report, a precursor to the Indian Constitution adopted in 1950. Gandhi embodied a dynastic nepotism that irked India's burgeoning middle class. His only qualification for leading the Congress Party, and India (if he won the 2014 elections), was this lineage. And to Indians aspiring for improved economic prosperity and higher social status, that was simply not enough.

Utterances by Congress Party leaders did little to help their cause. One senior leader dismissed Modi as no more than a chai-wallah (vendor of tea), a comment which the BJP immediately latched onto in a bid to demonstrate the Congress's elitism. Priyanka Gandhi-Vadra, Rahul Gandhi's sister and an emerging leader of the party, called Modi's remarks on nepotism within the Congress Party as 'lowly'. Modi promptly complained on TV:

> Don't I have the right to at least state the truth? Is it because I come from a humble background, from a humble family? Has this country become like that? Has my democracy submitted itself to one family? And when a poor man says something, there is uproar.[2]

Modi went on declare at subsequent election rallies that the coming decade would belong to men and women like himself, members of communities that were historically oppressed as 'low caste' and 'untouchable'. Such declarations endeared Modi to people like Kumar, who were reminded time and again of their socially subordinated status. By contrast, Gandhi's claims, at rally after election rally, that the Congress Party had 'lifted people out of poverty' appeared patronising to Kumar.

In the ensuing electoral battle, Gandhi's Congress Party proved no match for the BJP under Modi. Promises of economic growth and the provision of jobs were a big part of Modi's electoral campaign. Along with that, he made much of his own 'low caste' origins. These were infused by his commitment to Hindu nationalism, a century-old idea that Hindu ideals ought to be the bedrock of politics in the country. The stage had been set in an interview to Reuters, when he was pointedly asked if he was a Hindu nationalist, Modi glibly replied: 'Well, I am a Hindu and I am a nationalist, so yes, I am a Hindu nationalist.'[3] In the same interview, he was asked whether he felt any remorse for the violence unleashed on Muslims in Gujarat during the spring of 2002 while he was the chief minister. His reply was chilling:

> [If] someone else is driving a car and we're sitting behind, even
> then if a puppy comes under the wheel, will it be painful or not?
> Of course it is. If I'm a chief minister or not, I'm a human being.
> If something bad happens anywhere, it is natural to be sad.

His Hindu nationalist credentials firmly established even before the formal campaign took off, Modi left it to his followers and party leaders to emphasise that he was indeed 'emperor of Hindu hearts'. In the storm that followed, the BJP pulverised its rivals in the Lok Sabha, securing 282 out of 543 seats, thereby winning an absolute majority on its own—it was an achievement unmatched in three decades. Along with its allies, it enjoyed 336 seats, a crushing majority. Meanwhile, despite being the second-largest party, the Congress only managed to scrape a mere forty-four seats, which were not even enough to host the leader of the opposition.

Modi's election elated many of India's leading commentators. One, the head of a thinktank based in the heart of aristocratic Delhi, welcomed him as 'an embodiment of the desire for change'.[4] Another, an expatriate academic, then based in London, hailed him as 'a democratic asteroid'.[5] A third, one of India's best-selling authors, celebrated the attainment of 'an all-time high of Hindu power' and advised the BJP to use it wisely.[6] The few intellectuals who worried that Modi's victory threatened the country's secular identity[7] were nevertheless confident that at least India's democratic institutions would survive.[8]

Transitioning Away from Democracy (2014–19)

India's shift away from democracy became palpable during the BJP's first term. The Lok Sabha was decisively disempowered. It was allowed to scrutinise only 26 per cent of all bills, a fall from

60 per cent and 71 per cent in the two previous governments[9] led by the Congress. Cabinet ministers learnt about their policies from their bureaucrats, who in turn received their instructions from the Prime Minister's Office (PMO). The government made considerable headway in its attempts to achieve judicial compliance. Media proprietors were tamed by a combination of carrots and sticks. Laws were passed to enable greater executive control over the National Human Rights Commission (NHRC) and to cripple the Right to Information (RTI) Act, 2005. Amnesty International, winner of the Nobel Peace Prize, was targeted for portraying what the government considered an unfavourable view of India. India's ranking of academic freedom plummeted during these five years, lower than Somalia, Ukraine and Pakistan. Corporate executives murmured of an atmosphere of fear and complained that captains of industry were being treated as pariahs.

On Diwali Day, 8 November 2016, as the world was engrossed with the much-awaited elections in the USA, Prime Minister Modi addressed Indians over television at 8.00 p.m. He began with, 'Friends, the country is going through grave crisis, which makes it imperative for us to take some difficult yet important decisions.' Over the next one hour, in a speech marked by pauses and flourishes, the prime minister announced that high denomination currency notes (over ₹500) would be invalid from midnight. In less than four hours, Indians would find most of the currency they held to be worthless. They had until the end of the year to exchange the currency notes they held for new ones printed by the Reserve Bank of India (RBI), with limits imposed on the amounts they could exchange every day.

The BJP argued that the suddenness with which currency notes were 'demonetised' was justified as an assault on corruption and black money. Fed on the narrative that corruption was rife, Indians largely complied with the decision. But such compliance often came at grave personal cost. Daily wage labourers found themselves waiting in queues before banks when they needed to be at work to earn a living. Elderly people waited for hours in such queues as well, sometimes failing to reach the end of the line because of the heat, a heart condition or some general weakness. But there was little opposition since the move was considered well-intentioned, if somewhat rushed.

Kumar and I found ourselves standing in the same queue outside the State Bank of India (SBI) branch in South Delhi's Zamroodpur area. His evaluation of Modi's announcement was decisive: 'It's for the good of the country, so we must all make sacrifices.' Nodding in agreement, a neighbour added, 'Yes, Modi has taken a decision, so it must be in the best interest of the country.'

But this move to demonetise certain currency notes foreshadowed India's drift away from democracy. By all accounts, few people had been taken into confidence. A public assault on private property, the decision had not even been discussed in Parliament, the wellspring of democracy to which Modi had bowed in reverence when he entered the Lok Sabha for the first time in 2014. Cabinet members reported being informed, not consulted, a mere few hours before the announcement.

Despite the hardships people experienced because of demonetisation, BJP under Modi was re-elected in 2019 with an even larger majority than before. Not only did the party increase its tally of seats in the Lok Sabha but it also bettered its vote share—no mean feat given the array of opposition forces Modi faced. As per the final results declared by the Election Commission of India, the BJP had acquired a total of 303 seats in the 545-member Lok Sabha, up from the 270-odd seats it had held in the previous term. The results suggested that 45 per cent[10] of all Indians had reposed faith in the prime minister and his coalition partners in the National Democratic Alliance (NDA), the highest in thirty-five years. Around 67 per cent[11] of all registered voters cast their ballots, surpassing voter turnout in an industrialised democracy such as the United States (2016 turnout: 56 per cent). For an election that had been billed as 'The Battle for India's Soul', the verdict was decisive indeed.[12]

Modi's resounding victory was widely interpreted as an endorsement of his muscular nationalism and aggressive stance against neighbours Pakistan and China. But if nationalism resulted in a surge of support for Modi, Hindutva—the ideology that Hinduism, India's majority faith, ought to be the bedrock of Indian nationalism—provided much of the basis for that support in the first place. Results from the national election surveys, conducted among a random sample of 24,236 voters as they left the polling stations in 211 parliamentary constituencies,[13] suggested an unprecedented degree of Hindu consolidation behind the BJP and its allies: for the first time ever, over half of all Hindus reported voting for the BJP or its alliance partners, while the majority of Muslims reported voting opposition parties.[14] During election speeches, Modi invoked 'Hindu anger' against the opposition parties who had once accused Hindu radicals of fomenting terror. He carefully crafted a Hindu persona and assiduously courted the Hindu vote. Indeed, the BJP fielded a Hindu radical accused of plotting terror attacks on Muslims, promised to implement the National Register of Citizens (NRC) that threatened (albeit obliquely) Muslims with detention and deportation and pledged to build a temple to honour Ram in the northern Indian city of Ayodhya where Hindutva activists had demolished a sixteenth-century mosque back in 1992 under the party's leadership. A rightward shift towards Hindu majoritarianism in India's political pathway was unmistakable. This shift has continued unabated.

Modi in Power

Soon after being anointed India's fourteenth prime minister in 2014, Narendra Modi took the unprecedented step of celebrating his victory on the banks of the Ganga in the holy town of Varanasi. Varanasi was the parliamentary constituency that elected him, so it was to be expected that he would thank his voters. However, the spectacle of the prime minister accompanied by senior colleagues, who would go on to hold key cabinet portfolios, unapologetically flaunting his Hindu nationalist credentials, was a clear break with the past. To be sure, India's heads of government—even when personally agnostic—frequented places of worship on key occasions and regularly greeted the country on religious occasions but political association with religion as an inaugural act was rare. A few weeks later, while addressing India's Parliament for the first time as head of state, Modi referred to the '1,200 years of servitude' that Indians had suffered, making a not-so-subtle reference to accounts of conquest, plunder and domination by invaders of the Islamic faith. His words and deeds within the first month of his election as prime minister set the stage for a fundamental reconfiguration of politics in India.

Contrary to expectations that Modi's ascendance would usher in a period of stability and development, the BJP lurched from crisis to crisis during his first term in office. Much of their efforts were spent campaigning in one state after another to achieve electoral victory. Early in 2016, with less than two years into office, the BJP stirred up 'war hysteria' ahead of the 2017 elections in key states.[15] The government announced that it had attacked terrorists based in Pakistan to avenge the murder of Indian soldiers in the border state of Jammu and Kashmir. While functionaries of India's ruling BJP gloated, several opposition politicians questioned the truth of the government's claims. Nationalist passions were whipped up again on the eve of the 2019 elections. Terror attacks on military personnel in Jammu and Kashmir killed forty soldiers in February 2019. India retaliated through much-publicised attacks on alleged terror camps in Pakistan-controlled territory of Balakot, killing 300 terrorists affiliated with the dreaded Jaish-e-Mohammed group. Modi's approval ratings soared by as much as 7 per cent[16] after these events, suggesting that nationalist fervour may have contributed to his emphatic win in the subsequent elections held through April and May.[17]

The BJP's rule has also emboldened the proliferation of 'cow protection vigilantes' across the north and west of the country. Various people accused of slaughtering bovines or eating beef have been harassed, humiliated, beaten and killed since 2015. Most of the victims were from Muslim or Dalit communities, both of which depend on cows for their livelihood and sometimes food. A horrifying episode of lynching took place in September 2015 when Mohammed Akhlaq, a Muslim man in Dadri village of western Uttar Pradesh, was lynched on the suspicion that he had stored beef in his fridge.[18] The allegations were later found to be false as the meat stored in the fridge was not beef but goat; the attackers were taken into custody not because they killed Akhlaq but because they killed him for the wrong reason. Another ghastly episode emerged in July 2016 when seven Dalit labourers who were carrying cattle carcasses in the village of Una were rounded up by cow protection vigilantes,[19] stripped, dragged through the streets and thrashed with iron rods. In a telling measure of the impunity they enjoy, some of the vigilantes filmed the entire episode and uploaded it on social media as a warning to all those who slaughter cows and eat their meat.

Complementing such vigilantism were BJP-affiliated student organisations, such as the Akhil Bharatiya Vidyarthi Parishad (ABVP),[20] that took the battle to India's university campuses. In 2015, high-caste ABVP students at the University of Hyderabad complained about a Dalit student at the university, Rohith Vemula, who regularly organised readings and seminars on social justice and human rights. Vemula had been involved in a campus beef festival and funeral prayers for a terrorist convicted of the Bombay blasts of 1993. His activities got him suspended from the university along with three other Dalit students, and he eventually killed himself in January 2016.

Consolidating Power

Since its re-election in May 2019, the BJP under Modi has sought to make good on several key promises it has made to constituents over the last three decades. These promises resonate with views of Indian society and polity held dear by the RSS which strives to organise society in accordance with (and to ensure the protection of) the Hindu dharma, or way of life.[21] The RSS, BJP's parent body, was set up in 1925. In 2019, the RSS claimed to have 85,000 shakhas or cells where members are trained in physical combat and RSS ideology, and over fifteen formal affiliates, including the ABVP and Bharatiya Mazdoor Sangh (BMS), which are the largest students' and workers' unions in India, respectively. While the RSS has traditionally tapped into 'upper-caste' Hindus motivated not just by anti-Muslim hate but also by a fear of any defiance shown by 'lower-castes', in recent years, it has expanded its outreach.

In August 2019, barely three months after returning to power on the back of a landslide electoral win, Modi's government abolished Article 370[22] of the Indian Constitution which guaranteed a semi-autonomous status for the northern state of Jammu and Kashmir.[23] Politicians across the state (including supporters of its accession to India) were placed under house arrest, the internet was suspended and people were placed under a lockdown that continues till this date. Even as critics challenged the new law as unconstitutional,[24] the nationalist overtones of the move promised to unite the country behind a single idea of India where there is no special dispensation for different areas.[25] This was backed not only by BJP's allies but also by political parties that had bitterly opposed the BJP during the 2019 elections.[26]

The BJP government further burnished its credentials of uniform nationalism in September 2019 when it successfully spearheaded the abolition of the triple talaq, a practice which had hitherto permitted Muslim men to divorce their wives through mere verbal instruction. Long a subject of criticism, not least by Muslim women themselves, the practice had survived under successive postcolonial governments wary of being seen as interfering in Islamic religious customs. The bill was passed without much opposition in Parliament. While critics pointed to the Hindu nationalist undertones that accompanied the official narrative, supporters (again, not all of whom may have been BJP voters) hailed the move as a step towards the attainment of uniform civil code across India.

In November 2019, the BJP's Hindu nationalist agenda received a major fillip when India's Supreme Court proclaimed in their favour while announcing a verdict on the 150-year-old dispute in the northern town of Ayodhya. The dispute was over a tract of land believed to be the birthplace of Ram, hero and deity to many Hindus. A mosque had been built on that land by a Mughal general back in 1528; Hindu nationalist mobs exhorted by BJP leaders had pulled the mosque down in 1992. The Hindus claimed the land as theirs and demanded the right to build a grand temple to honour Ram, while the Muslims insisted it was theirs so they could rebuild the demolished mosque. Through its ruling, the Supreme Court effectively legalised mob vandalism against the mosque and, in doing so, handed over a carte blanche to the Hindus. The chief justice of the Supreme Court responsible for the verdict was subsequently rewarded by being selected as a BJP nominee to India's upper house of Parliament.

Riding on a wave of successful legislation with little resistance in Parliament, the Modi government legislated the Citizenship Amendment Act (CAA) in December 2019. Under the provisions of CAA, Hindus, Buddhists, Jains, Christians, Sikhs and Zoroastrians from Muslim-majority neighbours such as Afghanistan, Pakistan and Bangladesh would find their applications for citizenship fast-tracked. By explicitly omitting Muslims, Jews, Bahais and atheists from its purview, the CAA introduced a religious filter that struck at the heart of the secular principles enshrined in the Constitution. Home Minister Amit Shah promised the Indian Parliament as well as audiences during political rallies and press conferences that the amendment will be followed by the enumeration of a controversial NRC, adding to popular anxiety. Indians would now have to prove their citizenship by providing certain documents so they could be enlisted in the registry—failure to do so could result in detention as an 'illegal immigrant' and possibly deportation.[27]

By March 2020, the COVID-19 crisis had exploded in

India. The leader of the world's largest democracy announced the world's largest lockdown with a mere four hours' notice. The worst hit were the country's estimated 14 crore migrant workers, many of who lost their jobs and were evicted.[28] Several crores of them began journeying back to the villages they call home, often on foot since public transport was suspended. India's opposition parties demonstrated their utter ineptitude by failing to mobilise resources and provide relief in order to ensure dignity and justice for the millions of migrant labourers. The stringent lockdown also provided a convenient cover[29] for the BJP to muzzle the growing dissent[30] against the CAA. As protestors wound up their campaigns in keeping with social distancing regulations, police in Delhi erased protest graffiti to remove any trace of the demonstrations. Dissidents were rounded up and imprisoned under draconian colonial-era laws. The respected scholar-activist Anand Teltumbde was one such case in point.[31] Student-protestor Safoora Zargar was another.[32] Although India's thriving civil society protested vociferously, it was effectively curtailed to online forums.

On 5 August 2020—exactly one year after the Indian government repudiated the autonomous status of the state of Jammu and Kashmir—Modi personally consecrated the Ram temple in Ayodhya. In a spectacular ceremony televised across the world, he performed the bhumi poojan, a ritual to worship the land on which the temple was planned to be constructed, led by Hindu priests and accompanied by other legislators, including the chief minister of Uttar Pradesh, the state in which Ayodhya is located. The sight of the head of government of a secular democracy performing foundational rituals at a religious site that had been the bone of contention between the country's principal religious communities exemplified the distance India had travelled away from being a liberal democracy. From here on, India's democracy—nominally secular not because it enforced a strict separation between religion and state but because it maintained equidistance between the state and the country's numerous faiths—could be seen as firmly distancing itself from its liberal, pluralistic roots in favour of a more explicitly ethnic orientation.

In September 2020, the government introduced three legislations that collectively aimed at liberalising agriculture in India from state-guaranteed protections.[33] Together, the legislations signal the Indian government's long-standing attempt to lower restrictions in agriculture, perhaps the most protectionist sector of the Indian government. In response, over thirty farmers' unions mobilised their members to sit peacefully at protest sites on Delhi's borders towards the end of November. They were met with tear gas shells and water cannons. Although a 24-hour nationwide general strike involving 25 crore workers in support of the farmers passed without incident, the government was obviously rattled. Fearing a broader popular upsurge,[34] it sought ways to discredit the protestors, a large number of whom were of the Sikh community in Punjab. Pro-government blogs started peddling conspiracy theories,[35] linking the farmers' protests with Pakistani machinations to support an independent Khalistan, invoking memories of the bitter Hindu–Sikh conflict that rent Punjab asunder during the 1980s. Tactless remarks by individual protestors, from which the unions quickly distanced themselves, were cited as supporting evidence.[36]

Matters came to a head on Republic Day in January 2021 when a small section of protestors clashed with the police and sought to occupy the iconic Red Fort. Ignoring how peaceful the majority of the protests had been so far, India's pliant media lost no time in condemning the entire swathe of protestors, accusing them of conspiring to defame India and to damage the country's reputation.[37] TV anchors outdid one another to shame the farmers and their allies, urging the government to take strict action against all protestors. The general population, which is easily influenced by media sensationalism, decried the protests as damaging to law and order. Some actively encouraged police to beat and even shoot the protestors.[38] Even as the farmers pressed on with their peaceful protests, state repression continued. Internet connectivity was disrupted in the vicinity of Delhi and war-like fortifications were installed.[39] Journalists covering the protests faced charges and arrests if they were known to be sympathetic to the farmers.[40] As the Modi government continued to criminalise peaceful dissent and condemned global solidarity with such neologisms as 'foreign destructive ideology', its authoritarian tendencies were further exposed.

Hollowing Out the World's Largest Democracy

India shares the degradation of its democracy with many other countries across the world. This process has been variously described as authoritarian, populist, ethnocratic, exclusionary and fascist. An exclusionary nationalism pervades political discourse whereby internal enemies are as extensively targeted (if not more) than external ones: not only do Muslims and (to a lesser extent) Christians find themselves at the receiving end but anyone who does not conform to the image of a good Hindu can find themselves singled out as the internal enemy. In recent years, the list of internal enemies has come to include Dalits who have been historically oppressed as 'untouchables'; liberals, leftists and activists who have raised issues of the environment and human rights as well as anyone else perceived to be 'anti-national'. Such internal enemies are demonised and vilified. Recent constitutional amendments have initiated a process that critics fear may well culminate in eventually stripping Muslims of their citizenship. People leading lifestyles not approved by the law and society are lynched. Dissent is muzzled, increasingly through official edicts: the list of people incarcerated on any flimsy pretext include the eighty-year-old human rights activist Varavara Rao and Disha Ravi, a twenty-one-year-old environmental activist, among others.

In the meantime, the BJP-led government encourages sections of Indian society to further propagate Hindutva ideology. Old controversies over temples and mosques are reignited, such as in Mathura[41] and Varanasi[42] where claims that mosques in the cities were built upon the demolition of temples have resurfaced. Old agreements negotiated and settled by Hindus and Muslims centuries ago are being challenged and new religious flashpoints threaten to rent asunder the social fabric knitted together by India's diverse communities.

The RSS's commitment to enforcing the Hindu dharma across India at the expense of religious minorities is clear from a reading of its 'vision and mission statement' that is publicly available on its website. Invoking the words of its founder, the statement declares:

> The Hindu culture is the life-breath of Hindusthan. It is therefore clear that if Hindusthan is to be protected, we should first nourish the Hindu culture. If the Hindu culture perishes in Hindusthan itself, and if the Hindu society ceases to exist, it will hardly be appropriate to refer to the mere geographical entity that remains as Hindusthan. Mere geographical lumps do not make a nation. The entire society should be in such a vigilant and organised condition that no one wuld dare to cast an evil eye on any of our points of honour.

Strength, it should be remembered, comes only through organization. It is therefore the duty of every Hindu to do his best to consolidate the Hindu society. The Sangh is just carrying out this supreme task. The present fate of the country cannot be changed unless lakhs of young men dedicate their entire lifetime for that cause. To mould the minds of our youth towards that end is the supreme aim of the Sangh.

This statement endorses their founder's reference to India as 'Hindusthan', a cultural term used to refer to the land of the Hindus. Of course, this use of spelling cleverly manipulates the more common use of the term 'Hindustan', which is of Persian origin and also one that refers to India as the 'land of the Hindus' but in a geographical rather than cultural sense. That Hindu culture is celebrated as the 'life-breath' of the country which privileges it over other cultural influences that have shaped the country. The statement then goes on to identify Muslims and Christians as potential threats to the nation.

> Conjointly with Independence, parts of Punjab, Bengal, Sindh and the Frontier areas [a reference to Muslim-majority areas that were awarded to Pakistan under the terms of India's violent Partition] were sundered from Bharat [the Sanskrit term for India]; and, four and a half decades after the nation's attaining freedom, [Muslim-majority] Kashmir remains a thorn in the flesh.

> Continuous efforts have been there to make Assam a Muslim majority province. Likewise, no-holds-barred efforts to proselytize by Christian missions continue unabated. Even armed revolt has been engineered (e.g., in Nagaland) to carve out independent Christian provinces. Such activities receive ready support and unlimited funds from foreign countries and agencies keenly interested in destabilizing Bharat for their own ends.

Such actions and statements illustrate the surreptitious hollowing out of the world's largest democracy rather than a spectacular suspension. There does not appear to be any immediate or even long-term threat of democracy being formally dismantled. The prime minister does not tire of proclaiming India's democratic lineage, unlike interwar European fascist demagogues who pointedly reject democracy. Indeed, he has gone on to extol India as the mother of all democracies.[43] His utterances are not just for the strategic benefit of Western audiences that might be worried about political unrest in India—Modi has even repeated such claims of democracy being a quintessential Indian tenet in mass election rallies and in both the houses of Parliament as well as at global forums. This suggests that convincing domestic audiences of such narratives is as important as persuading the international ones.

The Modi regime has so far respected the mandate of the numerous provincial elections held across the country since its ascendance to power, including the ones where the BJP was routed (Delhi in 2015 and 2020; Bihar in 2015; West Bengal, Kerala and Tamil Nadu in 2016 and 2021; Jharkhand and Maharashtra in 2020). Although it has manipulated legislative rules to outmanoeuvre opponents and install friendly governments in states (Bihar in 2017; Madhya Pradesh in 2019), it has, by and large, accepted electoral mandates even when results have been unfavourable.

Modi has also declared himself at the service of his people rather than proclaiming himself as the equivalent of a Führer or Duce. He remains committed to the RSS Hindutva agenda. Modi's BJP-led government is even subject to checks and balances by its ideological fount, the RSS. Indeed, such checks and balances are likely to prevent as charismatic a leader as Modi from assuming absolute power.

Checks on a possible personal concentration of power are critical for the continued functioning of democracy. In this respect, the RSS enforces a degree of accountability over Modi and his cabinet colleagues[44] to which few other dictators have been subjected. At least thirty-eight of fifty-three members of the cabinet in Modi's second government have a background in the RSS. That proportion has increased from the first government, when forty-one of sixty-six cabinet members were from the RSS. An example of the perverse accountability of the government to the RSS was displayed when Modi rebuked the cow protection squads that lynched Muslims and Dalits in 2015-16. Modi's criticism invited prompt rebuttal from the RSS, which spoke out in favour of the squads[45] and the prime minister was compelled to back down and dilute his censure.[46] This subservience to the RSS exemplifies the peculiar ways in which the executive continues to be accountable, if only to a specific section of the population.

The way in which democracy is being hollowed out in India is, therefore, far from the textbook case of despotic rulers seizing absolute power. Rather, you would find that key elements of both authoritarian rule and democratic politics are being skilfully blended in such a way that opponents are struggling to mount a frontal challenge since defenders of the regime are able to easily highlight its democratic characteristics while also deflecting attention away from its authoritarian ones. India today exemplifies the tangled entwinement of authoritarianism and democracy, making it even more dangerous than situations where there is a forthright clash between the two.

Mobilising Against Caste

'Only Two Castes in India'

The BJP's headquarters in Delhi's ITO area wore a festive look. Supporters had been thronging the place for hours as news emerged of its decisive victory in the general elections of 2019. The party had improved both its seat and vote share from 2014. Narendra Modi had been elected once again as prime minister, with an even larger mandate to rule than the last time. A dhanyawad samaroh (gratitude ceremony) was organised that evening for Modi to thank the nation for repositing its faith on him for a second time.

Dedicating his victory to the poorest Indians over the course of his forty-minute speech, Modi declared:

> Now, there are only two castes living in the country and the country is going to be focused on these two castes.

> In the twenty-first century, there is a caste in India, the poor, and other castes in the country who have some contribution to free them of poverty.

> There are the ones who want to come out of poverty and the one who wants to bring people out of poverty. We have to empower these two.

> We have to walk with this dream.[1]

Modi's reference to two castes in India was an attempt to simplistically reframe the country's staggeringly complex social hierarchy while ignoring the oppression embedded within it. It was a general tendency among proponents of Hindutva to neglect the realities of caste-based discrimination in the structures of Indian society—its politics, economics and culture. For example, Madhav Sadashiv Golwalkar, who led the RSS from 1940 to 1973, decried criticisms of the caste hierarchy in his *Bunch of Thoughts* without mincing words:

> The ... main feature that distinguished our society was the Varna-vyavastha. But today it is being dubbed 'casteism' and scoffed at. Our people have come to feel that the mere mention of Varna-vyavastha is something derogatory. They often mistake the social order implied in it for social discrimination.

> The feeling of inequality, of high and low, which has crept into the Varna system, is comparatively of recent origin. The perversion was given a further fillip by the scheming Britisher in line with his 'divide and rule' policy. But in its original form, the distinctions in that social order did not imply any discrimination such as big and small, high and low, among its constituents.[2]

Golwalkar went on to celebrate caste as serving a great bond of social cohesion in the country. In his own words:

> Castes, there were in those ancient times too, continuing for thousands of years of our glorious national life. There is nowhere any instance of its having hampered the progress or disrupted the unity of society. It, in fact, served as a great bond of social cohesion.

Other proponents of Hindutva have taken care to distance themselves from being viewed as supportive of caste. In fact, some, like Vinayak Damodar Savarkar, even led initiatives against the practice of untouchability. But, by and large, they have sought to ignore the injustices of caste, choosing to focus instead on reviving the alleged glories of India as a Hindu nation.

But by the 1980s, such oppression was impossible to ignore. A combination of state policy, political action and public protest began to foment popular assertions against caste hierarchies. These assertions were often led by people who had historically been at the receiving end of caste violence. Their refusal to bow down to the strictures of social order worried the self-styled 'high castes' among the Hindus, not least the leadership of the RSS as well as the BJP that had been newly minted in 1980.

It all began in an obscure village in Tamil Nadu early in 1981.

A Conversion and Much Frenzy

The morning of 19 February 1981 promised new beginnings for the hundreds of people in Meenakshipuram who had assembled that morning in the village square. They were members of the village's Pallar community who were tired of being routinely harassed and stigmatised as 'untouchables' by the dominant Thevars. The Pallars had had enough. They were going to convert to Islam, which held an egalitarian promise, one that offered them hope for a dignified life. As the day wore on, the Ishaadul Islam Sabha of South India welcomed the Pallars into the Muslim faith.[3]

The conversion of a few hundred Pallars that morning catapulted Meenakshipuram to the national spotlight. It was not the first time that people stigmatised as 'untouchables' were leaving the Hindu fold and converting to other faiths, embracing Buddhism, Sikhism and Christianity as more egalitarian alternatives to Hinduism's caste-based hierarchies. But the conversion to

Islam was deemed a troubling step too far,[4] not only by locally dominant groups but also by 'high castes' across the nation. The conversion fuelled anxieties borne out by the realisation that the 'high castes' were, after all, a demographic minority.

Within days, a religious conference held in Meenakshipuram declared that untouchability found no mention in the Hindu texts. A few months later, the apex body of the RSS passed a resolution against proselytisation (though not against caste discrimination).[5] Before the end of the year, a hitherto obscure body called the Virat Hindu Samaj (VHS) convened members of sixty different sects in a huge rally that inundated Delhi's Boat Club loans and painted the city saffron. The 550 RSS shakhas across the capital offered their full support to this rally: 'Not since the Mahabharat war,' a participant gloated, 'had so many Hindus gathered in one place.'[6] Although the rally was presided over by Karan Singh, the son of the last Hindu king of the state of Jammu and Kashmir and hailed as a Suryavanshi Kshatriya (a warrior caste said to have descended from the sun god himself), the organisational influence of the RSS was evident. Two RSS stalwarts, Prem Chand Gupta and Hansraj Gupta, involved themselves as working presidents. Crucially, speakers at the rally included representatives of what the organisers called 'Indo-Gangetic religions', that is, Sikhism, Jainism and Buddhism. Even more crucially, Congress ministers from various states were in attendance. Speaker after speaker reiterated the same point: that untouchability did not stem from Hinduism.

A parallel rally held the very same day just a few kilometres away exposed the fault lines VHS had tried so hard to conceal. Jagjivan Ram, an erstwhile Congress stalwart and now a towering opposition politician, thundered against the joint efforts being made by the RSS and the Congress to disguise the religious sanction to untouchability. Untouchability was a product of varnashrama. It was enshrined in the Manusmiriti, the religious and moral code of the Hindus. Jagjivan Ram refused to express any opinions on the event in Meenakshipuram; the converts had exercised their constitutional right and that was that. A few months earlier, he had questioned the motivations of the VHS in a twelve-page letter: 'You are going to hold a rally which has been prompted by the mass conversion in Tamil Nadu but not by any of the incidents of atrocity on the Harijans,' referring to continued systemic violence suffered by Dalits across India.[7] If the Hindus did want to abolish untouchability, they ought to disband the caste system. And there was only one way to do it: ban endogamous marriages. Children of marriages within a single caste would neither be recognised as successors to property nor as legitimate children. Needless to say, such radical suggestions fell on deaf ears.

Before the end of the year, the RSS had activated the Vishwa Hindu Parishad (VHP) to galvanise Hindu opinion in favour of consolidation. A metallurgical engineer from Allahabad, Ashok Singhal, was pressed into service and he took up the issue with unprecedented enthusiasm. The VHP soon organised its own programme against proselytisation by non-Hindu religions. Under the aegis of the Sanskriti Raksha Nidhi Yojana, a name that signalled that it was launching a programme to protect culture, the VHP adopted a two-fold strategy: consolidate a solid Hindu identity and scapegoat non-Hindu 'others'.

Within two years, the VHP organised a Hindu Sammelan in the northern town of Muzaffarnagar. The star speaker was former Congressman Dau Dayal Khanna. Muslim rule had destroyed Hindu culture, Khanna bellowed, by building mosques over shattered temples. The time had come to reclaim these temples and demolish the mosques in turn. Khanna demanded that the VHP begin the process by focusing on Ayodhya where a temple marking the birthplace of the mythical god-king Ram had allegedly been destroyed in the sixteenth century on the orders of the Mughal king Babur. A mosque commemorating the marauding invader, the Babri Masjid, had been built in its stead. The masses were to be mobilised to demolish the masjid and restore the temple. On cue, the VHP adopted a resolution that would shape Indian politics for decades: a mass agitation to construct a temple dedicated to Ram after tearing down the Babri Masjid. The Ram Janmabhoomi movement had been born.

The broad template of deflecting demands for caste equality by sowing Hindu–Muslim divisions was being fashioned. In the meantime, challenges to the dominance of the 'high castes' continued to grow.

Bahujan Samaj

Protests against caste hierarchies have been a part of Indian society for centuries. From the Buddha's teachings over 2,500 years ago, to the prose and poetry produced by the Bhakti saints in early modern India and the anti-caste movements of the nineteenth and twentieth centuries, the system of social stratification has faced countless challenges. Rarely though did such contentions portend to unite the vast majority of Indians branded as 'lower caste', 'untouchable' and 'primitive' as did the efforts of a researcher at the Pune-based Explosive Research and Development Laboratory (ERDL), now known as the High Energy Materials Research Laboratory.

Kanshi Ram took the lessons from centuries of mobilisation against caste hierarchies across the country very seriously. Born into Dalit family, Kanshi Ram graduated with a bachelor degree in science and was recruited by the Indian government to one of its most sensitive research facilities. He was now a government employee, hired under the provisions of constitutionally mandated affirmative actions for members of Scheduled Castes and Scheduled Tribes. One year, the ERDL cancelled the official holidays meant to commemorate the birth anniversaries of the Buddha and B.R. Ambedkar, a Dalit icon, replacing these instead with a commemoration for the fiery nationalist Bal Gangadhar Tilak, and an additional holiday for Diwali. An enraged Kanshi Ram joined fellow Dalit colleagues to protest this decision. An altercation with his 'high-caste' supervisors ensued, following which he was suspended. Kanshi Ram eventually resigned from the ERDL.

Resignation from government service allowed Kanshi Ram more time for public service. In 1973, he convened the Backward and Minorities Employees Federation (BAMCEF). BAMCEF was intended as a platform for employees from 'low caste' social backgrounds. The platform thus brought together members of groups designated as Other Backward Classes, Scheduled Castes and Scheduled Tribes. Additionally, religious minorities from these backgrounds were also welcomed to BAMCEF. In 1981, the organisation was complemented by the creation of its agitational wing, the Dalit Shoshit Samaj Sangharsh Samiti (DS-4). DS-4 convened cadre camps, awakening squads and bicycle marches among Dalits and Muslims[8] across northern India in an effort to forge social unity between members of such marginalised communities against the dominance of the 'upper castes'.

Kanshi Ram was keen to craft a political identity that would further cement the sense of social unity between members of oppressed groups. On 14 April 1984, he proclaimed the formation of the Bahujan Samaj Party (BSP). The term 'bahujan' in this context had a very specific connotation. As Kanshi Ram put it succinctly and unambiguously in his 1985 publication titled *Oppressed Indian*, 'Bahujan Samaj is comprised of Scheduled Caste, Scheduled Tribe, Other Backward Classes and converted minorities.' To put it another way, 'bahujan' literally means majority. Kanshi Ram's usage referred to the majority of the Indian population that was not 'upper caste'.

It was easy to perceive the formation of the BSP as a concerted move against the 'upper castes'. Never before had a union across oppressed communities been so explicitly attempted. Never before had a singular political identity been claimed to encompass the members of such communities. Bahujans, as defined by Kanshi Ram, comprised almost 85 per cent of India's population, if not more. At 15 per cent, the 'upper castes'[9] were clearly identified as dominant minorities whose control over the country's economic, social and political resources far exceeded their ratio in the population.

To be sure, Kanshi Ram was not advocating the exclusion of the 'upper castes' from the Indian polity. Nor did he call for reversing caste hierarchy. He explained his ambition for the BSP using a pen and his characteristic flourish:

> The Brahmanical social order is like this pen held vertically with the Brahmins, Kshatriyas and Vaishyas dominating the top. The rest is dominated by the Shudras, the Ati-Shudras, the lowest castes and the Bahujan Samaj. And see the manipulation of the Brahmanical order. The Shudras and the Ati-Shudras are further divided into 6000 castes. It is time this pen is held horizontally.[10]

But this call for social equality was perceived as a threat by those at the apex of the social order. The choice of 14 April as the date to inaugurate the BSP was not lost on them: it was the birth anniversary of scholar-statesman Bhimrao Ambedkar. Born into the Mahar community whose members were classed as 'untouchables', his championship of civil rights and social justice called for a thorough interrogation of the very principles that framed Hinduism. As chairman of the committee that had penned India's Constitution, Ambedkar was largely responsible for institutionalising provisions for the affirmative actions that would ensure mandatory reservations for Dalits and Adivasis in the legislature, bureaucracy and institutions of higher education. Towards the end of his life, he led over five lakh members of his community to Buddhism, comprehensively denouncing and renouncing Hinduism. By launching the BSP to coincide with Ambedkar's birth anniversary, Kanshi Ram was making clear his own ideological affinity as well as the social moorings of his party in favour of an egalitarian society. This signalling and its implications for their inherited privileges began to worry members of the 'upper caste'. Their anxieties reached tipping point in faraway Gujarat where the social alliance envisioned by Kanshi Ram was about to gain political power, not under the aegis of the nascent BSP but because of a skilful political coalition stitched together by the ruling Congress.

Violence Against Subaltern Assertion

It was 11 March 1985. Madhav Singh Solanki had every reason to be ecstatic. As chief minister of Gujarat and the leader of its ruling Congress Party, he had just led his party to a massive electoral victory. The party had won 149 of the 182 seats in the state's Vidhan Sabha elections. This win had been the largest in the state's history till then and would remain unmatched for decades.

Beyond the scale of the electoral mandate, the social basis of the Congress's massive triumph was noteworthy.

Solanki was born into the Koli community, categorised in Gujarat's complex social hierarchy as a 'lower Kshatriya'. He had been appointed the leader of the party's Gujarat unit in 1975 and was immediately faced with the party's electoral collapse due to corruption in the state and the excesses of the Emergency between 1975 and 1977. As the Congress's electoral fortunes continued to dwindle, Solanki formulated a new strategy that would not only win it votes but also reconfigure the social coalition on which it was based. And so was born the Gujarat Congress's KHAM strategy.

As an acronym, KHAM stood for a consolidation of Kshatriya, Harijan (the term used to describe Dalits those days), Adivasi and Muslim. Each cluster was socially marginalised but also numerically significant. As such, Solanki's strategy involved recruiting prominent politicians from these communities within the Congress. This strategy sidelined the 'upper castes' as well as the 'middle caste' Kunbi-Patidars who had so far controlled the Congress and, in doing so, won the party rich dividends in the 1980 elections—its vote share increased from 40 per cent in 1975 to 51 per cent and seats won rose from 75 to 141 (out of a total of 182).[11] The political strategy of aligning socially marginalised communities had paid off handsomely. Solanki went on to become the first chief minister of Gujarat to complete a full term.

And it didn't stop there. While in power, Solanki sought to consolidate the KHAM strategy. Almost 70 per cent of his ministers were derived from KHAM communities.[12] Within a year, he appointed a commission to explore the possibility of extending affirmative actions to 'lower-caste' groups; these would be in addition to the affirmative actions for Dalits and Adivasis for whom such provisions were constitutionally mandated. The commission recommended an increase in backward class reservation to 28 per cent over and above the existing 21 per cent allocated for Dalits and Adivasis.[13] A total of 49 per cent of seats would be reserved for members of what Kanshi Ram would call Bahujan communities. Solanki's government accepted this recommendation early in January 1985 with barely two months left for the next elections. When accused of employing underhanded electoral tactics, he replied, 'Other communities have had their say for centuries. It is now time for the lower and underprivileged classes to come up.'

The electoral response to Solanki's announcement was emphatic. The Congress increased its huge vote share by a further 4 per cent and added eight seats to its kitty, surpassing its own expectations. Over ninety of the 149 Congress MLAs belonged to KHAM communities.[14] The lower and underprivileged classes had unequivocally registered their support for extending affirmative action. When Solanki announced his cabinet, few could ignore the fact that fourteen of the twenty ministers holding major positions had KHAM backgrounds. There seemed to be no way to prevent the extension of affirmative action.

But Gujarat's 'upper' and 'middle' castes were anxious at the prospect. To be sure, they would continue to enjoy access to jobs that was disproportionate to their share of the population. The 1931 census recorded them as 27 per cent of the state's inhabitants. The government's proposed expansion would still effectively reserve 51 per cent of all public jobs for them.[15] But this figure was much less than the 79 per cent they enjoyed. Anxiety quickly transformed into fury.

Violence erupted in Ahmedabad soon after Solanki and his cabinet of ministers took the oath of office on 11 March 1985.

Protestors stoned state transport buses. Some of these buses were set ablaze; in one grisly case, the bus conductor was tied up and burnt alive. A week later, students announced a general strike across the state. Violence intensified when the new assembly convened later that month. The walled city's famed pols (housing clusters) witnessed anarchic orgies of stabbing, stoning and police firing. In April, strikes by doctors and closure of banks added to the turmoil. Early in June, the Gujarat Chambers of Commerce called for a five-day strike. Ahmedabad ground to a halt.

Meanwhile, inter-caste conflict between 'upper' and 'lower' castes within the Hindu community swiftly transformed into inter-communal violence between Hindus and Muslims. The state's 8 per cent Muslim minority population, which had no stakes whatsoever in the dispute over affirmative action and would neither benefit from its extension nor be adversely affected, became an easy target. The Dave Commission of Inquiry, which later investigated the violence, noted that Muslims were its main victims. Indeed, by the time the violence calmed down in July 1985, the number of inter-communal rioting cases (743) had exceeded the incidents of anti-reservation protests (649).[16] 'Upper-caste' Hindus tried their best to splinter Solanki's alliance with the underprivileged. Furious at the challenge to their dominance and desperate to preserve it, they deflected attention away from their own privilege towards Muslims, blaming them for the country's problems. Hindutva and its ideology of Hindu unity proved handy.

Revolt Against Reservations

Following such events, from a mere two seats in 1984, the BJP increased its Lok Sabha tally to eighty-five in five years!

Its embrace of Hindutva endeared it to 'high-caste' voters who were threatened, worried and infuriated by the growing assertions being made by 'lower-caste' communities. The 1989 Lok Sabha elections dislodged the Congress from power but did not throw up a clear winner. The BJP extended support to V.P. Singh's Janata Dal-led National Front coalition when it became clear that neither could form the government on its own. The bonhomie was short-lived.

On 7 August 1990, Singh announced the implementation of the Mandal Commission's recommendations. Around 27 per cent affirmative action in public sector employment was now extended to the 'lower castes' across India, adding to the 24 per cent that was constitutionally guaranteed to Dalits and Adivasis.[17] The announcement provoked outrage among 'upper-caste' students across the country. I was an eleven-year-old student at a school in Delhi when the announcement was made. Drawing rooms across the city erupted in a volcanic angst against Singh's perceived betrayal of his fellow Savarnas. As students, we were mostly pleased that our school, like many across north India, was forced to close during the agitations. But when I saw older students as well as friends and neighbours in college furious at the prospect of their access to government jobs being threatened, I could not help but feel sympathy. 'What will happen to meritorious students?' I heard this question asked time and again. In their eyes, Singh was not only betraying his fellow Savarnas but he was also about to destroy India.

The RSS demanded the suspension of the recommendations. *Organiser* thundered: 'What V.P. Singh through Mandalisation of society intends to achieve is a division of Hindus on forward, backward and Harijan lines.'[18] The 'high-caste' leadership of BJP vacillated on a response. It privately agreed with the RSS but did not want to alienate the 'lower castes'. A way out was provided on 26 August 1990 when the RSS called for a meeting to coordinate support for the VHP's demand for the Ram temple in Ayodhya. Seizing the opportunity, the BJP's national president L.K. Advani embarked on a rath yatra (chariot procession) to drum up support for the temple, thus hijacking the VHP's agenda. What Advani called 'the greatest mass movement in history' was thus born.

Advani began the yatra on 25 September 1990. Commencing, somewhat unsurprisingly, in Gujarat, the procession would traverse through ten states to culminate in Ayodhya on 30 October 1990 when the VHP planned a kar seva (ensemble of rituals) that would consecrate the temple. By galvanising public opinion in favour of the temple, the BJP hoped to overcome the division of Hindus feared by the RSS without also alienating the 'lower castes'. However, the 'lower-caste' leaders of the Janata Dal were unimpressed. The procession left a trail of bloodshed, rioting and wrecked communal relations in its wake, jeopardising national security from within. On 23 October 1990, Lalu Prasad Yadav, the 'lower-caste' chief minister of Bihar, arrested Advani under the National Security Act. That very evening, the BJP withdrew its support for the government. A week later, the VHP cadres descended on Ayodhya to perform the kar seva. Mulayam Singh Yadav, the 'lower-caste' chief minister of the Uttar Pradesh, ordered the police to fire at the gathering, killing half a dozen kar sevaks. The sordid drama was repeated three days later, inflaming 'high-caste' opinion against the Janata Dal and crystallising Hindu support in favour of the BJP.

When fresh elections were called the following summer in 1991, the BJP emerged as the second largest party, winning 120 seats in the Lok Sabha. The 2014 elections paled in comparison to the bombardment launched by the BJP under Advani's leadership.

I even vividly remember the summer vacation project I did that year as a school student in Delhi. Recordings of speeches demanding the demolition of the Babri Masjid, the construction of a Ram temple in its place and the restoration of Hindu pride blared from loudspeakers in local markets. These broadcasts were cheered on by people I knew, some as mere acquaintances, others more closely. I was, of course, smugly unaware of how extremely tiny the circle, almost entirely in South Delhi, was within which I was located. But even within the tiny circle, the number of people who switched their support from Singh (whom they had enthusiastically supported just the previous year) to the BJP was striking.

The BJP increased its vote share from 11 per cent in 1989 to an impressive 20 per cent in 1991.[19] It was difficult to ignore that this coincided roughly with the proportion of the 'high castes' to India's population. They have since remained solidly supportive of it and its allies. Table 1 shows the consistently high support enjoyed by the party among the 'high castes'.[20]

To be sure, the party has since expanded its social base and increased its vote share across castes and communities. Its spectacular success is a testament to the resilience of the Hindutva narrative. But the contradictions cloaked by Hindutva cannot remain camouflaged for long.

Counting the Uncounted

On 7 January 2023, over 5 lakh surveyors fanned out across the state of Bihar. Armed with tablets, the data they were to collect would be deposited into a centralised database in real time. The core information they were after had last been compiled ninety-one years ago: the caste of their respondents. Additionally, they

TABLE 1

	1991	1996	1998	1999	2004	2009	2014	2019
'Upper caste'	32	51	54	62.5	56	35	57	59
OBC[21]	34	35	38	44.6	39	28	42	54
				44.2	39			
Dalit	8	10	11	25.6	23	15	30	40.5
Adivasi	5	6	7	34	33	26.5	41	46
Muslim	1	2	2	14.7	11	6	9.5	9

were to enquire about economic status. The data thus gathered would make it possible, for the first time in over ninety years, to connect caste status with occupations, income, wealth and educational attainments. Unlike sample surveys that only covered a slice of the population, this mammoth exercise would encompass the entire population of over the 10 crore who call Bihar home.

Population surveys tend to be rather banal exercises. Surveyors tally the social and economic characteristics of their respondents. Governments then publish those records in a plethora of reports. Barring a handful of bureaucrats, politicians and statisticians, few people care about their findings. A niche group might dabble in examining select data points. A bunch of public policy podcasters may argue over methods and results. But, by and large, population surveys barely generate public interest. Like unremarkable columns of ants that go about routine chores, surveyors are generally ignored by others around them. Hope is not something we attribute to them or their exertions.

But the survey being undertaken in Bihar was different. It followed decades of demands by political workers and social activists for a reliable database that would expose the caste-based inequalities which had marred the state's development. The resulting data would lay the foundation for a fairer allocation of resources and representation that could redress the balance of caste power in Bihar. For example, the expansion of affirmative actions, hitherto clouded by competing claims, could be based on statistics rather than speculation. Disagreement over such contentious issues were unavoidable, of course. But at least there would now be official data against which the veracity of claims and counterclaims could be gauged.

This possibility excited Gunvati Yadav who, together with her husband Narendra Yadav, owns and cultivates a small plot of land in a village in north Bihar some forty kilometres away from the border with Nepal. Her husband and son regularly travel to Delhi, Punjab and western Uttar Pradesh for work. The day after the caste census was announced, she called me on WhatsApp, more animated than I had ever seen or heard her. 'Have you heard?' she began without the usual queries about my well-being. 'We are finally being counted. Now, everyone will know how many of us there are, and who has what.' Her excitement mounted as she spoke. Despite their limited socio-economic resources (or perhaps because of them), the Yadavs, like several other people of modest means, took official actions such as censuses, surveys and sundry other activities very seriously. They had hoped for a long time that a caste census be conducted. 'This is very good,' she repeated several times during our conversation.

Hope involves a resolve to not give up. It involves a determination to not be overwhelmed by oppression but instead to confront it. Confrontation does not always entail violent or revolutionary activity. Instead, it spans a spectrum of practices that blunt, and eventually undermine, the structures of oppression. Hope's work against oppression often resembles the waves or winds that wears stone down rather than dynamite that blasts it away. Its glacial progress is often frustrating, especially to those of us excited by spectacular feats of heroism. But if you are inattentive to the consequences of incremental change, you risk an unwarranted hopelessness that insults the quiet fortitude of those who have been chipping away at oppressive structures.

Bihar's Chief Minister Nitish Kumar explained the purpose of the caste-based survey in an interview[22] with NDTV: 'Our intentions are clear. We want to undertake this survey that will benefit all.' Critics have accused him of using the exercise to shore up his dwindling support ahead of the general elections in

2024—their argument is that by decisively enumerating 'lower castes' as the majority in his state, Kumar is hoping to consolidate an electoral majority that would win him seats. Wearing a brown pullover and checked muffler, the canny seventy-one-year-old politician who has ruled Bihar almost uninterrupted from 2005 appeared unfazed with these allegations: 'Our intentions have been clear from the beginning. We want this survey so that government can function in a better way.'

Many critics have long considered Kumar to be nothing more than a rank opportunist. During the 1980s, he created and strengthened the Janata Dal in Bihar alongside emerging politicians Lalu Prasad Yadav and Ram Vilas Paswan. However, he parted ways with them in 1995 to join forces with the BJP. Although born into the Kurmi community, ritually stigmatised as 'lower caste', he appeared to have no compunctions dealing with the BJP, a party towards which the 'higher castes' easily gravitated. In 2005, he led his coalition with the BJP to electoral victory and became chief minister of the state for the first time. He consolidated his grip in 2010 when the coalition won an even larger mandate. By 2013, however, the emergence of Narendra Modi as the BJP's star campaigner and prime ministerial candidate unnerved him. He ditched the seventeen-year-old coalition and rejoined Yadav in 2015 to decisively win state elections under the aegis of a grand alliance of centre-left parties called Mahagathbandhan. But by 2017, he dumped the Mahagathbandhan and teamed up with the BJP again. Together, they won the 2019 general elections as well as the 2020 state elections. And then, by August 2022, Kumar once again jumped ship, returning to the Mahagathbandhan. Uncannily, with a brief exception of a few months, Nitish Kumar managed to retain the seat of the chief minister throughout this period.

Despite his political dexterity, Kumar's position on the caste survey was remarkably consistent. Even when in alliance with the BJP, he had sought to convince them of the efficacy of such a move. Indeed, cabinet approval to the exercise was granted in June 2022, when both Kumar and the BJP had been coalition partners. Before that, in 2021, Kumar had led an all-party delegation to Delhi in a bid to convince Prime Minister Modi of the merits of undertaking the caste survey on a national level. Predictably, the prime minister gave short shrift to the suggestion. His government averred that such an exercise was not administratively feasible.[23] But buoyed by support from friends and foes alike, Kumar decided to implement the survey despite the Centre's opposition. His task became easier when he severed ties with the BJP and allied with the Mahagathbandhan, whose leaders were committed to the caste survey.

Kumar's deputy Tejaswi Yadav echoed his boss. As chairperson of the Mahagathbandhan and Nitish Kumar's deputy, he appreciated the historic nature of the survey being carried out in the state. As Yadav told *The Economic Times*[24] in an interview, 'This survey will help us help the poor.' He went on to remind his audience about the long-standing demand for the caste survey in the state and the ways in which the central government had sought to scuttle the exercise. His critics accused Yadav of indulging in caste politics to remain politically relevant. To them, Yadav offered lessons in Indian history, culture and socio-economics. He reminded them of the persistence of caste-based discrimination in everyday life which debilitated social opportunities.

Tejaswi Yadav was the youngest of nine children. His father Lalu Prasad Yadav had been Bihar's chief minister from 1990 to 1998. His mother Rabri Devi took over the position when his father was accused of corruption in what has come to be called the 'fodder scam'. The senior Yadav then allied with the Congress-led United Progressive Alliance (UPA) in 2004. He had strongly advocated, alongside like-minded coalition partners, for a Socio-Economic Caste Census (SECC) that would tally the population of different caste groups and relate them to social and economic indicators. The SECC had been undertaken in 2011, but the UPA government fell before its findings could be made public. In 2015, father and son took to the streets in Patna, demanding that the new BJP-led government release the SECC data. The government's response was that the data was riddled with errors (a swipe at the previous government's alleged incompetence) and could not be used. Unfazed, the duo demanded that caste data be collected when the next census would be undertaken in 2021.[25] The commitment of the leaders of the Mahagathbandhan to the caste survey can barely be exaggerated. Theirs was a demand no political party in Bihar could ignore, not even the BJP.

Lalu Prasad Yadav and Nitish Kumar had both established track records of crafting novel alliances. Schooled in the socialist politics of the 1970s, they had both watched in alarm as Hindu nationalists gradually began setting the political agenda across the country through the 1980s. By the end of that decade, Bihar appeared to follow India into the spiral of anti-Muslim hatred. The cauliflowers planted on the outskirts of a small Bihari town in the winter of 1989 bore testimony to the outcomes of hatred spawned by Hindu nationalism. They also paved the way for the innovative social coalitions that came to define Bihar's politics through the next three decades.

Bhagalpur, 1989

Bhagalpur is a small town straddling the Ganga in the eastern part of Bihar. In October 1989, it was abuzz with excitement. The agitation for the Ram temple in Ayodhya was gathering momentum and its votaries in Bhagalpur did not want to be left behind in the demonstrations of their fervour. They began collecting bricks to be transported to Ayodhya, where they would be donated for the purpose of constructing the temple. Processions were organised to appeal for donations across town. These appeals quickly degenerated into genocidal calls to either kill Muslims or deport them to Pakistan. The consequences were ghastly. Over a thousand Muslims in the town and its vicinity were butchered within a span of three days. In one grotesque instance, about twenty Muslim men and boys were marched off to the countryside, hacked to death and buried in the fields.[26] Cauliflowers were then planted over their corpses. At the time, the Bhagalpur violence was recognised as the worst instance of anti-Muslim rioting in independent India. It almost broke Bihar.

Yadav and Kumar were both colleagues in the newly minted Janata Dal alongside Ram Vilas Paswan. Heirs to a vibrant socialist tradition, they refused to let the conflict fester. In the national elections held barely a month after the violence, they reached out to Bihar's beleaguered Muslims and promised to protect them from the growing menace of Hindu nationalism. Breaching religious polarisation, the Janata Dal forged a social coalition unheard of between Dalits, 'lower castes' and Muslims. Not only did this coalition deliver massive electoral victories, it, more importantly, protected Muslims from the depredations of Hindu nationalism that had ripped apart the delicate social fabric elsewhere in northern and western India. Unlike those regions, 'lower castes' and Dalits in Bihar refused to become the foot soldiers of Hindutva. Instead, they rose to defend their Muslim neighbours whenever the 'high castes' in their neighbourhoods attempted to instigate a riot. As mentioned earlier, the Janata Dal government famously arrested Advani when his rath yatra entered Bihar, thereby preventing Hindu–Muslim strife from spilling over into the state.

This alliance continued long after the trio parted ways politically. Even as he aligned with the BJP, Nitish Kumar assiduously sought to cultivate peace between Hindus and Muslims. Early in his tenure as chief minister, he had ordered the mostly Muslim victims of violence to be compensated. His party's social base comprised communities further discriminated against within the broader 'lower caste', Dalit and Muslim groups. To emphasise, groups designated as Extremely Backward Classes, Mahadalit and Pasmanda Muslims suffer dual oppression: while belonging *to* marginalised social groups, they are marginalised *within* those groups. Kumar's coalition of such communities balanced his party's alliance with the BJP without compromising protection for the state's Muslims from the resurgence of Hindu nationalism. The cheques of compensation that his BJP home minister dispersed among Bhagalpur's riot victims supported some of the most impoverished households within the Muslim community.[27]

Beyond the Confines of Community

Demanding and executing a caste survey was nothing less than a gamble. As mentioned, critics alleged that Kumar and Yadav were undertaking the survey to consolidate their support among the state's OBCs, estimated at between 50 to 60 per cent of the population. But the Kurmi community to which Kumar belonged was likely to account for less than 5 per cent of Bihar's people. The Yadav community into which his deputy was born was unlikely to exceed 15 per cent.[28] The caste survey could well result in their political dominance being challenged, rather than endorsed, by members of other OBC communities who might feel underrepresented despite their larger numbers. Despite these potentially adverse outcomes, Kumar and Yadav committed themselves to the exercise since it offered opportunities for both politicians to build alliances with members of other OBC communities.

The creation of new alliances that promise to lay the foundations of a good life in the future is integral to hope. It widens horizons and allows people to consider the ambitions of others and recognise them as legitimate. As an emotion that enables people to reach out to others, hope also helps them to critically reflect on shared understandings and ambitions. What would a good life in the future look like? Who would it be 'good' for? How would it be different from (and better than) the present moment? Collective reflections on these questions encourages realistic consideration of the possibilities and limitations of emerging alliances.

In September 2013, a public meeting was organised in Patna by a nascent network of Dalit social activists to discuss proposals that would help address the socio-economic ostracism of the Rishdeo community, one of the state's twenty-two Dalit groups. I witnessed speaker after speaker marshall detailed statistics from successive census reports that testified to the overlapping disadvantages suffered by members who had recently been disparaged as Musahars or 'rat-eaters'. Towards the end of the meeting, the discussion turned to the need for collecting similar data for the state's OBC communities. 'Would the activists support the collection of such data for OBC groups who were often complicit in, or instigators of, violence against Dalits in the state?' one of the activists was pointedly asked. Without batting an eyelid, Ram Sada, the convener of the meeting, replied in the affirmative. 'Yes, the OBCs have been cruel to us,' he said, but immediately added, 'That cruelty cannot justify not collecting such crucial information about them.'

We are once again reminded of the historian Ernst Bloch's insistence that 'the emotion of hope makes people broad instead of confining them'. By supporting the enumeration of individual castes under the OBC category, the Dalits rose above their own mutual disagreements with the OBCs. By embracing the caste survey and the uncertainties it was sure to produce, both Kumar and Yadav accepted the possibility of their dominance being challenged by members of other communities that had hitherto been ostracised in their state. They were open to the likelihood that the days of wielding power were numbered. Neither leader refused to remain confined to the society with which they were affiliated, preferring instead to craft an alliance between communities that had historically been branded as 'lower caste'. As we have seen, such an alliance was hardly novel, building as it did on the template of OBC mobilisation of the 1980s.[29] But while that mobilisation floundered due to Yadav and Kurmi aggrandisement, the data promised by the caste survey was likely to reduce, rather than enhance, their dominance.

Hope Against Hate

Less than a week after the caste survey commenced, the Bapu Sabhagar in Patna was abuzz with excitement. The auditorium was hosting the convocation day for Nalanda Open University, Bihar's only university that imparts distance learning. Education Minister Professor Chandrashekhar was to address the freshly minted graduates. A committed leader of the Rashtriya Janata Dal (RJD), he used only one name.

Over the course of his speech,[30] Professor Chandrashekhar stressed the importance of education in achieving national greatness: 'A country can only become a great nation through education. Let me ask you—will India become great through education or through stupidity?'

His audience responded with one voice: 'Education.'

'Thank you,' the minister replied. He continued:

Unfortunately, in this country, there are views emanating from Nagpur [where the RSS headquarters are located] that education breeds arrogance … [T]here are those who believe in fomenting hatred and believe that hate will make our country a great nation. This is not a new phenomenon. The Manusmiriti did the same thing three thousand years ago. A few decades ago, the learned Babasaheb Ambedkar burnt copies of this text. Do you know why he did that? You can search online in your smartphones. He burnt the Manusmriti because that text bans education for marginalised people and for women. They had no right to education as per the authors of that text.

Professor Chandrashekhar paused as if to consider his next words. He then continued:[31] 'Nearly 700 years ago, Tulsidas wrote the Ramcharitmanas [referring to the Hindi-language rendition of the Ramayana created during the sixteenth century]. The text tells us "पूजिए विप्र शील गुण हीना … पूजिए न शूद्र ज्ञान प्रवीणा" [referring to a verse that urges followers to worship a Brahmin irrespective of how poorly they are educated but forbids them from worshipping a Shudra, no matter how well-educated they may be]. If such thoughts prevail, our dream of making India great cannot be fulfilled. It means that Dr Bhimrao Ambedkar, who was a learned man, is not worthy of reverence. Such texts spread hatred in our society.'

The minister quoted another reference from the Ramcharitmanas: जे बरनाधम तेलि कुम्हारा स्वपच किरात कोल कलवारा, and explained its explicit reference to communities such as Teli, Kumhar, Kahaar, Kol, Kalwar, Adivasis and Dalits as 'low-born'. The text further instructs followers as: अधम जाति में विद्या पाए ... भयहुं यथा अहि दूध पिलाए which means that 'lower castes become venomous once they are educated in the same way that a snake rears its fangs once it has drunk milk'.

The minister said, 'Such religious texts spread hatred. India cannot become great by spreading hatred. God and education are not beholden to any caste. Conservatives, status quoists and flawed pandits have labelled some castes as low, others as untouchable. But we were blessed to have had Babasaheb Ambedkar born among us. He liberated us from the shackles of caste.' He then went on to tell his audience of Ambedkar's extraordinary life and the hope it had offered millions of oppressed people.

Hope entails challenging hate. 'The struggle for hope,' the educator Paulo Freire insists, 'means the denunciation, in no uncertain terms, of all abuses.' To be hopeful is to expose and dissolve hatred. It involves questioning our most stubborn beliefs which, often unknown to us, perpetuate hate. Beliefs that some people are 'high caste', 'low caste', 'untouchable' or 'primitive' are what birth and sustain hatred. Hatred prevents solidarity.

Hope's work is strengthened by awareness. The knowledge that discrimination, segregation and hierarchy are not the natural order of things is essential in challenging hate. An awareness of the machinations through which some people seek to manipulate religious beliefs in order to subjugate others is necessary. Not for nothing did Ambedkar urge his followers to 'educate, agitate, organise', emphasising the foundational aspect of awareness to hope.

Being mindful that social hierarchies are human flaws, not divine ordinance, isn't just liberating—it also generates confidence in your identity. It offers a collective self-assurance that makes you proud of who you are. You no longer accept stigmatising narratives of your identity. Just as the dawn of day brings into perspective the frightening silhouettes that mark the night, an informed acknowledgement of the constructed nature of prejudices exposes them for what they are.

Professor Chandrashekhar's speech to students predictably riled 'upper-caste' commentators. Media reports condemned him for his 'obnoxious' remarks against a popular author and a divine epic. Demands were made to arrest him for offending the religious sensibilities of the Hindus. These calls were countered by a groundswell of support from the rank and file of the RJD. Alliance partners refused to condemn him. In neighbouring Uttar Pradesh, workers and politicians of the opposing Samajwadi Party came out in support of his remarks. A few days after the minister made his original remarks, a host of banners appeared in Lucknow. One simple message was emblazoned across them: *Garv se kaho hum Shudra hai*, a proclamation of pride in being Shudra.

Such a declaration was not one to be taken lightly. Shudra had historically been a demeaning term intended to humiliate members of communities considered 'low caste', 'backward' and 'impure'. It was now being reclaimed by the very same people. These appropriations helped cock a snook at the self-styled 'upper castes' and the disparaging vocabularies they had hitherto embraced. Shudra was no longer a term that would foment embarrassment, self-loathing and shame. It was something to be proud of.

The Great Chamar

An unassuming signboard appeared at the entrance to Ghadkoli village in Uttar Pradesh's Saharanpur district. The white text across its blue background greeted passers-by in the name of 'The Great Chamar', a reference to a leatherworking community historically labelled as untouchable. On the top left, the text read 'Jai Bhim', the standard Ambedkarite greeting that invokes the memory of Bhimrao Ambedkar, mirrored on the top right with the text 'Jai Bharat' as a mark of patriotism. The media reported the signboard as the first of its kind. As a marker of untouchability and pollution within the carefully graded caste hierarchy, the term 'Chamar' was associated with vulnerability, exploitation and discrimination. The signboard subverted that hierarchy and reclaimed 'Chamar' as an honorific, as a marker of pride rather than pity. 'The Great Chamar Ghadkauli *aapka abhinandan karta hai*' was what the signboard proclaimed to one and all. The Great Chamar Ghadkauli village greets you.

The proclamation of Chamar pride sparked a frenzy among the Thakurs, the dominant community in the village. Their agitation could be calmed down, they said, if two problematic words could be removed. 'Delete the word "great",' one proposed. 'Even better to remove the word "Chamar",' offered another. Both words suggested that Chamars were superior to members of other communities, they argued. 'Rubbish,' the Chamars retorted. 'They can put up boards declaring themselves as "Great Rajputs" and get on with it. This board and its words are not going anywhere.' After days of intense negotiations, the police were called. Led by a Brahmin, the police team agreed to the Thakurs' suggestions. The board could stay, but the two words offensive to the Thakurs would be blackened out. Under the watchful eyes of the Brahmin policeman, the Thakurs dutifully smeared out 'Great Chamar'.

It was at this point that someone made an urgent call to an outfit called the Bhim Army. Named after Bhimrao Ambedkar, the Bhim Army proffered a commitment to defend the constitutional principles of equality enshrined in the Indian Constitution. Unlike Ambedkar, however, the Bhim Army was willing to resort to violence if necessary. Within minutes, a phalanx of buzzing motorbikes vroomed into Ghadkauli. They confronted the policemen with a cultivated confidence. Their leader was a muscular man sporting a pair of shades, a handlebar moustache and an ink blue scarf. His name, like Bihar's education minister who was to rile the sentiments of the privileged castes a few years later, was Chandrashekhar. He also added the sobriquets Azad and Ravan: the former an Urdu word for freedom and the latter a reference to Ram's worthy antagonist in the much-loved epic Ramayana.

As the assembly around the signboard swelled that afternoon, the police called in reinforcements and assaulted the protestors. The Bhim Army stood alongside the Chamars and defended them ferociously. The ensuing fracas stunned the police and the Thakurs alike: cowing down the Chamars could no longer be taken for granted. The text that had been smeared out on the signboard was restored, the Thakurs made peace and the police were sent packing. Ravan's timely intervention had subverted Thakur dominance in Ghadkauli.

If social hierarchies are crafted by people, they can also be challenged by people. The very possibility of a contest, that something can be done about injustice, offers a vision for redressing the imbalance of power between those at the opposite ends of the social hierarchy. It also builds confidence among members of oppressed communities. This sense of pride and confidence offers people the hope that a new social order unencumbered by past hierarchies is in the offing. Assertions of Shudra pride and Chamar greatness are crucial to such hope.

The incident at Ghadkauli had not been the Bhim Army's first brush with authority. It was not going to be their last. A few years prior, Dalit students at a local college, funded and run by Thakurs, had complained of discrimination.[32] They were expected to sweep benches in the classrooms and sit in the back rows during the lessons. One Dalit boy had his hands broken because he had dared to drink water from a handpump while Thakur boys were waiting in a queue. After the Bhim Army intervened, such incidents reportedly declined. But the standoff at Ghadkauli proved to be a turning point.

In April 2017, members of the Chamar community attempted to erect a statue of Ambedkar at the entrance to the village to commemorate the scholar-statesman's birth anniversary. Thakur men objected, saying that the statue's finger pointed to a road used by Thakur women. They insisted that permission be sought from the district administration. A few weeks later, the Thakur community sought to take out a procession to commemorate the medieval Rajput hero Maharana Pratap. This time, members of the Chamar community objected. Had the Thakurs taken permission from the district administration, they asked. The Thakurs would have none of such impertinence. They retaliated by torching Chamar homes. The Chamars hit back by burning Thakur motorcycles. Full-blown rioting occurred across Saharanpur on

5 May 2017[33] during which one Thakur man died, asphyxiated by the fumes of a hutment to which he had set fire.

The Bhim Army was widely suspected of having instigated the members of the Chamar community. The Uttar Pradesh state government slapped cases against Ravan under the National Security Act. He was found guilty and imprisoned, ostensibly to 'prevent him from acting in any manner prejudicial to the defence of India, the relations of India with foreign powers, or the security of India'. However, such efforts to constrain Ravan were soon exposed as delusional. By September 2018, the state government was compelled to release him as no concrete evidence against him could be marshalled. Nevertheless, the spell in prison added to Ravan's mystique. Membership of the Bhim Army surged beyond Ravan's own Chamar community.

Ravan envisages the Bhim Army as an inclusive force that would be open to Bahujans of all communities. A votary of Dalit–Muslim unity, he has been especially eager to recruit members of Uttar Pradesh's largest religious minority to the Bhim Army. Although historical experiences of Dalits and Muslims in the region certainly differ, members of both groups suffer discrimination in the present time. Their shared experiences offer possibilities for mutual solidarity. While it is difficult to achieve, mutual solidarity allows people to support each other, to develop shared strategies and, at the very least, hear each other out.

It also widens people's perspectives. They realise that they are not alone. Although individual experiences may indeed be unique, they are not the only ones facing difficulties. It enables people to reach out to one another in times of trouble and lays the foundation for the creation of a collective identity that allows people of diverse backgrounds to work together. Rather than suffering alone in silence, mutual solidarity offers the possibility of raising one unified voice against the perpetrators of injustice.

Reclaiming Memory

On New Year's Day in 2018, approximately 2,00,000 people gathered before an obelisk in Bhima Koregaon village on the outskirts of Pune. They were part of an event organised by the Elgar Parishad that commemorated the bicentenary of the Battle of Bhima Koregaon. This battle had been one of the most decisive ones during the Third Anglo-Maratha War as it had established the East India Company's supremacy over western and central India. The war resulted in the defeat of the Peshwa, whose influence over eighteenth-century India was second only to that of the Mughal emperor. This defeat cleared the decks for the eventual establishment of the East India Company's rule and, subsequently, the British Raj. Fighting on the side of the Company were 800-odd members of the Mahar community who had been pilloried as 'untouchables' during the Peshwa's rule, and whose names were recorded by the victorious Company on the obelisk before which people had now assembled. This had been an annual gathering since at least 1927 when Bhimrao Ambedkar first led a commemorative meeting to celebrate the battle of Bhima Koregaon as not merely yet another chapter of British conquest over India but as a symbol of Dalit assertion against Peshwa rule.

The annual commemoration quickly became an important event in the calendars of Maharashtra's Dalits. As a symbol of successful assertion against Peshwa rule which had rigorously upheld Brahmanical values, the Battle of Bhima Koregaon was a matter of pride for a beleaguered tribe whose members were routinely disparaged as untouchables. Recognising its symbolic value as bolstering Dalit self-respect rather than as celebration of British conquest, postcolonial governments permitted the commemorations. Speeches would be made by Dalit leaders, young people would be able to bond with others and find confidence and the possibility of overturning unjust power hierarchies would be appreciated. The event on New Year's Day in 2018 should have been no different.

Except, three days before the event, a signboard materialised in nearby Vadhu Budruk at a site believed to be the grave of a seventeenth-century farmer, Govind Gopal Mahar. The signboard celebrated Mahar as having dared to defy Emperor Aurangzeb. The Mughals had defeated and killed the Maratha sovereign Chhatrapati Sambhaji Maharaj in battle and Aurangzeb had prohibited his brave adversary's cremation. Flouting this proclamation, Mahar performed the last rites of the dead sovereign, which the signboard celebrated over three centuries after the event. Its emergence provoked resentment among members of the village's dominant Maratha community. Mahar was untouchable, they claimed. How could he have performed their sovereign's last rites? In their version of history, it was their ancestors—Padmavati and Bapuji Buva, not Govind Gopal Mahar—who had stepped up to oppose the might of the Mughal emperor. The Marathas allegedly defiled the signboard. The Dalits filed cases against the Marathas. The Marathas seethed with resentment.

The gathering on New Year's Day offered the Marathas the opportunity to retaliate. On 31 December, the Elgar Parishad organised a conclave where prominent activists and leaders from across India were invited as speakers. Rohith Vemula's mother, Radhika Vemula, was present. As was Jignesh Mevani, a young Dalit politician from Gujarat, elected as an independent member of its legislative assembly. JNU student leader Umar Khalid was another speaker. Soni Sori, an Adivasi activist, also addressed the gathering. The speakers' support for subaltern assertions and the equation of the Hindutva with the Peshwai is said to have annoyed the Marathas who took it upon themselves to teach the Dalits a lesson. On 1 January 2018, 200 years after the Third Anglo-Maratha War that had extinguished the Peshwai in western India, a mob of Marathas attacked a section of the Dalits gathered at Bhima Koregaon.

The Dalits responded by filing legal complaints against the instigators of the mob. But the authorities dragged their feet. Eventually, when the police did swing into action a few months later, they arrested not the instigators of the mob but the individuals who had convened the Elgar Parishad! These included scholar Anand Teltumbde, researcher Rona Wilson, academic Shoma Sen, poet Varavara Rao, activists Arun Ferreira and Mahesh Raut, lawyers Sudha Bharadwaj and Surendra Gadling, journalist Gautam Navlakha, publisher Sunil Dhawale, priest Stan Swamy and others. They were accused of having Maoist links and being involved in a plot to kill Prime Minister Narendra Modi.

The individuals arrested in the aftermath of the Bhima Koregaon events exemplify a commitment to the solidarity which motivates and sustains hope. That individuals from relatively privileged social backgrounds were willing to stay in jail without pleading for mercy conveyed the conviction they harboured towards the cause of social justice and anti-caste politics. Stan Swamy died while in prison. Wilson, Sen, Gadling, Raut and Dhawale are still in prison at the time of writing. On the fourth anniversary of their arrest, they issued an open letter[34] through their lawyers, excerpts of which are reproduced below:

> ... Today, we wish to make it clear that what happened to us
> is not exceptional. Workers, students, writers, poets, scholars,
> journalists and even common people who have chosen to fight

against the ruling powers in the country on behalf of Dalits, tribals and the underprivileged, are all being targeted. Many are being put behind bars to stifle their dissent ...

... We all are committed to the same thought, same sensitivity. Unlike the rulers we have not abandoned our conscience. Even in the darkness of our confinement, our conscience is wide awake; on the contrary, our confinement has helped make it sharper.

All of us are committed to take up the cudgels for the labourers, the underprivileged and the downtrodden. From time to time we have raised our voice and have battled injustice, exploitation, plunder, discrimination and inequality. We know this ruthless world gives nothing without a fight and so our struggle has been first for food and then for liberation. We are proud inheritors of the thoughts and ideas of Charwak, Buddha, Kabir, Tukaram, Shivaji Maharaj, Bhagatsingh, Phule, Ambedkar and so on. Our history is full of a radiant fire which is the source of eternal inspiration for us. Naturally, we cherish being a part of this glorious heritage. We have not and we will not deviate from our course because we have unflinching faith in our ideas and our actions.

Is it any wonder that we have become like a thorn in the tender flesh of those who follow in the path of Brahminism, of Peshwa spirit, of the English and the Hitlerite imperialism? The irony is that those who are destroying the nation are being hailed as patriots and those who have toiled selflessly for the country are labeled as traitors. Logic has been abandoned to let loose the hysteric mobs. Religious polarisation is being promoted by spreading lies left right and centre. This hysteric nationalism is dragging the nation towards autocracy. In such a poisoned atmosphere, we are bound to be called traitors and jailed with the help of a web of untruths.

They think they can destroy us by imprisoning us; this hope of theirs of course, is futile. After four years, we have stayed alive and lively. In our confinement, there have been occasions when despair suffocated us momentarily; but never have we begged for mercy, nor cried nor written apologies. On the contrary, among us, one wrote poems on defiance, another composed songs on love, on freedom and we all sang them. We are writing stories and essays and books. One of us is busy exposing the sham of the case against us and another one is meticulously preparing our defence. Our counsels have demonstrated what steely resolve is. And there are those who have befriended other inmates in the jail and are working to create awareness and enlightenment among the prisoners.

A prison is a symbol of repression practiced by an anti-people regime and it automatically lacks the basic facilities which are considered by tradition as measures of development. It then follows that agitations and fights against injustice are frequent. You have to create your own space to make life in the prison bearable, humane. This is our constant fight ...

The period of four years we have spent here seems little before the long years some of the prisoners have behind them. Yet they smile through their hard days and nights, they have hope in their hearts even as they face inhuman conditions. Their indomitable hope, as also the books and other reading material breathes life into us.

These compassionate and sensitive people become our solace in the midst of the terrible violence that the newspapers report ... all of us are sensitive and emotional human beings of all ages from young, to middle-aged to old. And because we are human beings, we practice politics of transformation and that is why we continue to fight for humanity even inside this prison ...

It is now four years since we have been detained and are deprived of the love, the company and the attachment of our near and dear ones. Our hearts too beat for love and liberty. But it is your steadfastness, your courage, your strength and your patience with which you too endure our absence; which are a great source of resolve for us. You set an example for us to understand the nature of trust and closeness of relationship; we learn from you how fight and love coexist ... you show us that it is love that is being reflected in togetherness, in unity, in people's voice and our voice.

... It is a fact that we have entered an age of darkness, yet history bears out that the empires built on the foundation of oppression did exist and did flourish; but in the end, all were reduced to rubble. This one too will have to go one day. It is the call of the time that we join hands to create a better world. As we will fight the attacks on our fundamental rights, we also shall fight to create a better, just, equitable and compassionate world. Millions suffering from injustice and oppression are coming together to give shape to a force that will break the shackles of those who think differently; because the oppressive regime and their white lies themselves are feeding power to the people's resolve. Let us look forward to the day when Sahir's prophesy comes alive.

We await the dawn when the earth stirs and the prisoners are out the abodes of sin crash and chains of injustice break and the rulers of that world will have no use of jails. We shall create that dawn.

We shall create that dawn. With that, the prisoners invoked the poet Sahir Ludhianvi's memorable couplet to remind their readers that no regime, however unjust and tyrannical, lasts forever. They recognised that the hardships they were enduring paled in comparison to what others are being subjected to. Above all, they appreciated the solidarity they had been offered and highlighted that as the strength that saw them through their confinement.

Generating solidarity is, however, not always possible. The networks required to build it can be a luxury few can afford. After all, such networks assume that oppressed communities possess, or can mobilise, adequate reserves of social capital. Solidarity relies on the compassion of others, their kindness and a shared conviction that working together is not merely strategically viable but morally imperative. Its creation is no easy task. In its absence, communities often have little option but to soldier on by themselves, spurred singularly by the conviction that they are doing the right thing.

Striking for Hope

Through the monsoon season of 2016, India was rocked by chilling images of seven Dalit labourers who had been lynched by cow protection vigilantes. They had been skinning cattle carcasses in the village of Una, Gujarat, when they were brutally beaten to death on the street. The vigilantes even filmed the entire episode and uploaded it on social media as a warning to all.

As the video went viral, Dalits across the state of Gujarat were furious. They responded with unprecedented protests. A fortnight after the lynching, social workers Nathubhai Parmar and Maheshbhai Rathod along with businessman Hirabhai Chawda obtained permission for a rally that would culminate at Una's apex district office. The administration was reluctant at first but gave in. On the afternoon of 18 July, when the rally was to converge on the district office, the authorities encountered a rude shock. Using Facebook, WhatsApp and other social media, the trio had mobilised almost 1,500 Dalits to travel to the district office with as many carcasses of dead cattle as they could find.

'The district superintendent of police was shocked to see the carcasses but then I just showed him the permission letter for the rally—it didn't say you can't bring carcasses!' the trio chuckled when *Scroll* reporter Shoaib Daniyal asked them about their daring.[35] The rallyists began dumping the carcasses they had brought with them in front of the district office and left. The alarmed officials pleaded with local Dalits to clear out the carcasses but to no avail. Over the next few days, Dalits across Gujarat struck work and refused to clear out the carcasses of dead cows. 'The cow is your mother, you better look after it,' they declared. As carcasses piled up, the administration pressed earth movers and chemicals into the work of carcass disposal. In the meantime, rallies and protests against the Una lynching continued, culminating in an assembly of thousands of people in Una on India's sixty-ninth Independence Day.[36] Gujarat's chief minister was ultimately forced to resign.

Two social activists I met in Ahmedabad a while after these events gushed about the importance of the strike. Neither of the two activists were Dalit, nor had they been involved in organising it. 'There are few things in Gujarat about which we are hopeful,' Maniben told me. 'Actually, we were beginning to think that hope was the problem. People believe that things will magically improve. But they don't, do they?' she continued, her words reminding me of Hannah Arendt's warning against hope, how it deludes people into believing that things will become better when, in fact, they only become worse. Tears welled up in Mirzabhai's eyes. 'We really were starting to think this was all pointless. And then the manual scavengers show us the way. They took matters into their hands. They showed us the light.'

The myriad mobilisations against caste across India have understandably generated mixed results. Caste manifests differently in different regions, shaped by demographic balance, socio-cultural histories and political economy. Any attempt at airbrushing these complexities with simplistic formulations of 'two castes' risks neglecting the rich tapestry that constitutes the mosaic of Indian society. That tapestry is not always pretty. But it is what makes India what it is.

Mobilisations against caste have punctuated Indian society for as long as caste has existed. Contemporary mobilisations against caste draw on this dynamic heritage with the added leverages of electoral democracy and affirmative action. These leverages spur anxieties among privileged communities who worry about their impending loss of dominance. The overwhelming support enjoyed by the BJP among members of these communities suggests that they view the party as a conduit for preserving their caste privilege while consecrating a broader Hindu identity. However, contrary to expectations that such an identity will contain anti-caste assertions, the last decade has witnessed the proliferation of popular movements as well as official policies to make the voices of historically oppressed people count.

The hope fostered by such mobilisations against caste offers important lessons for students across the country. Many among them face discrimination based on their caste identity on a daily basis. Others cope with different varieties of discrimination, anchored in gender, ethnicity, religion and political beliefs. It is to the hopes harboured by India's students that we now turn.

Students on the Streets

Death in the Hostel

In the early hours of 17 January 2016, a twenty-six-year-old student was found hanging in room 207 of the Hyderabad Central University. He had been enrolled in the university's Centre for Knowledge Innovation and Culture Studies as a doctoral student and had been a recipient of the prestigious (and highly competitive) Junior Research Fellowship for his research on science, technology and society. The student had topped the PhD interview and had been awarded the fellowship by the Council of Scientific and Industrial Research (CSIR), India's largest research and development organisation overseen by the Ministry of Science and Technology. His name was Rohith Chakravarthy Vemula.

As a doctoral scholar, Vemula refused to be confined to his books and laboratories. He was also a social activist, keen on making India a better place for members of its historically oppressed communities. He joined the Students' Federation of India (SFI), a union affiliated with the Communist Part of India (Marxist), or the CPI(M), but was quickly frustrated with its abstract theorisation of Indian society and politics. Along with his friend Chintagada Ramji, he became a member of the

Ambedkar Students' Association (ASA), a politically unaffiliated organisation committed to the social assertion of marginalised communities across India. As vice-president of the ASA, Vemula was often involved in events to provoke discussion, debate and introspection among members of the general public.

One such event was a prayer meeting held on 30 July 2015 in memory of Yakub Memon, who had been hanged a few hours prior. Memon had been accused of organising funds that led to the infamous Bombay bombings, a series of twelve bomb blasts that had ripped through India's financial capital in March 1993, killing over 250 people. His execution prompted nationwide debate on the continuation of capital punishment and the death penalty. Vemula's participation in the prayer meeting prompted his rivals in the ABVP, the student wing of the BJP, to accuse the ASA of harbouring anti-national sentiments. They alleged that the prayer meeting was designed to whip up communal passions and could have been a threat to public order (it wasn't).

The ensuing war of words between the ASA and the ABVP quickly led to fisticuffs. The exact sequence of events is hotly contested, but one of the ABVP students alleged that Vemula and four of his friends in the ASA assaulted him. This allegation spurred a flurry of letters exchanged between the university administration, the incoming vice-chancellor and the union Ministry of Human Resource Development which oversaw the disbursement of the fellowship to Vemula. All agreed that a suspension was needed to teach the 'anti-national' students a lesson. The university administration suspended Vemula and his friends from the university, barred him from using hostel accommodation and stripped him of his fellowship. In desperation, Vemula took his own life.

'I believe that I can travel to the stars'

Desperation would hardly appear to be the place to look for hope. It is, after all, the very opposite of it. When desperation leads you to take your own life, it is usually because you feel there is no hope. Nothing seems worth living for.

When desperation is wrought by institutional violence, as was the case during the winter of 2015 in Hyderabad, hopelessness looms even larger. By rescinding his fellowship, Vemula's university systemically targeted him, intending to teach him a lesson for falling out of line. The aim was to discipline him for indulging in activities that university authorities and its majoritarian students did not approve of. A plethora of rules, norms and actions were invoked, designed to subdue Vemula and his friends into submission.

Vemula preferred to die than to be thus disciplined. In his suicide note, he writes:

> People may dub me as a coward. And selfish, or stupid once I am gone. I am not bothered about what I am called. I don't believe in after-death stories, ghosts, or spirits. If there is anything at all I believe, I believe that I can travel to the stars. And know about the other worlds.[1]

Death was freedom. Vemula had declared his independence.

Individual Failure or Institutional Murder?

Vemula's death, and the eloquent suicide note he left behind, sparked public outrage. The institutional response—from the university, the police, the ministry—was to pin the blame on the troubled mind of a struggling student. Smriti Irani, the union minister for Human Resource Development under whose remit the educational institutions fall, constantly referred to Vemula as a child. Urging people not to politicise the death of a 'child', Irani pointed to the parts of his suicide letter in which he had urged readers not to blame anyone else for his death. In speeches infused with theatrics that drew on her dazzling career as the lead star in one of the most successful Indian soap operas, the minister admonished those demanding an institutional inquiry into Vemula's death as playing politics over the corpse of a 'child'.

Such repeated attempts at infantilising Vemula failed miserably. As a doctoral scholar, Vemula had led a famously political life espousing a range of progressive causes, from upholding transgender rights to abolishing the death penalty. As a member of the ASA, he had frequently clashed with the ABVP, leading them to label him 'anti-national'. Above all, Vemula had relentlessly battled caste discrimination within the campus and outside of it, demanding that institutions of higher education treat members of India's historically oppressed communities with dignity. Born to and brought up by a Dalit woman, Vemula was all too familiar with the insidious ways in which caste operated. The humiliation wrought by caste—not only against him and his mother as individuals but also against Dalits as a collective—further politicised him.

The University of Hyderabad had witnessed eight suicides by students of Dalit backgrounds over the previous decade. These deaths were not merely caused due to discrimination by fellow students. Rather, they bore the brunt of institutional indifference, if not hostility. Back in 2008, for example, doctoral scholar Senthil Kumar found out that he was the only student who had not been allocated a supervisor even after being enrolled in the programme for a year.[2] The university also halted his scholarship on grounds that he had not cleared his backlog of exams and assignments. Staring into the abyss, Senthil Kumar died by suicide. The university's fact-finding committee reported that the institution had, in fact, relaxed its rules about scholarship a week before Senthil Kumar's death but wilfully withheld this information from him! It was into this callous institutional milieu that Vemula had enrolled, fully aware of the struggles that awaited him. To dismiss him as a 'child' despite his political awareness represented a blatant attempt at undermining his understanding of the world around him.

Ferment in Hyderabad

Defying the minister's command, and consonant with his short political life, Vemula's death sparked immediate outrage among students across India. In Hyderabad, hours after news of Vemula's death trickled out, batches of students began a relay hunger strike,[3] demanding the removal of the Vice-Chancellor Appa Rao Podile for failing in his duty of care. They called for him to be booked under the Prevention of Atrocities Against SC/ST Act (1989), more popularly called the Atrocities Act, for his role in facilitating institutional discrimination against Dalit students such as Vemula and his friends. Finally, they demanded the introduction of a Rohith Act, which would prevent discrimination against students from marginalised communities across the country.

Students at the University of Hyderabad convened a joint action committee to coordinate these demands. Over the next few months, more joint action committees mushroomed across India, with students, teachers and workers combining forces to intensify protests. They rebutted allegations that Vemula's suicide had resulted from his loneliness rather than the institutionalised discrimination to which he was subjected. Even more importantly, they sought to dispel the canard that Vemula was not Dalit. This was crucial to their claim that he and his friends had been discriminated against because of their caste. The Atrocities Act could not be invoked if it could somehow be proved that the victim was not Dalit.

Supported by sympathetic journalists, committee members assembled evidence of Vemula's caste identity. Vemula's mother Radhika was born into the Mala community, designated as a Scheduled Caste, or Dalit, in Andhra Pradesh. She was adopted by a family from a privileged caste, which provided her shelter but treated her as a maidservant.[4] Her adopted mother arranged her marriage to a man of the Vaddera community, classified as OBC in the state. However, the man turned out to be an alcoholic and a wife-beater, so Radhika left him soon after Rohith was born and returned to live in her adopted mother's home. Rohith Vemula was brought up by his mother and shared in her joys and sorrows, including the experience of discrimination she faced due to her identity. Rohith's upbringing as the son of an 'untouchable' maidservant in a privileged caste household proved his Dalit identity, committee members contended.

These efforts hit a brick wall of official antipathy. The Roopkanwal Commission constituted by the university in the wake of the suicide exonerated the institution of any responsibility. It declared that Vemula's frustration with worldly affairs led him to end his life. The suicide note in which he refused to blame anyone for his decision was used by the Commission against him. The Commission went beyond its mandate and claimed that Vemula was not even Dalit since his father was OBC! Its conclusion defied a Supreme Court judgment from 2012 which decreed that the caste of a child born of inter-caste marriage could not automatically be derived from the caste of the father but would instead depend on the circumstances in which they were brought up. As K. Laxminarayana, former president of the University of Hyderabad Teacher's Association, noted in an article for the *Economic and Political Weekly*, Vemula's 'lived experience, his social identity and his membership of the Ambedkar Students' Association affirm his Dalit identity beyond a shadow of doubt'.[5]

Official antipathy could not stonewall the outpouring of support and solidarity. Students at the university turned to art as a medium for expressing their outrage.[6] The campus was awash with murals, graffiti and posters. One mural was especially poignant. It portrayed Vemula with a cheerful defiance, looking squarely into the eyes of the beholder. Drawn by Sreelakshmi, a student at the university, the mural departed from tropes of sympathy and pity that are all too commonly associated with Dalit life. Instead, Vemula is presented as confident, his eyes containing a vision of a hopeful political future. Poignantly, as well as presciently, Sreelakshmi titled her work of art *1989–forever*.[7]

Reverberations

Vemula's suicide galvanised the nation.[8] Students at Hyderabad's Osmania University went on a hunger strike. Their counterparts at the city's Maulana Azad Urdu University took out a candlelight march. In nearby Nizamabad's Telengana University, they burnt effigies of the Human Resource Development minister. A Joint Action Committee for Social Justice (JAC) was formed by students, academics and social activists. Committee members called on students, teachers and allies from across the country to support the protesting students in Hyderabad. Students from as far as Calicut, Delhi and Kolkata responded and converged on the city in a massive show of solidarity.

Beyond Hyderabad, people from across social backgrounds poured out onto the streets. In South Mumbai,[9] students from Tata Institute of Social Sciences, Indian Institute of Technology-Bombay, Tata Institute of Fundamental Research and colleges affiliated with Mumbai University rallied alongside workers and social activists in the southern and central parts of the city. Vemula's friends addressed the rallyists, as did social activists from the city along with Prakash Ambedkar, B.R. Ambedkar's grandson. Students of Delhi University and Jamila Milia Islamia organised rallies in support of their peers in Hyderabad and Mumbai.

In Phule Nagar, a low-income neighbourhood in north Mumbai, community members pooled resources to establish a small one-room library and education centre, which they named after Vemula.[10] In a community where private space is at a premium, this one-room centre offers students the opportunity to study in peace and quiet, away from the hustle and bustle of their homes. The wooden cupboard in the centre doubles as a library. In it are some books that help young people in the community prepare for school, college and competitive exams. Also featured are works of literature that children can read for leisure. Finally, students use the blank notebooks that the coordinators regularly provide to take notes as they reflect on their lessons from school. For a people whose marginalisation has hinged on preventing their access to education, Vemula's spirit infuses the centre and every individual who passes through it.

Students living as far afield as Kolkata and Delhi undertook hunger strikes to protest Vemula's institutional murder. Deborshi Chakaraborty, a Kolkata-based research fellow at the University of Berkeley, was one such student.[11] Pabitra Das, pursuing a PhD in computer science from the University of Calcutta, was another.[12]

In an open letter, Das wrote: 'With the injustice done to Rohith Vemula by the BJP ministers and the Hyderabad University VC, the entire Dalit student community is feeling humiliated and alienated. The only ray of hope is that students are protesting all over the country against this.' Chakraborty and Das were joined by three students from Delhi's Jawaharlal University (JNU). V. Lenin Kumar was a former president of the JNU Students' Union. Shubhanshu Singh was studying for a degree in political science and, like Vemula and Das, was born into a Dalit community. Suchishree was a second-year master's student in geography.[13] She signed off her note outlining the reasons for refusing food: 'This indefinite hunger strike I do not see as an appeal to the state but as a means to regain from the state the basic human dignity that is rightfully ours.'

I was in Patna a few weeks after Vemula's suicide, scoping out a research project on migration. In that context, I met some stellar university students to understand their perspectives on leaving their homes in rural Bihar to study in its capital. The city's students called out the stench of institutional discrimination against their peers in no uncertain terms. With backgrounds in very different communities, classes and regions, they saw through the obfuscation attempted by rival students, the university management and the ministry. They did not always agree with Vemula's politics. Some of them suggested that his brilliance was overstated. But that the torture to which he was subjected could only be attributed to his background as a Dalit was a common refrain.

The outpouring of solidarity in support of Vemula revealed the unlikely pairing of pain and hope. Vemula's suicide certainly crushed many aspirations as it exposed institutional antipathy towards students who dared question the status quo. They sought solace in each other's company under the shroud of grief. Thinking beyond themselves, reaching out to each other, comforting one another to mitigate the collective pain they were enduring, they mourned. This not only helped them cope with their immediate loss but it also helped them to think about what they could do to address the injustice of Vemula's death. Eventually, rays of light pierced through the pall of gloom as students from across the country organised and agitated together, beyond their institutional affiliations, social backgrounds and economic circumstances.

Hope begets togetherness. It helps us pick up the shards of the present and piece them together to produce something entirely new and unexpected. The students mourning Vemula's suicide did not allow their grief to turn them into inert repositories of fear. Instead, they channelled their sorrow in the benefit of a broader cause: the reclamation of human dignity. Few had expected the death of a Dalit student in southern India to galvanise students across the entire country. By defying such expectations, the students and their allies embodied and enlivened hope.

Vemula would have celebrated his thirtieth birthday on 27 January 2016, nearly two weeks after his death. To commemorate the occasion, nearly 8,000 people congregated in Nagpur,[14] a city famous for its oranges and host to two of India's political icons. Towards the east of the city sits the headquarters of the RSS, the paramilitary organisation that has sought to mould India into a Hindu rashtra since 1925. Six kilometres to its west, across the River Nag that flows through the city, lending it its name, is the four-acre Deeksha Bhoomi, a public park where Ambedkar led over 5 lakh of his followers to Buddhism in 1956. The people gathered in Nagpur in the wake of Vemula's death had dressed themselves in white, the colour of the Navayana Buddhist sect to which Ambedkar and his followers converted, and marched silently from the Deeksha Bhoomi to the RSS headquarters. No slogans were raised, no speeches made. Just a quiet protest against the caste discrimination that symbolised the 2,500-year-old clash between Buddhism and Brahmanism in India—a discrimination that has taken Vemula's life. Vemula's mother and brother returned to Deeksha Bhoomi later that year on 14 April to celebrate Ambedkar's 125th birth anniversary and follow in his footsteps to renounce Hinduism and embrace Buddhism.

Sedition in the Capital

Within weeks of Vemula's death, JNU found itself engulfed in controversy. No stranger to contentious politics and well-known for the numerous shades of left-wing politics among its members, the institution was faced with an unprecedented threat from the central government. This threat would, ironically and unintentionally, strengthen the bonds of solidarity among students across the country.

Located in south-western Delhi, abutting the urban village of Munirka and the plush residential colony of Vasant Vihar, JNU is a world apart from its surroundings. Its leafy campus hosts student housing and staff quarters, academic departments and lecture rooms, as well as a variety of dhabas, or eateries. The dhabas offer sustenance to the students by providing low-cost meals and the opportunity to gossip as well as debate the contours of socialist revolution, if and when it arrived. Posters and banners bearing revolutionary slogans condemning capitalism and oppression of all sorts overwhelm the visual senses on a typical day. The vibrant nightlife on campus contrasts with that of the rest of Delhi, which is dull at best and threatening at worst. Like any campus-based university, JNU's sprawling estate housed a universe of its own, operating according to its own distinct rhythm that was usually unaffected by its surroundings.

The controversy that erupted in JNU in February 2016 smashed that idyll. On 9 February, students organised a rally to commemorate the third anniversary of the execution of Afzal Guru. Guru had been convicted for his role in an attack on the Indian Parliament back in 2001, although human rights activists believed that his trial was flawed. Guru's death was condemned as a judicial murder in his home state of Jammu and Kashmir, where politicians and protestors alike celebrated him as a hero. The event in JNU had been planned as a cultural evening by students associated with the ultra-left Democratic Students' Union (DSU). Titled 'The country without a post office' after a collection of poems by Kashmiri-American poet Agha Shahid Ali, the event's poster styled itself as:

> Against the Brahmanical 'Collective Conscience'!
> Against the judicial killing of Afzal Guru & Maqbool Bhatt
> In solidarity with the struggle of the Kashmiri people
> For their democratic right to self-determination.[15]

ABVP, the right-wing student branch of the BJP, called on the university administration to ban the event. Fearing clashes, the administration caved in and withdrew permission for the event barely twenty minutes before it was to commence. The DSU complied. Members agreed to convene a meeting at one of the campus's famed dhabas rather than a political rally, as had been originally planned. They sought help from the JNU Students' Union (JNUSU) as well as other leftist student groups to gather in support of their democratic right to hold peaceful meetings. Members of these unions agreed immediately and assembled not so much in support of the meeting's agenda (with which many of them may well have dissented) but to defend the democratic freedom of expression. Meanwhile, the administration banned the use of microphones in a bid to literally mute the voices of the students. ABVP students also arrived at the venue. They began shouting slogans reiterating the official claim that all of Kashmir belongs to India: *'Ye Kashmir hamara hai, sara ka sara hamara hai.'*

'Hum kya chahte? Azadi!', the organisers of the meeting chanted in response. What do we want? Independence. The slogan, a popular intonation used in protests, was meant to resonate with Kashmiri demands for autonomy and signalled student solidarity with the people of Jammu and Kashmir. It was an important message conveying a modicum of support from a slice of the Indian population for their struggles. The slogan acknowledged the troubled history of the state, its emergence as a battleground between India and Pakistan, and the repression meted out to its people. The call for azadi or independence echoed a yearning among many people in the state to live their lives unencumbered by what they perceived as military occupation. Such yearnings are met with little sympathy and plenty of hostility from other Indians, enlarging the gulf between the state and the rest of the country. Kashmir's issues are largely viewed through the prism of national security. Instead of appreciating the rich cultural tapestry that runs through the state linking it to the rest of the country, most Indians perceive their fellow citizens in Kashmir to be potential incubators of terrorism.

'Tum kitne Afzal maaroge, har ghar se Afzal niklega,' the organisers amped up their challenge. You can kill as many Afzals as you want, every house will produce an Afzal. This slogan was undoubtedly provocative for nationalistic Indians but signalled

an understanding of Kashmiri resentment against the excessive militarisation of their state. This militarisation was enabled by the Armed Forces (Special Powers) Act (AFSPA), which allows the government to hold prisoners without trial. Civilians are known to have been detained for as many as two years without charges,[16] prompting concerns about the violation of human rights by international observers as well as domestic critics. The Indian government justifies the Act on grounds that its repeal would embolden terrorists. Whatever be the merit of such justifications, its existence alienates civilians who may not otherwise harbour separatist sympathies. The students at that meeting recognised these realities. In a short note published in *Scroll* within a week of the event, JNU student Harshit Agarwal—who professed no sympathy for either Afzal Guru or the cause of Kashmiri separatism—wrote that '[the students] are not carrying guns, they are carrying ideas'.[17]

Ideas are more than the words we speak or the thoughts we think. They convey the imagination of the worlds in which we live, and of the worlds in which we would like to. They challenge us to be adventurous, to think beyond the confines imposed by authority and to question assumptions we all too often take for granted. To be clear, not all ideas are good: the world is awash with terrible ones that have inflicted immense harm on humanity. However, the ideas conveyed by the slogans at that meeting at JNU provoked their audience to think about the troubles visited upon the people of Kashmir, their collective aspirations to lead dignified lives and, above all, their humanity. Unshackled by the dominant nationalistic presumptions that sought to suppress any alternative political attachments, JNU's students amplified opinions that jarred the jingoism of the time. A tiny corner of India's national capital was voicing ideas in support of a beleaguered minority that accounted for less than 2 per cent of the country's population.

Two further slogans were now heard. One of these claimed 'Bharat ke barbadi tak jung rahegi' which mainstream TV media promptly reported as 'We will fight till India is destroyed'. Distasteful as it sounds, this slogan represented the opinions of a section of the population in the Kashmir Valley. Indeed, it was subsequently suggested that this slogan was not raised by JNU students at all but by Kashmiri students unaffiliated with JNU who were in attendance. The other slogan heard was 'Pakistan zindabad', translated simply as 'Long live Pakistan' to celebrate India's western neighbour. This last slogan, it later emerged, was shouted by the activists of the ABVP to incite public opinion against the organisers of the meeting.

The ABVP pounced on the sloganeering with glee. Within days, they had lodged formal complaints against the organisers of the meeting as well as the JNU Students' Union. Complaints were filed with the university administration, the Delhi Police and the Ministry of Human Resource Development. India's Home Minister Rajnath Singh tweeted out condemnations of the event. Misinformed by 'inputs' from party colleagues, he alleged that the event and the associated sloganeering had been orchestrated by terrorists based in Pakistan.[18] Soon after, the police swooped down on the campus and arrested Kanhaiya Kumar, the president of the JNU Students' Union. He was charged with sedition and criminal conspiracy, invoking a law that had been promulgated under British colonialism way back in 1860 and had been used to suppress Indian nationalism. In essence, the current government enthusiastically deployed a tool from the era of the British Raj upon Indian students.

Reclaiming Nationalism

Nationalism is a potent force. It can be a soothing balm as well as a toxic potion. On the one hand, it can generate a political inclusion that regards every human living within the territory of a nation state as worthy of equal respect, thus dismantling hierarchies such as caste, class, gender, religion and sexual orientation. On the other hand, it can create a political exclusion that demands total obeisance to the imagined territory of a nation state with little or no regard for the human beings that dwell in it. As a soothing balm, it can heal wounds inflicted by historical inequalities. As a toxic potion, it can inject poison into those very same wounds, resulting in festering sores. Nothing about harbouring nationalist pride necessitates the subordination of other viewpoints or the demonisation of dissenters. Yet, it is easier to do exactly that in order to prove one's own nationalistic credentials.

A view of nationalism was offered by Kanhaiya Kumar himself. The evening before his arrest, Kumar delivered a stirring speech at the steps of one of JNU's campus buildings. Ignored by the mainstream media but recorded on mobile camera, the JNUSU president reminded Indians that the nation is not a piece of territory. It is made up of real people. Patriotism is not about chest-thumping against imagined 'anti-nationals'—it is about treating people as equals, including the poor, the marginalised, Muslims, other minorities and women. It is about respecting the Constitution, which promises freedom of expression. 'You have killed Rohith [Vemula]. But we will not let that happen here. We will not let Rohith's sacrifice go in vain,' he vowed. Closing his speech with the twin salutations of 'Jai Bhim' and 'Lal Salaam'—entwining the emancipatory greetings associated with Ambedkarites and leftists—Kumar made the case for a less inflammatory sort of patriotism.

But on the other side of the fence, the toxicity of nationalism was amplified by India's mainstream English-language media. They especially hounded Umar Khalid, who had initially conceived the idea of a meeting to commemorate Guru's death anniversary. A staunch communist, Khalid is atheist. But that did not deter the Indian media from latching on to his Muslim name to portray him and his friends at JNU as 'anti-national'.[19] Arnab Goswami, host of *The Newshour* programme, told Khalid on the show, 'You are more dangerous than the Maoist terrorists.' *News X* host Rahul Shivshankar proclaimed Khalid to be a sympathiser of the Jaish-e-Mohammed, a terrorist group that seeks the secession of Kashmir from India and its merger with Pakistan. *India Today* claimed that Khalid made '800 calls to Jammu and Kashmir' in the week before the meeting, insinuating that he had encouraged the Kashmiri students to join the meeting and chant anti-India slogans. They aggressively targeted a lone student bearing a Muslim name among the five charged with sedition. It was, after all, much easier to display one's nationalist credentials in Hindu India against a Khalid than against a Kumar.

Against these canards, students across the country rallied to reclaim nationalism. Students and staff at JNU held a public meeting to 'save JNU' and to protest the inability of the vice-chancellor to protect their university as a site of dissent.[20] Students at Kolkata's Jadavpur University took out rallies in support of their comrades at JNU, shouting slogans demanding azadi not just for Kashmir but also for the north-eastern states of Manipur and Nagaland.[21] In Hyderabad's Osmania University, students gathered in front of the Arts College to protest Kumar's arrest and defend the right to dissent. Students and faculty at the Aligarh Muslim University organised a protest meeting in support as well. Universities as far apart as Panjab University in Chandigarh and University of Kerala in Thiruvananthapuram witnessed an outpouring of encouragement in favour of the beleaguered students at JNU.[22] In Mumbai, the Joint Action Committee for Social Justice amplified the protests, drawing parallels between Vemula's institutional murder and the crackdown on JNU's students. While Khalid and the other students charged with sedition were forced into hiding and Kumar was arrested and sent into custody, students across India's universities were reminding everyone else about the value of criticism in strengthening, rather than weakening, a nation.

Raids continued across Delhi as the city's police hunted for the five JNU students as if they were hardened criminals.[23] Umar Khalid and his friend Anirban Bhattacharya came out of hiding, surrendering to the police within ten days, and were taken into custody. Three others—Rama Naga, Ashutosh Narayan and Anant Prakash—refused to surrender but remained available for questioning as and when required.[24] Kumar, who was already in custody, was accosted by lawyers in court and physically assaulted for his allegedly 'seditious' speeches. The police, who were responsible for his safety, looked the other way.

Since the charges against him couldn't stick, Kumar was granted bail on 2 March 2016. The following evening, he addressed a packed audience at JNU, a black jacket over his white vest.[25] The atmosphere was carnivalesque, replete with drumbeats. Aeroplanes flying overhead to and from the nearby Indira Gandhi International Airport added to the din. Standing tall despite his diminutive five feet six inches, Kumar spoke over the hubbub, commanding the crowd's complete attention despite the commotion. At once jocular and grave, the mischievous glint in his eyes added vitality to his cast. Despite his deadpan expression, he spoke animatedly, with an eloquence. Those in attendance listened to his speech as if inhaling a long-awaited breath of fresh air. The Indian Tricolour fluttered proudly, nodding its assent to the words being uttered, endorsing every emotion that was felt by the audience.

Reaching Out

'As JNUSU president, I want to thank everyone in this country and all over the world for standing by us,' his opening words met with thunderous applause. He continued, 'In addition, I want to thank everyone in the media, in civil society, among the political persons and also among non-political persons, for standing with us in our battle to save JNU, for standing up to demand justice for Rohith Vemula. I want to offer them the red salute, and to thank them profusely. In prison, I was given food in two bowls—one blue, and one red. I smiled. I don't believe in destiny, but here it was, right before me, the solution to India's problems. The blue bowl symbolising Ambedkarite thinking and the red one representing leftist ideas.'

It might appear like a simple call for Ambedkarite solidarity with the left-wing, a possible means of addressing the political crisis of the country. But the significance of Kumar's pronouncements on such a union must be appreciated following decades of mutual suspicion between the two political formations. Both claimed universal relevance: the Ambedkarites emphasised caste as the organising principle of social life while leftists have highlighted its salience. Ambedkarite leaders were typically drawn from Dalit backgrounds, while leftist leadership was usually concentrated among the Savarna communities. Ambedkar himself faced political opposition from the (mostly Savarna) leaders of the Communist Party of India, who accused him of splitting the working class. The Bhumihar community into which Kumar was born in Bihar's Begusarai had spearheaded peasant movements across northern India through the All-India Kisan Sabha while also zealously guarding the state's otherwise fluid caste hierarchies—the founder, Swami Sahajanand Saraswati, had also been a leader of the Bhumihar Brahmin Sabha, a caste association preoccupied with promoting the interests of its own members as Brahmins. Begusarai was called the 'Leningrad of the East' for decades because of its commitment to leftist politics, yet its leaders tended to be drawn almost entirely from among the Bhumihars, including Kumar's distant relative, Chandrashekhar Singh. As such, Kumar's recognition of the need for Ambedkarite–left solidarity to defend Indian democracy was a tiny, but welcome, step in this context.

Kumar invoked Vemula's institutional murder at least three times over the course of his forty-five-minute speech. Indeed, it was entirely possible that the controversy in which JNU found itself embroiled was a distraction from nationwide demands to bring Vemula's killers to justice. But Kumar assured his audience, 'The dream of Babasaheb [Ambedkar], the dream of Rohith Vemula, will live on. This fight was started by Rohith Vemula. It will be continued by all progressive forces in the country.'

Freedom Fighters

The speech was punctuated with cries for azadi, for freedom. Nobody wanted freedom from India, Kumar made it clear. People wanted freedom within India. Politically, azadi meant independence from the RSS agenda that was being dictated from Nagpur and was being implemented by the BJP, ABVP and other organisations that made up the Sangh Parivar. Socially, azadi meant freedom from hunger, from corruption and from casteism. It was interesting how RSS's collaboration with

British colonialism was often forgotten and, as such, ironic that collaborators of colonialism were issuing certificates of patriotism and determining Indians' nationalist credentials.

I happened to be at JNU one evening a few weeks after Kumar's address. Sipping chai by myself at the dhaba that had been witness to the kerfuffle in February, I could not help overhearing the detailed analysis to which it was subjected by fellow students. As the spring dusk fell, the conversations became more animated but never bitter. Should he have used the word 'azadi' as much as he did, given its associations with secessionism, some argued. To say that was to miss the point, others countered, since he was reclaiming the vocabulary of 'azadi' from being appropriated by jingoists. Although the debate remained inconclusive, it was a measure of the seriousness with which the term 'azadi' was being taken as India neared seven decades of independence from colonialism.

In Allahabad, Richa Singh had already discovered how difficult the pursuit of azadi in postcolonial India was. In October 2015, she had become the first woman to be elected the president of Uttar Pradesh's Allahabad University Students' Union after Independence. Although supported by the student body of the Samajwadi Party which then ruled the state, she was unaffiliated with any political party and found herself presiding over a students' union that was otherwise dominated by ABVP students. Within a month, Singh faced her first major political test when Yogi Adityanath, the firebrand BJP politician and chief priest of the Gorakhnath monastery, was invited by the ABVP to inaugurate a new building on campus.[26] Singh objected on grounds of Adityanath's controversial statements on women, caste and Muslims.[27] 'Here we have Muslim students too in the university. If any riot-like situation occurred after his speech on the campus, who will be responsible? The ABVP members invited Adityanath without consulting me and that is against the Allahabad University Students' Union constitution,' she told the *Indian Express*.

Under Singh's leadership, students of Allahabad University collectively protested the invitation to such a divisive figure as Adityanath. Placards declaring 'Go back Yogi, spreader of communalism' and 'Anti-woman Yogi, go back' sprang up all over campus, held by students who resisted the idea of their campus becoming a platform for hate-mongering. Adityanath had questioned Muslims' loyalty to India, justified violence against them and had floated the Hindu Yuva Vahini back in 2002 as a militant outfit of young Hindus. His conservative perspective of women was made obvious through his reactionary opinions about people conforming to gender rules and women needing protection rather than independence.[28] The university's women organised a sit-in protest at the administrative block, holding placards which said 'Yogi Adityanath *campus chhodo*' (Yogi Adityanath, leave the campus). They were surrounded by hordes of ABVP students proclaiming '*Campus mein rehna hoga toh* Yogi Yogi *kehna hoga*' (Anyone living on the university campus has to chant Yogi's name). But Singh and her comrades remained undeterred. Weathering the violence unleashed against them— Singh's right wrist was broken in a scuffle with the ABVP—they had succeeded in keeping Adityanath out of the campus, at least for the time being.

The ABVP neither forgot nor forgave.[29] On 19 January, they threatened Singh in the presence of the vice-chancellor, the proctor and the dean of student welfare. News of Vemula's death was trickling in, leaving many students despondent. An emboldened ABVP successfully arm-twisted the university administration to ban a talk scheduled to be delivered by Siddharth Varadarajan, editor of the left-leaning *Wire*.

It was not only the ABVP which felt their feathers ruffled. Singh annoyed the university administration by directing attention to the regular harassment women faced on the campus. One area of contention was the appointment of an official tasked with the duty of care for the students. It turned out that the same official was facing charges of sexually harassing a Dalit girl. Singh raised the matter with the vice-chancellor and shot off letters to prominent government officials, including Prime Minister Modi. Although nothing came of it, her activism riled the university authorities up so much that the administration threatened her with expulsion.[30]

The commitment to defending Muslim students and promoting women's rights in the university necessitated a kind of freedom that was both inclusive and egalitarian. Of course, Singh's pronouncements barely received the sort of media coverage that Kumar's did, likely because mainstream news outlets found it easier to scrutinise every move of students in JNU than faraway Allahabad. It is also possible that the rough and tumble of student politics in Allahabad left Singh with little time to make eloquent speeches like her counterpart in JNU. But if actions can be taken as evidence, her campaign to ensure that Allahabad University was a safe space for Muslims and women certainly represented a view of the nation in which people from all backgrounds would be free to lead lives of dignity.

Students at Manipur University have faced daily assaults on their dignity for far longer than their counterparts in either Allahabad or Delhi. After all, their university has an army camp on its campus, a distinction no other university enjoys.[31] The Assam Rifles, established by the East India Company way back in 1835 to protect the British-owned tea gardens from so-called 'unruly tribes', set up base on a hillock overlooking the campus as part of the operation to enforce the Armed Forces (Special Powers) Act, better known as AFSPA.

Less than ten days after the fateful event in JNU, retired army man Major-General G.D. Bakshi broke into tears live on television.[32] He was a guest on the *Newshour Debate* hosted by Arnab Goswami. They were arguing over the union government's directive to universities to fly the national tricolour 'prominently and proudly'[33] with the aim of 'instilling nationalism and pride' among students. Hurt by the arguments of those opposing the diktat, the Major-General lashed out at them and burst out crying. Livestreamed to living rooms across the country, his tears won him instant accolades among the middle class. However, not everyone was impressed. Chinglen Kshetrimayun wrote an open letter to the retired Major-General. It started with: 'My name is Chinglen Kshetrimayum, I am from Manipur and I am not a threat to anyone.' The letter then went on to discuss the impact of AFSPA on Indians living in Manipur, stating:

> General Bakshi, at Manipur University, there is something more than your national flag. There is an Assam Rifles camp inside the university campus. So don't worry, you are winning. There are also two Assam Rifles camps on both sides of my town ... I am pretty much under your control.[34]

The presence of an army camp in Manipur University represents just how militarised the state has been for decades. The underlying mistrust many Manipuris harbour against India dates back to 1949, when Maharaja Bodhachandra signed the Instrument of Accession to merge his state with the newly formed nation. However, Manipur had already become a constitutional monarchy the previous year, and many Manipuris believed that the state's elected legislature ought to have been consulted.[35] Without its ratification, they considered the state's accession to India illegal. To add insult to injury, Manipur was governed directly from Delhi, thereby stripping its nascent legislature of any authority. It was only in 1972 that Manipur was granted full statehood with an elected legislature. By then, however, it was too late.

The United National Liberation Front spearheaded armed insurgency against India in 1964. The People's Revolutionary Party of Kangleipak was formed in 1977. The following year, the People's Liberation Army was born. Early in 1980, the Communist Party of Kangleipak came into existence. By September that year, Indira Gandhi, re-elected as prime minister in January, declared Manipur a disturbed area and imposed the AFSPA. Over the next few years, internecine clashes among Manipur's different ethnicities erupted, offering the government a justification for the continuation of the draconian law. In turn, few issues united the otherwise disparate and often conflicting claims among Manipuris (and elsewhere in India's north-east) as did freedom from AFSPA.[36]

The resentment caused by AFSPA is understandable. Legally, the rule of law stands suspended. Curfews restricting the movement of people can be imposed at will. People can be picked up on the suspicion not just of being insurgents but of sympathising with the insurgency. Manipur University has been raided from time to time since the imposition of the AFSPA. Checkpoints across the state, sometimes within just two kilometres, subject its citizens to arbitrary and humiliating frisks by military personnel. Beyond this, the culture of impunity spawned by AFSPA has routinised rapes, violent encounters and extra-judicial tortures. Of course, the suspension of the rule of law means that military personnel are never held to account for the terror they unleash on ordinary citizens. Amidst the lush valleys of Manipur, freedom is merely a faraway word that sounds nice but is barely felt.

To Manipuris, however, it means a lot. They have protested the imposition of the AFSPA almost from the day it was implemented. Their protests have intensified when the act has been spectacularly abused, such as when thirty-two-year-old Thangjam Manorama was allegedly gang-raped and murdered by paramilitary forces in 2004.[37] Twelve women, mothers of boys and girls that had 'been disappeared' (the colloquial term for people who had been picked up by the military and were never heard of again), protested in the nude in front of the Assam Rifles HQ.[38] Pebam Chittaranjan, a student leader at Manipur University, immolated himself in protest.[39]

Early in December 2021, Vikramjit Thongjam found himself leading an All-Manipur Students' Union (AMSU) march through the streets of Imphal. They had gathered to protest the gunning down of innocent civilians by security forces in the neighbouring state of Nagaland, also suffering the imposition of the AFSPA. The AMSU had organised the march under the supervision of the North-East Students' Organisation (NESO), an umbrella body representing the seven north-eastern states. Addressing the students, Thongjam insisted on the need to repeal AFSPA, not only in Manipur, but across the entire north-eastern region. In a spectacular show of solidarity, AMSU vowed to support NESO regarding the abrogation of AFSPA. Setting aside inter-ethnic conflicts and inter-state claims and counter-claims, the AMSU unequivocally condemned the application of the brutal law and called for its complete rescindment. By demanding this, Thongjam and his comrades were demanding the very same freedoms that were guaranteed to their fellow citizens in 'mainland' India, nothing more and nothing less.[40]

The yearnings for freedom expressed by Vemula, Khalid, Kumar, Singh, Thongjam and thousands of other students mirror the chants of azadi that have echoed throughout the Valley of Kashmir since 1947. Long before terrorist groups infused the vocabulary of jihad into the region's political struggles, generations of students protested New Delhi's chicanery and manipulation of Kashmiri politics.[41] Rigged elections engineered by the Congress Party under Nehru himself, imposition of the infamous AFSPA and a humiliating military occupation that subjected people to arbitrary checks created a resentful public that look upon the Indian government as a brutal oppressor.[42] Aghast at the betrayal of the democratic promise made by the Congress leadership to Kashmir, its people were left with little option but to demand azadi. But the government repeatedly ignored those claims. To make themselves heard, the Kashmiri populace turned to the growing crop of young militant insurgents that mushroomed across the Valley since 1990. That is, of course, where the similarities end: where the Kashmiri insurgents received moral and material resources from elsewhere, the Vemulas and Khalids relied on little more than support from fellow students and sympathetic teachers for their cause.

Umar Khalid and Anirban Bhattacharya were rusticated from JNU shortly after the fateful events of February 2016.[43] Faculty members formed human chains to focus attention on the injustice done to the university's students.[44] Later that year, students were debarred from a protest taking place outside the administrative block. The following year, in 2017, nine students who disrupted a meeting of the academic council were suspended. In response to the suspension, their teachers started the azadi lecture series.[45] Despite the administration forbidding the event and warning retaliation, the series commenced as scheduled, inviting public reflections on the many meanings of azadi. Kathu Lukose, a graduate of the School of Arts and Aesthetics, produced a short film titled *March March March*, which was blocked by the Ministry of Information and Broadcasting.[46] Shehla Rashid, JNUSU's feisty vice-president who was in charge when Kanhaiya Kumar was jailed, mobilised fellow students and kept their morale high. Later that year, as Kumar, Khalid and Bhattacharya remained embroiled in legal challenges, Rashid coached the next generation of leftist students to carry forward the mantle of social struggle.

The quest for freedom imagines a life of dignity for the self and for fellow humans. Freedom can be a negative 'freedom from', in which case it can refer to liberation from state dominance and social control. Freedom can also be a positive 'freedom to', intimating people's ability to lead life in accordance with their hopes and plans. Endeavours that begin as attempts to seek freedom 'from' dominance and control not infrequently transform into efforts to achieve freedom 'to' shape collective life that supports solidarity and equality. Such freedoms offer us the chance to reinvigorate our belonging and membership in the political community, and to assert citizenship.

Asserting Citizenship

Ayesha Renna, Ladeeda Farzana and Chanda Yadav exemplified the quest for freedom to assert citizenship on a mild winter morning in December 2019.[47] Renna and Farzana were both from Kerala, one from Kandotty and the other from Kannur. Yadav's home was in Uttar Pradesh's Chandoli. They were all students at Delhi's Jamia Milia Islamia. Renna was a student of history, Farzana was undertaking a programme in Arabic and Yadav was studying Hindi literature. Together with their friends

Akhtarista Ansari (from Jharkhand) and Tasneem (also from Kerala) they had assembled near their campus in south Delhi to protest the Citizenship Amendment Act (CAA), which had been legislated in the Lok Sabha the previous day. The act introduced a religious filter into the process of acquiring Indian citizenship and led, as we shall see in the next chapter, to a storm of protests across India. Students of Jamia Milia Islamia, such as Renna, Farzana and Yadav, had already become the face of the protests in Delhi. That afternoon, they were joined by Shaheen Abdullah, a student of mass communications. As they marched, the students found themselves accosted by policemen as well as others wearing police uniforms. Uncertain about the wisdom of starting a full-scale confrontation with baton-wielding police personnel, the students sought refuge in one of the bungalows in the upscale neighbourhood of the leafy New Friends' Colony. That did not help, as the policemen spotted them and demanded they step out. The students refused.

The policemen then entered the property and tried to physically pull the students out of its precincts. Renna took the lead and dared the police to touch them. 'Go back, go back,' she screamed, and the policemen seemed to back off. But then a man wearing a police outfit over his red T-shirt grabbed Abdullah, pulled him out of the premises and shoved him to the ground. The policemen closed in on him and started striking him with their lathis.

The women rushed in to defend their friend. Four of them crouched by Abdullah and formed a protective ring around him to shield him from further blows. Renna stood next to them, demanding they leave her friends alone. Maroon headscarf firmly in place with a colourful printed shawl around her shoulders, she thundered, 'You won't do that again', looking the policemen in the eye. The police managed to land a few more blows on Abdullah and on Yadav but finally realised this was not going to be as easy as they had thought. They backed off.

It may appear like a small incident in the larger landscape, but Renna, Farzana and Yadav garnered a significant win that winter afternoon when they compelled the police to back off. That victory encompassed not only the successful prevention of their friend being physically assaulted and arrested but also for the assertion of their belonging to the political community. As we shall see in the next chapter, such actions will resonate with the collective expectations of their fellow citizens, who also protested the imposition of the CAA.

Reimagining Citizenship

The Citizenship Amendment Act

Union Home Minister Amit Shah looked very contented. A smug smile replaced the grim scowl he had been wearing for the last three days. The Lok Sabha had just passed the Citizenship Amendment Act (CAA) by an overwhelming 311 votes in favour and 80 against. His saffron-coloured Nehru jacket neatly buttoned up, he joined the chorus of legislators thumping desks and erupting in jubilation as the Lok Sabha speaker declared the results. Prime Minister Modi's Man Friday, a fifty-five-year-old politician from Gujarat, revelled in his success at chaperoning one of the most contentious pieces of legislation in recent years. Forty-eight parliamentarians had debated it over nine hours in the Lok Sabha and many more would discuss it in the Rajya Sabha over the next few days. For now, however, he was thoroughly pleased at the crushing win his legislation had secured.

To many, the CAA was extremely benevolent. I was in Delhi the day the debate on the legislation was introduced in the Lok Sabha. On the 724 from Bhikaiji Cama Place to Kailash Colony, a group of three men and two women gushed over its importance. It would allow religious minorities from three neighbouring countries to fast-track their citizenship applications in India. The law was framed as beneficial to communities who faced persecution in their respective countries. The choice of the three countries whose religious minorities were privileged by the legislation added to its alleged benevolence, since it named Hindus, Buddhists, Jains, Christians, Sikhs and Parsis as its beneficiaries. These three countries were India's Muslim-majority neighbours: Pakistan, Afghanistan and Bangladesh. Pakistan had been an Islamic republic since its constitution was adopted in 1956. Afghanistan had alternated between an Islamic republic and an Islamic emirate since 1992. Bangladesh had established Islam as the state religion in 1988. Because of its focus on religious minorities in Muslim-majority countries, the Act excluded Muslims from those countries as eligible for a swift citizenship approval process in India.

The CAA was a curious piece of work. Framed as a legislation to provide succour for religious minorities in the neighbourhood, it weaponised their persecution to determine inclusions and exclusions in India's political community. It applied provisions for protective discrimination within the Indian Constitution to religious minorities outside the country. Its framers consciously sought to expand the ambit of Indian citizenship and bring religious minorities persecuted by Muslim-majority countries within its embrace. It defied the logic of static citizenship based on birth and residence and embraced, instead, an expansive view of the political community that blurred national boundaries. On paper it seemed a progressive law that promised to ameliorate the condition of beleaguered communities.

But in Shah's utterances and given the BJP's ideological predilections, the CAA forebode disaster.

The CAA was to be followed by the enumeration of NRC. Indians would have to be prove their citizenship by providing certain documents so that they could be listed on the NRC. Failure to do so could result in detention as an 'illegal immigrant' and possibly deportation although no one quite knew to where. An enumeration of the NRC had already been undertaken in Assam, and the results published in August 2019 had confounded everybody.[1] Almost 20 lakh of the state's 3.3 crore residents had found themselves excluded from the NRC.[2] Hindus made up at least 40 per cent of the exclusions, running the risk of being designated 'illegal infiltrators'. Just over a quarter were Bangla-speaking Muslims, who were frequently accused of being 'illegal infiltrators'. The remainder of the exclusions were made up of Assam's myriad indigenous communities who shared syncretic practices that straddled various faiths. The BJP, which also ruled Assam, insisted that a fresh survey be conducted. The number of exclusions was too low for a state that had been flooded with illegal immigrants, the party's supporters claimed. Muslims, rather than Hindus and others, comprised these illegal immigrants, so how could they be a minority among the exclusions, they questioned. The CAA would ensure that Muslims were excluded, and everyone else included, whenever the brand-new NRC was launched.

Shah himself clarified the chronology with characteristic clarity.[3] On 11 April 2019, while campaigning for the Lok Sabha elections in West Bengal's Raigunj, Shah promised to implement the NRC across the country after Hindus, Buddhists and Sikhs had all obtained citizenship, specifically excluding Muslims. On 23 April, in a video released by the BJP, Shah clarified things again, urging his audience to understand the 'chronology' (using that specific word): 'First, we will bring forth the CAA, then we will implement the NRC', specifying that refugees had nothing to worry about, but infiltrators did. To everyone familiar with BJP-speak, 'refugee' was a coded term for Hindus and 'infiltrator' a similarly coded term for Muslims. On 1 May, at another election rally in West Bengal's Bongaon, Shah was at it again: 'First we will pass the Citizenship Amendment bill and ensure that all the refugees from the neighbouring nations get the Indian citizenship. After that, NRC will be made and we will detect and deport every infiltrator from our motherland.' In this speech, Shah added Jains and Christians to his original list of Hindus, Buddhists and Sikhs, but studiously refrained from including Muslims. For good measure, he added that infiltrators were like termites, sapping the vitality of the nation.

After the BJP's stupendous win at the Lok Sabha elections, Shah was anointed Home Minister. A principled politician, he kept his promise and never wavered from the path of introducing the CAA. Interviewed by a journalist of the *Ananda Bazar Patrika* on 2 October 2019 (which happened to be Mahatma Gandhi's 150th birth anniversary), Shah once again made it clear that refugees would be given citizenship once the CAA was introduced. 'We will walk up to them and gift them citizenship,' he told his interviewer, listing, yet again, that this gift would be extended to Hindus, Buddhists, Sikhs, Jains and Christians. By the following month, on 20 November 2019, Shah had added Parsis to the list, but still refrained from mentioning Muslims. He also went on to assure his audience in the Lok Sabha that the NRC would be conducted afresh after the laws amending citizenship were enacted. To his credit, he did say that no one from any religious community needed to worry and magnanimously added that anyone not listed in the NRC would have the right to appeal to a Foreigners' Tribunal and any expenditure incurred thereon would be borne by the state. Slowly but surely, the possibility of some residents being stripped of their citizenship and rendered stateless was being creepily normalised.

Votaries of Hindutva salivated at the prospects. The CAA would welcome Hindus, Buddhists, Sikhs, Jains, Christians and Parsis fleeing persecution from Afghanistan, Pakistan and Bangladesh as citizens. The NRC would classify citizens and foreigners based on documentation whose veracity would have to be approved by local officials. Being born in India was no longer enough to be classified a citizen. You would have to prove that your parents were not illegal infiltrators, for which documentation was necessary. And because it was possible for documents to have been forged or obtained illegally, their veracity would have to be established by a government official. The process was riddled with arbitrariness. With Hindus, Buddhists, Sikhs, Jains, Christians and Parsis categorically labelled as either citizens or refugees-about-to-become citizens, who would be the illegal infiltrators? It was an open secret.

The contentions around the CAA were almost surreal. Hearsay masqueraded as history. Jolly uncles and lovable aunts transformed into venom-spewing WhatsApp warriors circulating stories of atrocities real and imagined. Fragments of the past, long thought buried, were resurrected. As legislators discussed the nuances of amending India's citizenship laws, the country was reminded of such long-forgotten events as the 1946 elections, the travails of Jogendra Nath Mandal and the Nehru–Liaqat Pact. Framed as a legislation to right the wrongs of the past, the debates on the CAA degenerated into a series of recriminations and name-calling. What could have been a moment of reckoning for the nation, an honest appraisal of the nation's trajectory since Independence and the treatment of minorities, was quickly reduced to weaponising the persecution of some minorities against others.

Throwback to the Past

On 18 July 1947, an aeroplane landed in Delhi's Palam airport. The figure that emerged from it was an English barrister appointed by the British government at the special request of India's last viceroy and the squabbling leaders of its two largest political parties, the Indian National Congress and the Muslim League. Indeed, his appointment was one of the few things on which the Congress and League leaders could agree. The task before the barrister was enormous: to chart a line across two enormous Indian provinces that would minimise the population of religious minorities on either side. This line would become the international boundary between two independent nations, which were to be inaugurated in just over five weeks.

Sir Cyril Radcliffe set about the task assigned to him with as much earnestness as he could have possibly mustered in the Indian summer of 1947. Field surveys and public consultations were out of the question, given the tight deadline. Consequently, the fruits of his labour were bittersweet. Two new countries were born, eager to bask in the warm glow of freedom. But their religious minorities were under serious threat of violence on either side of the lines that now divided India from the two parts of Pakistan. Radcliffe had sliced through villages, communities and cultures across Bengal in the east and Punjab in the west, wrenching people apart and hurling them at each other's throats. The barrister's pen was supposed to have been a surgeon's scalpel. Instead, it had turned out to be a butcher's knife.

To be fair to Sir Cyril, the violence unleashed along the lines he had drawn was hardly his fault. He was merely the executioner of a will that had been drawn out by Mountbatten and the quarrelling leaders of the Congress and the Muslim League as they presided over the dying spasms of British India. Since at least August 1946, when the Muslim League had called for Direct Action Day to achieve a separate Muslim homeland, violence between Hindus and Muslims had escalated across India. Passions had first been ignited in Calcutta (now Kolkata) and spread first to the eastern districts of Bengal before turning westwards to Bihar and the United Provinces (now Uttar Pradesh). By March 1947, Punjab exploded as the province's multi-religious ministry collapsed, its Sikhs and Hindus banding together against the Muslims, who were in majority. Partition seemed to offer a way out of the violence. But its hasty execution, spurred by a megalomaniac viceroy and supported by politicians scrambling for the spoils of power, made it worse. Over 10 lakh people were killed and more than 1.5 crore people displaced, according to official estimates. The actual figures are likely higher.

As the dust was settling, India and Pakistan both vouched to protect their religious minorities. Jawaharlal Nehru, India's first prime minister, promised Muslims equal rights in addition to safeguarding their personal laws. Together with Home Minister Vallabhbhai Patel, Nehru successfully resisted demands from the Hindu Mahasabha, the RSS and sundry other Hindu conservatives to declare India a Hindu republic. Pakistan was less successful in protecting its minorities despite founder Mohammed Ali Jinnah's assurances. Jinnah's death within a year of independence and the diminishing commitment of Muslim League politicians towards either democracy or minority rights resulted in Pakistan eventually styling itself as an Islamic republic, where sovereignty belonged to Allah and only Muslims are allowed to hold the position of prime minister and president by law. Pakistan's failure to secure equal rights for its minorities would go on to provide a convenient excuse for Hindutva supporters to harass India's Muslims.

Punjab bore the brunt of the violence during the Partition. Since the fall of the elected ministry in March, it was placed under the rule of a British governor. The departing British had little interest in preserving peace. Without political commitment to harmony, the 55,000 military personnel deployed in the province failed spectacularly to stem the communal bloodbath. Entire districts were emptied of their minorities on both sides of the Radcliffe line as Hindus and Sikhs sped east while Muslims fled west. The exchanges of population in the two Punjabs decimated religious minorities on both sides of the border. Hindus and Sikhs, who, in 1941, had comprised about 21 per cent of the population that went on to form West Punjab, constituted less than 1 per cent of the population in 1951. Likewise, the population of Muslims in the Punjab districts that remained in India fell from 31 per cent in 1941 to under 4 per cent in 1951.[4]

Bengal, which was similarly partitioned and where communal unrest the previous year had triggered the entire chain of violence in the first place, was relatively less tumultuous during the time of Partition. It was possible that Gandhi's presence had a soothing effect on the province as he and Huseyn Shahid Suhrawardy, the Muslim League's chief minister of the province, lived together in Calcutta's Hyderi House to demonstrate that Hindus and Muslims could co-exist. The Congress and League governments in the two halves of the province remained committed to keeping the peace in the regions they governed. The scale of population transfers in the immediate aftermath of the Partition was less than in Punjab. Nevertheless, the Hindu population in the province's eastern districts declined from 28 per cent in 1941 to 22 per cent in 1951, while the share of the Muslim population in the west fell from 26 per cent in 1941 to less than 20 per cent in 1951.[5]

Subsequent decades were not so kind to the eastern half of

the province, rechristened as East Pakistan after 1955. As the military, bureaucratic and religious elites of the western side of Pakistan consolidated their rule, communal violence against the province's Hindus intensified. The pact to protect minorities that had been signed between Prime Ministers Nehru and Liaqat Ali Khan was quickly forgotten. The ferocity of anti-Hindu rioting shook the topmost non-Muslim leader and law minister of the fledgeling nation, Jogendra Nath Mandal, who resigned his post in despair and disgust. Other Hindu leaders such as Kiran Shankar Roy, leader of Pakistan's opposition, had already left for Calcutta to join the new provincial government. However, anti-Hindu sentiment propagated by West Pakistani rulers could not prevent Hindus and Muslims in the east from jointly demanding democratic rule in Pakistan, which would have shifted the locus of power to their more populous province, whose people comprised over half the population of the new country.

For West Pakistan's rulers, the prospect of relinquishing power to the east was unthinkable. Deluded by colonial-era notions of being a 'martial race' and fed the narratives of having 'ruled' India for centuries, they could not fathom the political aspirations of the peasants, labourers and artisans—mostly 'lower-caste converts'—who occupied East Pakistan. Moreover, the Bangla spoken in East Pakistan was very different from the Urdu they wanted to promote as the national language of the new country—to them, Bangla was too Hindu, not Muslim enough. But the Muslim majority of East Pakistan refused to fall for such propaganda and joined forces with the Hindu minority to defend their language. The authoritarian rulers of West Pakistan intensified the targeting of Hindu minorities in East Pakistan even as Muslim leaders of the province sought to preserve communal amity. As democratic demands for universal adult franchise gained ground, Hindu minorities found themselves to be the victims of violence engineered by West Pakistan elites. Their share in the population of eastern Bengal fell further, from 22 per cent in 1951 to 18.5 per cent in 1961—a trend that was to intensify in the following decade.[6]

Overseen by a military regime led by Yahya Khan, Pakistan eventually held its first general elections based on universal adult franchise on 7 December 1970. The Awami League, led by Sheikh Mujibur Rehman and representing the Bangla-speaking Muslims and Hindus of East Pakistan, won 167 of the 300 seats in the National Assembly. The Pakistan People's Party, founded by Zulfikar Ali Bhutto, came a distant second, winning a majority of seats in Punjab and Sindh. Bhutto and other West Pakistani politicians refused to accept the results as they mistrusted the Bengalis. They persuaded Yahya Khan to delay convening the national assembly. Unrest brewed in cities across East Pakistan and the countryside turned restive. On 25 March 1971, the Pakistan army launched 'Operation Searchlight', a military operation that cracked down on Awami Leaguers. Sheikh Mujib was arrested without charges and flown over to West Pakistan to be imprisoned in solitary confinement. One of the worst genocides of the twentieth century followed.

Over the rest of that year, crores of Bengalis—Muslims, Hindus and others—were tortured, maimed, killed, raped, dispossessed, or otherwise died of hunger and disease. Almost 1 crore Bengalis crossed the border to seek refuge in India, a huge majority of which were Hindus, but also consisted of Muslims. Bangladesh eventually liberated itself to form South Asia's youngest nation. Sheikh Mujib returned home to become the new country's first prime minister, but not before stopping by in Calcutta with an appeal to the refugees to return home and rebuild their land. Many refugees heeded his call—others chose to stay back, anxious about economic and social prospects if they returned. A Bangladesh census of 1974 revealed the Hindu population of the new country was less than 14 per cent.[7]

Bangladesh's constitution enshrined nationalism, socialism, democracy and secularism as its four pillars. These lofty ideals could not, however, prevent the new nation from lurching from one crisis to another. A fearsome cyclone ravaged the land on the eve of the 1971 elections. In 1974, famine killed over 10 lakh people. The following year, Sheikh Mujib was assassinated in a military coup. The army took over. In 1988, Islam was declared the state religion of Bangladesh, although, importantly, the four founding pillars were never formally relinquished. As the state privileged one religion over others, its emboldened fundamentalist adherents actively began to harass Hindus and other religious minorities. The situation continued to deteriorate even after democracy was re-established in 1991. Although the Awami League was elected in 2008 on a secularist plank, it has so far refrained from repealing Islam as the country's state religion. The share of Hindus to the total population has continued to fall.[8]

This last-mentioned fact is marshalled repeatedly by proponents of the CAA in its defence. But an obsession with this statement neglects the historical fight for democracy, linguistic rights and national liberation waged by Muslims, Hindus and others. This is repeatedly ignored to claim religious persecution as the singular experience of Hindus and other minorities in India's neighbouring countries. Doing so brushes aside their contributions to the making of Bangladesh and their identity as a proud people is reduced entirely to that of victims in need of rehabilitation. Bangladesh's protracted struggle against religious nationalism, waged by its Muslims no less, has become conflated with an Islamic identity seen as antithetical to Hindus and Hinduism.

Indeed, the Islamisation of Afghanistan, Pakistan and Bangladesh did not spare the Muslims of their lands. Those who fall short of being 'good Muslims' face discrimination, harassment or worse. Hazaras in Afghanistan, Shias in Pakistan and Ahmadiyyas in Pakistan and Bangladesh—all Muslims— have found themselves victims of persecution for decades. Muslim women suffered Pakistan's Hudood Ordinance, which enshrined gender inequality into the law for nearly three decades. But the CAA makes no provisions for Muslims persecuted by harsh Islamic regimes. Shah's retort to legislators who pointed out these omissions was telling: all three countries were created for Muslims, he insisted, so they do not face structural persecution there. His response failed to consider the censoring, bombings and executions of Muslims not considered Muslim enough in such regions.

The claim that Pakistan or Bangladesh was founded for and by Muslims is also insubstantial. While it is certainly true that Pakistan's founders emphasised their Islamic identity to distinguish themselves from Hindu-majority India, the extent to which Muslims supported its creation will never be known. The 1946 provincial elections, which powered the Muslim League's claims for the establishment of Pakistan, allowed only a quarter of the Indian population to cast their vote. Although the League secured 87 per cent of Muslim seats (elections were held on the basis of separate electorates where you could only vote for a candidate of your religion), no more than a quarter of the total Muslim population was eligible. Of a total population of approximately 9.4 crore, less than half a crore Muslims voted for the Muslim League.[9] The claim that Pakistan was created by the subcontinent's Muslims is untested at best.

Defending Identities

Relying on distorted interpretations of the past, protagonists of the CAA were unprepared for the vehemence with which it would be opposed in the present. Opposition erupted in Assam as soon as the proposal to amend citizenship laws was cleared by the cabinet for debate in Parliament.[10] Defying the curfew imposed by the BJP-led state government, people spilled out onto the streets in protest. Led by diverse organisations such as the All-Assam Students' Union and the Krishak Mukti Sangram Samiti (KMSS), the former a well-established students' body and the latter a newly formed peasants' association, massive protest meetings were organised. The largest one was held in Guwahati's Latashil playground and attended by hundreds of people. The day the new law was slated to be enacted (12 December) was to be declared a Black Day.

It was not only Guwahati that witnessed popular anger against the CAA. Elsewhere, protestors blocked key nodes in Assam, such as the Guwahati–Shillong Road, which now resembled a war zone. Entire districts witnessed complete shutdowns against the CAA: schools and shops closed down and tea garden workers went on strike. Police fired at unarmed crowds, killing scores of people that included Dipanjan Das, Sam Stafford, Ishwar Nayak and Abdul Alim. These names are a testament to the multi-religious composition of the people opposed to the CAA. Akhil Gogoi, the leader of KMSS, was arrested. Army columns were deployed across the state and conducted flag marches in major cities. Transport to and from Assam had to be suspended. Shah's gambit had spawned a general uprising, which the military now scrambled to contain.

The Assamese had good reasons to suspect the CAA. A tapestry of different languages, ethnicities and religious affiliations, they worried that the CAA would disrupt the intricate social mosaic of their state.[11] About 1.5 crore of the state's 3.1 crore spoke Ahomiya. Roughly 90 lakh spoke Bangla, 2 lakh spoke Hindi and 14 lakh spoke Bodo. The remaining 35 lakh people spoke a range of languages that included Mishing, Karbi, Dimasa, Rabha, Tawa, Deori and others. While the shares of Bangla and Hindi speakers in the state had increased over time, the proportion of other languages had fallen. In 1991, Assamese speakers comprised well over half the state's population; by 2011, they were less than 50 per cent. The CAA, they feared, would inundate their state with Bangla-speaking Hindu refugees who had been trickling into Assam from neighbouring Bangladesh since the Partition. The CAA also threatened the fates of Ahomiya Muslims who might not be able to supply the relevant documents to prove their citizenship, thus further reducing the numbers of Ahomiya speakers.

Fear makes strange bedfellows with hope. Afraid of being overwhelmed by foreigners, Hindus, Muslims and others in Assam made common cause. Overcoming their internecine squabbles of the last several decades, they united as one against the CAA. The spectre of losing their cherished ways of life haunted them all, to the extent that they closed ranks in their opposition to the divisive legislation. Despite having voted the BJP to power in the Vidhan Sabha twice, the Assamese now fiercely protested it. They refused to acquiesce with a legislative decision that would result in pitting one set of persecuted minorities against another.

Assam's anxieties about being overwhelmed by Bengalis were founded on the prospects, in 1946, of a union with their larger, more linguistically homogenous neighbour. The departing British had proposed a complex grouping of provinces for India that would bind Bengal with Assam as a federated unit. The Assamese, already worried about the migration of Bengali peasants (mostly Muslim) and professionals (mostly Hindus) since the turn of the twentieth century, successfully resisted this grouping. They heaved a sigh of relief when the Bengali Muslim-majority Sylhet district narrowly voted to join East Pakistan in a July 1947 referendum. But the waves of refugees sent their way by political instability, religious persecution and, eventually, the genocide in East Bengal continued to threaten the precarious social demographics of their province.

As the weeks crept by, Assamese linguistic chauvinism, indigenous nativist ideas and religious prejudice against Muslims mixed with the population flow from eastern Bengal to produce a deadly cocktail that explicitly targeted foreigners. A concoction of hate exploded in February 1983 when at least two thousand Bengal-origin Muslims were butchered within a matter of six hours by gangs of caste Hindu Assamese, Tiwa, Karbis and others in fourteen villages around Nellie, a nondescript town in central Assam.[12] A new generation of Assamese leaders catapulted to political fame and fortune: they capitalised on the anxieties of the state's myriad communities by scapegoating hapless minorities such as Bengal-origin Muslims. Branded as outsiders, Bengal-origin Muslims found themselves singularly targeted despite learning and speaking Ahomiya. The CAA focused precisely on this demographic with the aim of first detaining them and then expelling them from the state. However, instead of celebrating it, protestors across Assam confounded their sympathisers and critics alike by pouring out onto the streets in protest.

Hope can be knotted. It can entwine with emotions that range from pride to fear and anger. Such a kind of hope was on full display across Assam through the December of 2019. Angry at being betrayed by the BJP and fearful of a demographic invasion from Bangla-speaking Hindus, the protestors collectively made their discontent clear. Protesting the CAA was integral to their collective cultural pride. Assam's recent mistreatment of its linguistic and religious minorities blurred the distinction between hope and hate in the eyes of observers who were not discerning enough.

No one understands the complexity of hope better than the Bengal-origin Muslims who confront ethnic, linguistic and religious prejudice daily. They have been imported as labourers to the districts that make up modern-day Assam since at least 1838. That was the year the British East India Company completed its annexation of Assam and attached it to the Bengal Presidency. Assam was then severed from Bengal in 1874 when it became a chief commissioner's province. It was again incorporated within the short-lived province of East Bengal and Assam created by Viceroy Curzon's infamous (first) Partition of Bengal that lasted from 1905 to 1912. In 1912, Assam became a full province of British India but retained the Bengali-speaking district of Sylhet till Independence in 1947. An administrative entwinement (of what became two different countries after 1947) facilitated a movement of labourers from East Bengal which was encouraged by colonial rulers and welcomed by caste Hindu Assamese landowners. However, Bengal-origin Muslims were belittled due to their ethnic, linguistic and religious identities despite their vital role in the development of the province and their best efforts at assimilating into the dominant Ahomiya culture. They were labelled 'Miya', an Urdu term used in northern India to refer to a gentleman, but which was repurposed into a slur in Assam to target Bengal-origin Muslims.

Against these quotidian discriminations and mindful of the historical twists and turns that produced them, Bengal-origin

Muslims turned to poetry as a form of protest. In May 2015, the state began to update the NCR amidst a growing cacophony calling for the deportation of 'foreigners'.[13] In 2016, schoolteacher Dr Hafiz Ahmed expressed his angst on social media through a short poem that was translated into English by Assamese researcher Shalim Hussain.

> I am a Miya
> My serial number in the NRC is 200543
> I have two children
> Another is coming
> Next summer
> Will you hate him
> As you hate me?[14]

Dr Ahmed was the founder-president of the Char Chapori Sahiya Parishad, a literary body that works towards preserving and promoting the culture of the chars (river islands) and chaporis (river banks) of the mighty Brahmaputra.[15] Growing up amongst the chars and chaporis of the region, he had experienced first-hand the dissolution of the syncretic culture of his land in the wake of the Assam agitation that had weaponised the insecurities of marginalised peoples against each other. His poem reclaimed the identity of the Miya and turned it on its head, transforming it from a slur to a symbol of collective recognition. It celebrated the Miya as an industrious worker, an enterprising peasant and a hardworking labourer who contributed to economic development. And, finally, it took pride in the languages spoken by the Miyas themselves, departing from the grammatical conventions of both High Ahomiya and High Bangla.

Even after being translated into English by Hussain, Dr Ahmed's verses shine a light on the long-standing prejudice faced by Bengal-origin Muslims in Assam. Despite their many contributions, they remain distrusted—their loyalties are questioned even when they have the documents to prove their citizenship, with officials labelling them as 'doubtful voters' in an effort to cast governmental suspicion onto their legal status.

'I am a Miya' took social media by storm. Over the next few years, people identifying themselves as Miya poets poured their hearts out against the discrimination to which they have been subjected, discrimination which now threatened to strip them of citizenship and render them stateless. Mirza Lutfar Rehman, Rehna Sultan and Kazi Neel were among the many poets who assembled their thoughts into verses that reflected their varying several dialects.[16] Inspired, as poet-scholar Dr Abdul Kalam Azad says, by Negritude and the Black Arts Movements as well as queer, feminist and Dalit literary movements, Miya poetry was similar to other movements in which the oppressed 'reclaimed the identity which was used to dehumanise them'.[17] Dibrugarh-based writer Jiten Bezbaruah hailed Miya poetry as 'a bridge of unity between the mainstream Assamese society and the Miya people'.[18]

Not everyone was impressed, however. In June 2019, a freelance journalist complained that the Miya poets were portraying the Assamese population as xenophobic. Another complaint was that Miya poetry was provoking sedition and harming Assam's fragile social peace. Assamese public intellectuals, otherwise renowned for their stand against Ahomiya linguistic chauvinism, worried that Miya poets writing in their own languages would cause social unrest. The Miya poets were better off, advised the intellectuals, writing in Ahomiya so they could appeal to the conscience of Assam's population rather than birthing further linguistic categories. In critical conversation with such perspectives, many

Miya poets emphasised their ambition of generating solidarity with members of other oppressed communities. In their contribution to an edited collection titled *Citizenship in Contemporary Times: The Indian Context*, scholars Abdul Kalam Azad and Gorky Chakraborty note the poet Aman Ali's commitment in this regard.

> Just assertion of Miya identity is not enough. We need to make a coalition with other communities on the common issues like employment, education, health among other things. When you speak twice about the issues of Miyas, you must speak once for the rights of the Adivasi community. They are also not less oppressed. We must speak about them as well.

Aman Ali's composition illustrates this commitment. In the concluding verses of his poem (whose title in English translates into 'Why do our poems scare you?'), Ali justifies the use of his language while reaching out to others:

> Why do you fear when we write poems
> In the language we weep in?
> The water in your eyes and mine is the same
> Your grief and mine bears the same address
> Your country and mine is bound within the same barbwires.

To remember is to resist. As Assam erupted against the CAA, members of its different communities made it a point to remind themselves (and others) of their tumultuous histories. They refused to be folded into the flat religious binaries that the CAA sought to institutionalise, and harked back to memories of their mobilisations—often against each other—to defend their way of life. Assam's defiance of neat labels confounded onlookers who expected the 'mainland's' binaries to be replicated across the state. Instead, they were offered a glimpse into the overlapping social contradictions that nevertheless held possibilities, however slim, of a solidarity that could yet resist Hindutva's juggernaut.

Insurgent Constitutionalists

Indians on the 'mainland' were slower to push back against the CAA. But push back they did. A few days before the debates on the CAA commenced, the soft-spoken Harsh Mander, a former bureaucrat, a social activist and India's foremost public intellectual, offered his strategy to resist its imposition. He would register himself as Muslim, he tweeted. He would refuse to submit his documents to the NRC. And then, he would demand the same punishment as any other undocumented Muslim: internment in a detention centre and stripping of citizenship. He ended his tweet by urging his fellow Indians to join him in his civil disobedience. Mander was joined by another former civil servant Sashikant Senthil who described the passage of the CAA as exemplifying 'the darkest day in the history of modern India'. In a public letter to Amit Shah, he declared:

> I refuse to accept the process of enumeration in NRC by not submitting the requisite documents to prove my citizenship and is willing to accept the action taken by the Indian State for my disobedience. If the state chooses to declare me as non-citizen, I would also be happy to fill up the many detention centres that you are building all over the country.[19]

Actioning these sentiments were people who poured out into the streets across India in the weeks that followed. The slogans they chanted, the placards they held and the demands they raised emphasised their belief that the CAA was a divisive piece of legislation that had no place in a civilised society.[20] Handmade placards held up by young women which read 'Grand-daughters of refugees against the CAA' and 'Not in my name' drove home the simple yet powerful message that many do not share the exclusionary aims of the legislation. Other posters played on versions of the 'It's so bad …' joke, that is, 'It's so bad, even the introverts are here', 'It's so bad, even cynics are here' and the extremely self-aware 'It's so bad, even the privileged are here', suggesting that anger against the legislation had managed to penetrate widely divergent circles of the population. Among the most evocative messages conveyed during the protests was the one held up by a young man proclaiming 'Hindu *hoon, chutiya nahin*' (I am a Hindu, not an idiot).

Folks from all generations, backgrounds and genders merged together to protest the weaponisation of minorities against each other. 'Fascism is achieved not when government oppresses half of its people but when the other half chooses to be silent,' screamed one vibrantly red poster that was inked in black. Another declared, 'We are Indians by blood, not by documentation,' asserting a civic conception of citizenship that rejected the religious divisions being floated by the CAA. A poster held up by three women dared, '*Isi mitti ke hai, isi mitti mein mil jaayeinge, kissi ke baap ka mulq nahin, ki Mussalman aise chale jaayenge*' or 'We are of this land and we will merge with its soil; this country is not the property of any single community that the Muslims will simply leave'.

The protests attracted all sorts—entrepreneurs, film-makers, students, professionals—who came together to defend the rights enshrined in the Constitution.[21] In Delhi, protestors converged on Jantar Mantar, an eighteenth-century open-air observatory built by Raja Jai Singh of Jaipur and installed in the capital by the reigning Mughal emperor. In Mumbai, they thronged the

August Kranti Maidan, where the All-India Congress Committee had, under the presidency of scholar-statesman Abul Kalam Azad, launched the Quit India movement against the British. In Kolkata, Chief Minister Mamata Banerjee herself led the protests against the CAA. In Chennai, women drew kolams (decorative patterns created using rice flour) in front of their houses to criticise the CAA and the NRC. But it were the convulsions beyond major metropolitan cities that took India by storm and the world by surprise. A truly nationwide movement had begun.

Large cities and small towns alike inserted themselves into the protests against the CAA. State capitals from Agartala to Bengaluru and Jaipur to Hyderabad witnessed large-scale protests. From Malerkotla in Punjab to Darbhanga in Bihar and Kalburgi in Karnataka, protestors claimed their Indian citizenship with one voice, urging the government not to go down a route that would inject religious identity into determinations of citizenship. Opposition parties struggled to keep pace. Where they were unable to lead the movements, civil society activists stepped up, as in Chhatisgarh[22] and Odisha.[23] The Nagrik Ekta Manch in Uttarakhand[24] and women vendors in Manipur's Ima market[25] led the protests themselves when political parties were missing in action. The crushing support enjoyed by the CAA inside Parliament was matched by a cornucopia of contention against it on the streets.

On 20 December, over a week after the CAA was made into law, Delhi's Jama Masjid was agog with anticipation. The Friday prayers had just concluded, and worshippers thronged its precincts to vent their frustrations at the new legislation. The city's police had denied them permission to formally protest in the area but could not prevent them from assembling inside the mosque. More people than usual had turned up, holding banners that condemned the legislation. The gathering was almost carnivalesque, with huge tricolours held aloft under the watchful gaze of the mosque's domes. All of a sudden, a wave of excitement rippled through the assembly as they spotted their leader.

Chandrashekhar Azad Ravan, chief of the Uttar Pradesh-based Bhim Army, emerged on the steps of the sixteenth-century mosque that had once symbolised Islamic glory in India. Built by Emperor Shah Jahan as the imperial mosque, it had witnessed the rise and fall of two of the world's mightiest empires as well as the emergence of the world's largest democracy—all within the radius of a few kilometres. It had been witness to unprecedented moments of Hindu–Muslim solidarity when it hosted the anti-colonial Arya Samaj monk Swami Shraddhanand in 1922 to deliver Vedic sermons. It was also witness to the tragedy of the Partition when thousands of Muslims fleeing Delhi were housed in transit camps as they waited for trains to Pakistan. Abul Kalam Azad, who combined his leadership of the Congress Party with an unmatched mastery of Islamic theology, had warned worshippers of the dangers the Muslim League's machinations would pose to them. After the Partition, he chided them for the course of their politics from those very steps where Ravan now stood:

> Think for one moment. What course did you adopt? Where have you reached, and where do you stand now? Haven't your senses become torpid? Aren't you living in a constant state of fear? This fear is your own creation, a fruit of your own deeds. It was not long ago when I wanted you that the two-nation theory was death-knell to a meaningful, dignified life: forsake it. I told you that the pillars upon which you were leaning would inevitably crumble. To all this you turned a deaf ear.[26]

His reminder of their follies was not meant to humiliate Delhi's Muslims. Far from it, the soft-spoken Maulana urged his listeners to repudiate the false promise of a Muslim Zion. Stay on and build the new India, he urged them:

> Where are you going and why? Raise your eyes. The minarets of Jama Masjid want to ask you a question. Where have you lost the glorious pages from your chronicles? Was it only yesterday that on the banks of the Jamuna, your caravans performed wazu? Today, you are afraid of living here. Remember, Delhi has been nurtured with your blood. Brothers, create a basic change in yourselves. Today, your fear is as misplaced as your jubilation was yesterday.

Holding up a copy of the Indian Constitution, Ravan walked down the same steps of the Jama Masjid as Maulana Azad had seven decades ago. Unlike the Maulana's dejected and despondent audience, Ravan's audience roared its approval. Photos of Ambedkar fluttered as the crowd chanted '*Inquilab Zindabad!*', that rousing chant which had inspired generations of patriots and revolutionaries. In a short speech punctuated with thunderous applause, the swashbuckling Ravan invoked the genteel Maulana several times, urging his audience to defend their rights in India shoulder to shoulder with its varied communities in defence of the Indian Constitution against unconstitutional laws like the CAA.

Policemen were swarming outside the gates of the Jama Masjid, waiting for Ravan to step out so they could arrest him for violating their orders to not protest. One of them managed to grasp his collar but he pulled away and escaped into the sea of humanity that had gathered. The police gave chase. Azad made good use of the compact neighbourhoods of Old Delhi. He was on the street one moment, inside a house the next, atop the roofs the third. The drama on the streets outside the Jama Masjid resembled a scene from a Bollywood action movie, except that the stakes here were a lot more real.

Ravan escaped that afternoon but surrendered early next morning before dawn broke over Delhi. His month-long detention in police custody established him as one, alongside scores of others, who insisted on defending the constitutional principles of equal citizenship. His actions—like that of the Nagarik Ekta Manch in Uttarakhand, the women vegetable vendors in Manipur and the Forum against the Constitutional Amendment Bill in Chhattisgarh—offered hope to India's Muslims that they were not alone. Indeed, he was willing to court imprisonment for a cause that did not directly affect him or his community, not as a favour or an act of charity but because it was the correct, constitutional thing to do.

Hope requires a shared commitment to work together through trouble. The attempt to overcome differences of opinion, mutual distrust and legacies of animosity is a necessary step to nurture it. Such attempts might not succeed in the first instance—as a matter of fact, they never may. But the experience of working together counts. That life is worth living, and that this worth is recognised by others who are willing to defend it with you is highly valued by those who are targeted on the basis of their identities.

That likely explained the visceral reaction of the government, the pliable media houses at its command and certain sections of society. Ravan was given gratuitous lessons on the alleged history of Dalit–Muslim conflict. Jogendra Nath Mandal's abject humiliation at the hands of the Muslim League in Pakistan suddenly became a topic of great interest on social media. Ambedkar's scathing criticisms of Islam and India's pre-Independence Muslim leadership were selectively appropriated. However, Ravan remained unmoved. His first action upon receiving bail after his illegal arrest was to turn up at the Jama Masjid again, copy of the Indian Constitution in hand, assuring Muslims that he and his Bhim Army would stand by them, come what may.

State Retaliation

The Centre and allied state governments lost little time in retaliating against the proponents of equal citizenship. Within days of the CAA's passage, Delhi's Jamia Milia Islamia was invaded by Delhi Police. The students' vociferous public protests, personified by Ayesha Renna, Ladeeda Farzana and Chanda Yadav, was the reason for this invasion, although the official pretext was that the police were chasing vandals who had entered the campus.[27] On the evening of 15 December, police swarmed the campus of the century-old university, barging into libraries and residential halls, beating up students, destroying equipment and shattering glass panes as if they were in battle against highly dangerous enemies. As weaponless students cowered before platoons of armed police, the state's attempts to instil fear in the hearts and minds of its opponents was on full display. Students were beaten with batons. Tear gas shells were lobbed into areas where they sought shelter, to flush them out. Even the library was not spared.

A few weeks later, on the first Sunday evening of the new year, masked miscreants attacked JNU. Armed with sticks, stones and iron rods, they went on a rampage, thrashing students as well as any staff members who tried to protect them. The left-wing SFI and the right-wing ABVP blamed each other for the violence, but more left-leaning students reported being assaulted and injured than right-leaning ones. Aishe Ghosh, then president of the JNUSU and member of the SFI, was beaten so brutally she had to be admitted into the All-India Institute of Medical Sciences for her head injuries. And bizarrely, she was arrested shortly afterwards on grounds of vandalism and fomenting violence! When the police named the masked assailants, the ABVP was forced to admit that at least one of them was a member. No arrests were made.

If the rule of law showed cracks in Delhi, it crumbled in Uttar Pradesh. State-backed lawlessness ruled the roost. Aligarh Muslim University (AMU) was raided by police: AMU students met a fate much worse than that of their counterparts in Delhi. At least sixty students were injured. Internet services were suspended. One independent team of lawyer-activists reported[28] that the police used the tactic of deceptive shelling: camouflaging explosives in tear gas shells to inflict maximum injury. Another independent team by the People's Union for Democratic Rights (PUDR) reported[29] that the police labelled students as terrorists and chanted slogans such as 'Jai Shri Ram' during their assault on the campus. When students of Lucknow's Nadwa College sought to show solidarity with their peers in Aligarh, police locked the gates of their university and prevented them from stepping out. Eventually, the campus was closed down and the students were asked to vacate it for a few weeks. Protests also rocked the campuses of Banaras Hindu University where some students were arrested for participating in rallies held against the CAA, and others refused to accept their degrees at the convocation.[30]

Small towns across Uttar Pradesh made common cause against the discriminatory law. The substantial Muslim minorities in Meerut, Saharanpur, Banda, Azamgarh, Rampur, Bijnor and Muzaffarnagar inserted themselves into national headlines by reminding everyone of India's constitutional guarantees that ensure equal citizenship. Though terrified that the law may eventually be deployed against them or their descendants, Muslim populations across the state refused to be paralysed by fear. They organised themselves or reached out to political parties to coordinate mobilisations of protest.

Hope is what underscores a kind of trust in life. It motivates us to think of the next step. It stems from a belief that our families, cultures and societies are important. It is based upon the conviction that civilisation is worth fighting for, that people's lives are precious. Some philosophers feel that too much optimism can hinder action, that it can cloud rationality and that relying on it reduces our chances of taking timely action. The protestors across Uttar Pradesh, however, reminded us that hope is about confronting oppression. Despite the dangers posed by the CAA and the desperate actions of a particularly hostile government, they believed there was a way out and opted to challenge an unjust law.

The state responded swiftly and brutally. Section 144, a colonial-era law banning public assembly, was pressed into service across towns in Uttar Pradesh (and elsewhere). Police firing on assemblies of protesters was rampant, which killed at least twenty-three people across the state. People were arrested for posting content on social media that was critical of the CAA and thus deemed inimical to public order. Mass First Information Reports (FIRs) were filed against protestors: police in the former industrial heartland of Kanpur filed fifteen FIRs against over 21,000 people over one weekend in December 2019.[31] Protestors in Meerut were told by the police to 'go to Pakistan'.[32] Shops were sealed in Muzaffarnagar, and houses of Muslims vandalised by police searching for protestors.[33] In Nehtaur, police stormed into Muslim houses and arrested people they thought were likely to be involved in the protests. This resulted in casualties—some bodies were recovered in neighbouring localities, while others simply went missing.[34] In Sambhal, twenty-six people received notices for their alleged involvement in protests: they were asked to either explain their position or cough up compensation for losses to public property valued at almost ₹12 lakh.[35] The chief minister himself threatened protestors that the government would auction off their belongings to recover losses to property.

Uttar Pradesh's citizens refused to be browbeaten. Braving the brutal Indo-Gangetic winter, hundreds of women assembled outside the Clock Tower in the heart of Lucknow, the state capital. The north Indian fog hung thick in the air, but did little to dampen the spirits of the women. Wrapping themselves in blankets, they huddled together night after night to register their protest against the CAA. One night, the city police swooped down on them and made off with their blankets, leaving them out in the cold. The women defiantly replaced their old blankets with new ones. The city police then hoisted hoardings that named the protestors in order to shame them. It was at this point that the Supreme Court intervened and declared the state government's actions a violation of protestors' privacy. The hoardings were dismantled but the blankets were never returned.

Tenacious Resistance

Across the country, resistance to the imposition of the CAA continued. Students of universities across the seven north-eastern states, including Gauhati University, Cotton University, North-Eastern Hill University, Dibrugarh University, Tezpur University, Assam Women's University, Nagaland University, Rajiv Gandhi University, Assam Agricultural University and North Eastern Regional Institute of Science and Technology abstained from their classes and participated in seven-hour-long hunger strikes.[36] Even the usually peaceful state of Meghalaya, which had separated rather cordially from Assam in 1971, saw mass rallies and demonstrations.[37] The army had to be deployed in Tripura[38] where Bangla-speaking supporters of CAA clashed with the Reangs and Tripuris who opposed it. The idyllic mountains of Arunachal Pradesh, land of the dawn-lit mountains, turned into fiery battlegrounds where protestors carried grim placards that declared '*Ai jui jolise, jolise jolibo, ai hongram solise, solise, solibo*'[39] (This fire is burning and will keep burning, this movement is on and it will continue).

Opposition to the CAA across the north-east was not merely a primeval reaction to the possibilities of a demographic invasion. As critics pointed out, the legislation does not only exclude Muslims—animists, ancestor-worshippers and other practitioners of the region's myriad faiths and traditions were also excluded. To avail of the CAA's provisions, they would have to identify themselves as Hindus or Buddhists rather than as practitioners of their specific faiths. Members of such trans-border communities as Khasis, Garos and Hajongs face persecution on account of their tribal identities and are often evicted from their lands, compelling them to seek refuge in India.

Indeed, Adivasi communities across the country balked at the prospects of having to pigeonhole their diverse beliefs and syncretic customs within the six religious categories approved by the architects of the CAA. Yamuna Murmu, a tribal rights activist in Bihar, summed up the resentment against the CAA among the Adivasis cogently. 'Our ancestors—Tilka Majhi, Birsa Munda, Sidhu-Kanhu—fought vehemently against the British for our rights and independence but sadly today, the government is seeking proof of relation and belongingness to our motherland,' he told the reporter of *Newsclick*, a left-leaning news portal.[40] The approved religious categories fail to reflect the diversity of faiths held by members of India's numerous Adivasi communities. This fuelled growing anxieties among them that their religious beliefs would disappear altogether from official enumeration.[41]

Cities in the south weren't far behind when it came to voicing their fury against the legislation. Tens of thousands of people in Hyderabad marched through streets, calling on the government to axe the act.[42] Over 2,00,000 people converged on Mangaluru in south Karnataka from road, sea and air to register their opposition.[43] Further south, nearly 70 lakh people linked together to form a human chain across the length of Kerala in protest, led by the chief minister himself. As elsewhere, these protests tended to be punctuated with collective readings of the preamble of the Constitution and slogans hailing the unity of India despite its religious diversity, concluding with the singing of the national anthem.

Smaller towns were as vociferous in the articulation of their anger. On Makar Sankranti, the sun festival, Gujarat's skies became a battleground as government-sponsored kites supporting the CAA were cut down by kites in opposition to it.[44] In February 2020, a sea of yellow flooded Punjab's Malerkotla town as farmers' organisations joined hands with religious associations to convene an 'invitation march' that sought to inform people about the divisiveness of the act.[45] Over 12,000 women marched through Malegaon in Maharashtra demanding its withdrawal.[46]

Harsh Mander eloquently captured the ethos of the protests when he suggested to students that the claims of equal citizenship had shifted from the Parliament to the streets.

> To do this, we have come out on the streets and will continue to occupy the streets.

This fight cannot be won in the parliament because our political parties, who declare themselves secular, do not have the moral strength to take up the fight.

This fight can also not be won in the Supreme Court because, as we have seen in the case of the NRC, Ayodhya and Kashmir, the Supreme Court has not been able to protect humanity, equality and secularism

Mander's call riled up right-wing commentators who misinterpreted it, as is their wont, as a call to arms. They lost no time in accusing the former civil servant of encouraging sedition, inciting violence and other fantastical nonsense. Mander was a perfect target for the wrath of the right. He had founded the Karwan-e Mohabbat, the Caravan of Love, in 2017 as a response to the spike in hate crimes against and lynching of Muslims after the BJP's ascent to power in 2014. The Karwan-e Mohabbat tours towns and villages ravaged by violence between Hindus and Muslims, seeking to heal old and new wounds. Their gesture of integrating love in Indian politics has been portrayed as hateful by the Indian media. Mander was well-linked to global circuits of social movements, which made it convenient to invent any number of allegations from the idiotic to the insidious. On this occasion, the accusations were based on badly doctored videos of Mander's speech.

Perhaps the most iconic and well-documented protest against the CAA was the one mounted by women on the south-eastern edge of Delhi, in a neighbourhood called Shaheen Bagh. Braving the bitter Delhi winter, hundreds of Muslim women undertook a continuous sit-in for over a hundred days. They blockaded a portion of Kalindi Kunj Road, a six-lane highway that connects the city to the south-eastern suburb of Noida and onwards to south-west Uttar Pradesh, in a bid to foreground their discontent against the divisive legislation. Over three iridescent months, the homemakers who assembled in this corner of Delhi taught their fellow citizens invaluable lessons about belonging and membership in the political community.

Shaheen Bagh, both literally and metaphorically, showcased the diverse arts of politics. Complementing the sloganeering and speech-making by prominent citizens were collective actions that were at once spectacular and banal. Thousands gathered on New Year's Eve to collectively sing the national anthem, a routine aspect of the discipline instilled by schools in India, as a chorus of defiance against divisiveness. On Republic Day, three dadis of Shaheen Bagh, grandmothers who won national affection and international fame for their tenacious commitment to the Indian Constitution, unfurled the national flag. While the national media framed the protestors as unruly saboteurs out to disrupt daily life in the capital, Shaheen Bagh transformed into an open-air exhibition centre with murals, posters and installations jostling for attention alongside politicians, singers, comedians, poets and even enthusiastic children. Enterprising people set up makeshift kiosks to serve snacks and drinks to the protestors. The effervescence of Shaheen Bagh dispelled the pall of dread that had crept over the city in the wake of the CAA's triumph in Parliament.

Harbouring hope can be extremely difficult when the odds are stacked against you. Fear, anxiety and anger feed on these odds and birth despair. There was ample reason to feel dejected during that bitterly cold winter. When protestors were not being harangued as saboteurs, they were mocked for being unable to achieve anything. But the women of Shaheen Bagh remained determined. The solidarity they received from civil society activists, students and artistes from across India strengthened their commitment. Radhika Vemula, whose son Rohith had died almost four years prior, joined the three dadis of Shaheen Bagh as they unfurled the tricolour. Sikh farmers set up community kitchens in the neighbourhood to cook for Muslim homemakers as they continued their sit-in. In turn, the Muslim homemakers observed a two-minute silence on 19 January to commemorate the thirtieth anniversary of the exodus of Pandits from the Kashmir Valley. Inspired by Shaheen Bagh, similar protests sprouted up elsewhere. Kolkata's Park Circus, Mumbai's Agripada and Bengaluru's Bilal Bagh saw comparable numbers of women expressing dissent against the CAA.

The carnivalesque ambience at Shaheen Bagh did not merely infuse hope in Delhi that winter. It spurred hope across the country, motivating many to speak out against what they considered an unjust law. That it would not last long does not dim its significance for igniting public debates on what it means to be a citizen. Although a global crisis quietly brewing in the background was soon to overwhelm one and all, the incandescence of Shaheen Bagh and the country-wide protests it inspired were to illuminate conversations on citizenship for years to come.

Pandemic Communities

Viruses, Old and New

A few hours before protestors gathered at Shaheen Bagh to sing the national anthem on New Year's Eve in 2019, the World Health Organisation (WHO) picked up an intriguing media report in its Beijing office. The municipal health commission of a little-known town in central China had posted reports of what appeared to be a viral pneumonia. Over a week later, as protests continued to rage across India and the government remained stubbornly committed to introducing the NRC, WHO reported that investigations by Chinese authorities had revealed an outbreak caused by a novel coronavirus. Two days later, Chinese media reported the first death caused by the virus. A week later, on 27 January 2020, India reported its first case. Early next month, on 5 February, the WHO began holding daily briefings on the subject. Within a week, as cases exploded beyond China in countries as far apart as Italy and Iran, the disease was given a name: COVID-19.

The BJP government had other priorities. It spent much of the last week of January and early February campaigning for the Delhi Vidhan Sabha elections scheduled for 8 February. The protests against the CAA quickly emerged as a convenient agenda to target. At an election rally, junior Finance Minister Anurag

Thakur urged: *'Desh ke gaddaron ko goli maaron saalon ko'* (Shoot the traitors to the nation). Similar slogans had been raised by BJP politicians such as Kapil Mishra over the previous weeks when they called for so-called 'traitors' at institutions such as JNU, Jamia and AMU to be shot. Although the hate speech arguably increased the party's vote share in Delhi, it failed miserably to dislodge the ruling Aam Admi Party (AAP)—the BJP won a mere eight out of seventy seats. Rankled by the defeat, the government was nevertheless quickly preoccupied with organising the state visit of US President Donald Trump. Trump was to spend two days in India—24-25 February—that included a public address at Ahmedabad's Motera stadium to approximately 1,50,000 spectators. The WHO's guidance on organising mass gatherings, published over a week before the event, was wilfully ignored.

In the meantime, a nationwide strike termed 'Bharat Bandh' was called by Ravan's Bhim Army. It was to protest a ruling by the Indian Supreme Court that states were not bound to guarantee reservations in appointments and promotions. Calling the court ruling an assault on the Constitution, Azad appealed to 'friends of the Bahujan Samaj':[1]

> Be it reservation, be it citizenship or employment; we have to work on these issues. We should protest peacefully and convey our message to the government as well as the Supreme Court.

The Bharat Bandh was called for 23 February, the day before Trump was scheduled to arrive. In solidarity with the bandh as well as to protest the imposition of the CAA, a group of between 500 and 1,000 people gathered in the Jaffrabad region of north-east Delhi to sit-in on the street in front of the metro station. Kapil Mishra, the BJP politician who had earlier called for 'traitors' at AMU, Jamia and JNU to be shot, arrived at the area and issued an ultimatum to the assembled policemen. Either they were to act against the protestors or Mishra and his followers would take drastic action, he warned. 'We will keep quiet till Donald Trump is in town. After that, please don't blame us for what happens,' he told the police in a public meeting.

What followed was mayhem. Drawing on Mishra's lead, supporters of the CAA set upon the protestors. Over the next couple of days, barely three kilometres away from where the Indian government was hosting Trump, north-east Delhi burned. The attacks on protestors against the CAA quickly spiralled into violence against the city's Muslims. At least fifty-three people were killed, of whom thirty-eight were Muslim and fifteen Hindu.[2] The 755 FIRs named 935 Muslims and 820 Hindus, suggesting that Muslims were to blame for the violence when they were clearly its victims. No FIR was filed against the politicians for making provocative speeches, leading the Delhi High Court to slam the police for its incompetence.[3] In response to an emergency plea filed by activists Harsh Mander and Farah Naqvi, the court convened a midnight hearing and ordered the police to help victims secure health and other facilities. Chandrashekhar Azad Ravan also filed an appeal with the Supreme Court, along with former Chief Information Commissioner Wajahat Habibullah and social activist Syed Bahadur Abbas Naqvi. The highest court in the land also criticised police failure to curb the violence.

The violence against Muslims ripped apart Delhi's delicate social weave. Not since the turn of the millennium had the city seen a communal conflagration of this scale. Although Muslims tended to be largely relegated to ghettos, violent conflict between them and Hindus had last occurred almost three decades ago, in the wake of the 1992 demolition of the Babri Masjid. In fact, in the working-class localities of north-east Delhi, members of the two communities had coexisted peacefully as neighbours, creating richly diverse pockets of humanity despite eras of mutual suspicion and distrust. The social fabric they had stitched together over decades of labour now lay in tatters.

This sudden assault did not, however, deter Hindus and Muslims from coming together to restore peace. They marched together to promote solidarity, grieved together when they lost their friends and neighbours and worked together to ensure calm. Members of the two communities in Jaffrabad and Maujpur prevented mobs from entering their neighbourhoods by barricading the gates. Hindu families opened up their homes to shelter Muslims from marauders in Hindu-majority areas, a gesture that was reciprocated by Muslims who protected Hindus in Muslim-majority areas. Muslims saved temples from attacks by their co-religionists while Hindus similarly defended mosques from assaults by fellow Hindus. The Sikh minority, despite being brutalised by Muslims in 1947 and Hindus in 1984, generously protected them both from each other. Unbeknown to them of course, a bigger crisis loomed ahead. Communal tensions would soon be overshadowed by the coronavirus.

On 29 February, as violence ebbed in India's capital, WHO published guidelines for quarantining individuals in order to contain COVID-19. A few days later, it called on governments and private sector manufacturers across the world to step up the production of personal protective equipment that would help healthcare workers deal with the growing crisis without endangering themselves. As the worldwide number of cases surpassed 1,00,000 on 7 March, WHO called for urgent action to stop, contain, control, delay and reduce the impact of the virus. Four days later, on 11 March, WHO formally declared that the world was in the throes of a pandemic.

The Indian government, hitherto oblivious to the ramifications of a brewing pandemic, awakened hurriedly from its slumber. Seven ministries collaborated to establish quarantine facilities across the country. Within a week, the union government urged state governments to enforce social distancing as a preventative strategy in their territories. Prime Minister Modi called for a Janata Curfew, a people's curfew, to be observed on 22 March. He urged citizens to conclude the curfew at 5.00 p.m. by banging pots and pans together, ostensibly in appreciation of the hard work being done by frontline health workers. Rich and middle-class Indians dutifully obliged. At 5.00 p.m. on Sunday, balconies and rooftops across the country erupted in one grand cacophony of obeisance to Modi.

Lockdown

Two nights later, the prime minister dropped a bombshell on national television. With the Indian Tricolour as the backdrop, looking directly into the camera, he announced his plans to stem the spread of the virus:

> The nation is going to take a very important decision today. From midnight today, please listen carefully, from midnight today the entire country will be placed under a total lockdown. To save India, to save every citizen of India, to save you, to save your family—there will be a complete ban on you stepping out of your homes. Every State, every Union Territory, every city, village, town, neighbourhood is going to be placed under lockdown ... With folded hands, I appeal to you to please remain wherever you are. Please do not venture out of your homes.[4]

The speech was delivered at 8.00 p.m. on the evening of 24 March. Modi allowed a mere four hours to his citizens to prepare for the world's largest lockdown and, arguably, the most stringent. For the rich and the middle class who had enthusiastically embraced the Janata Curfew, this was not entirely a serious predicament. But for working-class Indians engaged in informal employment across cities and towns, it spelt disaster. Reliant on daily wages rather than monthly salaries to feed themselves and their families, they found themselves staring into the awful abyss of certain unemployment. Unlike the joint or nuclear models that characterise middle-class households, families of working-class Indians are often trans-local—it is not uncommon for one member of the family to work in the city while others cultivate a small plot of land they might own in the village. Such a strategy helps them pool in resources and diversify risks during uncertainty. While more prosperous white-collar folks could work from home and learn new hobbies while they were at it, working-class Indians quickly realised that lockdown would also lock them out of the factories, firms and homes that provided them with pay. And above all, the lockdown would isolate them in the cities and towns where they lived, away from their families and friends. It was a dreadful prospect.

Cities across the world and over time have been hailed as repositories of hope. They have provided succour to populations fleeing hunger and famine in the countryside. Others have thronged to towns keen on making a fresh start or in search of dignified lives unencumbered by identities imposed upon them. India's cities have been beacons of light for its rural multitudes seeking deliverance from caste-based oppression in the countryside. The prospects offered by cities to the country's rural poor have been unprecedented. To be sure, cities remain segregated along lines of caste, class and religion while employment opportunities, where they exist, do tend to be precarious. But, all things considered, they have offered succour to those people who were no longer content with village life. In the last week of March 2020, and over the subsequent weeks and months, the prime minister's diktat turned these very same cities from repositories of hope and opportunity into dens of fear, anxiety and panic.

Workers across Indian cities thus made a determined bid to get back to their villages and re-join their families. Within the four hours Modi gave them to make alternative arrangements, they left the shanties and hovels in which they lived and headed to the nearest bus stands or railway stations to take the next available transport back home. Once the lockdown came into effect, that option was no longer available since trains, buses and other modes of transport ceased to operate. There was nothing left to do except walk. And walk they did. Through the summer of 2020, innumerable streams of people poured onto streets, roads and highways and walked back to the villages they called home. The cities in which they worked had betrayed them.

At least a crore people left India's towns and cities to return to their villages in the twenty-first century's largest mass migration so far. This figure was supplied by the Labour and Employment Minister Santosh Kumar Gangwar in Parliament; the actual numbers are likely to be higher than this official estimate. National and international newspapers reported horrifying stories of migrant workers being harassed, humiliated and brutalised by authorities. One video emerged of the police accosting migrant workers walking from Jammu to Bilaspur through Badayun in Uttar Pradesh, beating them and forcing them to continue their journey by leaping like frogs.[5] Another emerged of the police ordering migrant workers, returning to their homes in Uttar Pradesh's Bareilly district, to strip, and then spraying them with chemical disinfectants[6] purportedly to sanitise them. Many died trying to reach their homes.[7] Some, like thirty-nine-year-old Ranveer Singh, collapsed due to exhaustion, having walked more than 200 kilometres on foot in scorching heat.[8] Others, such as eighteen-year-old Lauram Bhagora, were run over by vehicles speeding on Indian highways. A one-year-old baby was among four people killed in a fire as they walked through a forest since no motorised transport was available.[9] In May, sixteen migrants were mowed down by a speeding train when they fell asleep on train tracks due to exhaustion.[10] Workers aboard the special Shramik Special trains initiated by the government perished of hunger and dehydration since neither food nor water was available. A woman on one such train died soon after alighting at her destination station due to hunger and dehydration—a gut-wrenching video of her little toddler trying desperately to wake her was widely circulated.[11] In contrast to the alacrity with which India airlifted hundreds of its citizens stranded abroad, the state's bias against labour migrants was glaring indeed.

The resolve of migrants to reach home in the face of hurdles was immense, with acts of courage and compassion rising to the surface amidst the chaos. On 15 May 2020, as dawn broke, a truck stopped at the outskirts of Shivpuri, a small town in Madhya Pradesh. Its passengers were a huddle of weary workers from Gujarat heading back to their villages in north India. One of them, twenty-five-year-old Amrit Kumar, who worked at a textile unit in Surat and was returning to his village in eastern Uttar Pradesh's Basti district, was suffering a high temperature. Fearing contagion, Kumar's co-passengers were growing jittery and instigated the truck driver to get rid of him as quickly as possible. The frightened truck driver ordered Kumar out of his truck on a highway some sixty kilometres away from the nearest hospital. To his bewilderment, Kumar's friend and neighbour in Basti, and roommate and co-worker in Surat, twenty-two-year-old Muhammad Saiyub, helped Kumar off the truck and insisted on staying with him by the side of the highway. Later that morning, a photograph of Saiyub cradling Kumar in his lap as his friend gasped for breath went viral. The image of the two desperate men—one struggling to breathe, the other struggling to help— towered over the religious identities which the Indian state was seeking to inscribe into the daily life of Indians. The photograph, most likely taken by one of the volunteers on the highway who were providing food supplies to migrant workers, offers one of the most enduring images of painful hope that came to epitomise the pandemic.

But as the state sought to barricade its population and cities betrayed their citizens, India's workers refused to be paralysed by inaction. Incurring huge costs, including the loss of their own lives and those they loved, they headed for their villages in the hope that if they could not live with dignity, at least they would not die in indignity.[12]

Stung by images of mass migration beamed across social and mainstream media, the Centre and some state governments sought to limit the damage to their reputation. Some areas, such as Karnataka, promised to make travel arrangements for migrants so they wouldn't have to walk. Others, such as Gujarat, offered food so workers would not starve. Yet others, such as Uttar Pradesh, simply imposed restrictions on migrants moving on foot. But all such promises or threats rang hollow. In early May, workers assembled on the outskirts of Bengaluru demanding that the Karnataka government arrange to transport them home, as they had been promised.[13] In the town of Surat in Gujarat, renowned world over for its diamonds, workers protested the poor quality of food offered to them throughout April.[14] In the middle of May, 2,500-odd people openly flouted Uttar Pradesh's no-movement-on-foot order when they tried to walk into their home district of Mathura. When the district administration and local police stopped them, the workers blockaded the arterial highway, disrupting traffic until the administration conceded defeat and provided them with food and transportation to take them home.[15] Over 6,000 Bihari migrants in Uttar Pradesh's Saharanpur poured onto the city's streets alleging negligence by their home as well as host governments, demanding to be transported home: the administration duly requisitioned buses for them so they could return to their villages.[16] Faced with the uncertainties wrought by a global pandemic and an inept state, workers turned to well-meaning members of an otherwise indifferent middle class for assistance.

Civic Action

Three days after the prime minister declared the world's largest lockdown, Sanjay Sahni reached out to some of his acquaintances who studied social welfare in his home state of Bihar. Sanjay led the Samaj Parivartan Shakti Sangathan (SPSS), a union of almost 50,000 workers who were drawn largely from Bihar and Jharkhand but worked all over the country. These workers, stunned by the sudden announcement of the lockdown, called Sanjay for advice, spurring him to activate his contacts with academics and researchers whom he thought might be willing to help. Food and cash were urgently required, as workers stranded across cities were staring not only at unemployment but also at starvation and illness. Sanjay's efforts were not in vain. His acquaintances responded as best as they could. As the frequency of calls and messages for help increased rapidly, Anindita Adhikari, a doctoral student at a US university, and Seema Mundoli, a staff member at Bengaluru's Azim Premji University, joined forces with Rajendra Narayan and Sakina Dhoraijiwala of Liberation Technology, a team of engineers, social workers and academics committed to improving public services in India, to form the Stranded Workers' Action Network (SWAN), a helpline platform that responded to requests for assistance across India. SWAN was convened by a network of zonal teams—staffed entirely by volunteers who worked in shifts—who responded to phone calls, WhatsApp messages and other requests and logged them onto an Excel sheet. Volunteers then followed up with the workers to determine their needs as well as that of their friends, families and neighbours. Based on the assessment of needs, volunteers linked the workers with local charities and/or government officers. Where such alternatives were not available, the volunteers crowdsourced funds and transferred them into workers' bank accounts. Between 27 March 2020, when Sanjay Sahni first called his acquaintances, and 3 July 2020, SWAN disbursed around ₹60 lakh into the accounts of almost 36,000 workers.[17]

A doctoral student at a university in Germany, Debojit Thakur was a member of a group of volunteers that had journeyed from Kolkata to Delhi in the wake of the February violence. They had collected funds from Hindu neighbourhoods in Kolkata to support the rehabilitation of Muslims who had braved the conflict and were struggling to rebuild their lives. They made it back to Kolkata right before lockdown was imposed. As the enormity of the lockdown's consequences sank in, he and his friends posted a message on Facebook, inviting donations to support those who had been rendered homeless and jobless by it. Overwhelmed by the response, mostly from students and other young people, Thakur and his friends formed the Quarantined Students' Youth Network (QSYN), a network of 650 volunteers across Delhi and West Bengal, to disburse the resources they received. They set up twenty-six makeshift kitchens, delivered over 10,000 ration packages and served over 1,00,000 cooked meals. In May, Cyclone Amphan battered West Bengal, which was already reeling from the onslaught of COVID-19. The QSYN volunteers mobilised their social connections and raised almost ₹1 crore in a matter of weeks. Their transparent use of the funds they received, under the supervision of Jadavpur University alumnus Nadia Imam, inspired confidence among donors who ranged from school children to Bollywood stars.[18]

For Jaywant Hire, who lived in Mumbai's Ramabai Nagar, the lockdown was a bigger disaster than the pandemic. He and his neighbours had few expectations from the state to begin with. After all, the memory of the 1997 massacre of fellow Dalits by the State Reserve Police Force and the subsequent inaction by the state and central governments was still alive. The stringent lockdown imposed without preparation meant that most people in the area who relied on daily wages rather than monthly salaries found themselves without money to buy food or procure other essential supplies. Ramabai Nagar's residents were faced with starvation, and worse. Recognising this, Jayawant Hire and his neighbours swung into action. They activated their networks through Yoddha Pratishthan, their residents' association, to mobilise funds and other resources that could help people obtain food, medicines and supplies, as well as blood donations. They also arranged quarantine facilities for people returning from other parts of the country. Yoddha Pratishthan had been formed sixteen years ago as an initiative for activists to work together with local politicians and bureaucrats to ensure that public services were provisioned for the area's population in line with official regulations. Now, as politicians and bureaucrats absconded, the Yoddha Pratishthan activists emerged as beacons of hope for Ramabai Nagar's beleaguered population.

By the time the Indian government had grasped the enormity of the exodus, volunteers across the country were already provisioning food and essential supplies. The central government instructed state governments to provide food and shelter to the workers in their respective jurisdictions. The governments of Delhi and Haryana fed as many as 30 lakh within the first fortnight of the lockdown, while the government of Kerala sheltered 3,00,000 migrants during the same period. Even so, in as many as twelve states, private charities outstripped state governments in provisioning basic supplies to the workers.[19] By the time the government started to lower restrictions, it appeared that India had indeed managed to contain the surge of the pandemic. Underpinning this achievement was the stellar role of volunteers and charities that anchored society at a moment of crisis. Their dedication and dogged efforts during those first few weeks must remain etched in social memory. While the pandemic pushed everyone to the absolute edge, these unnamed individuals had laboured away, holding together a society on the brink of implosion.

Politicising the Pandemic

Expectedly, the pandemic offered plenty of opportunities for politicians and supporters of the ruling party. The lockdown rendered illegal protests such as those in Shaheen Bagh. The city police seized the chance to clear out the demonstrators and bulldoze their way through the makeshift tents and camps.

This was well within the purview of the law. However, the zeal with which they whitewashed the murals and other works of art that had come to symbolise the effervescence of Shaheen Bagh suggested that they were not only imposing the lockdown but also cleansing all traces of the city's tryst with one of India's largest popular movements in recent years. A gathering at Delhi's iconic Nizamuddin Markaz of the Tablighi Jamaat, an Islamic sect that exhorts Muslims to be religiously observant, spurred a series of Islamophobic campaigns across national media that resulted in physical attacks on Muslims who were scapegoated for spreading the coronavirus.[20]

The announcement that the Ram temple at Ayodhya would be consecrated by the prime minister himself further excited Hindutva opinion; several BJP politicians fervently believed that its construction would end COVID.[21] On 5 August 2020, as the pandemic continued its slow but steady spread across the country, Prime Minister Narendra Modi performed the consecration ceremony for the temple to Ram in the presence of the governor and chief minister of Uttar Pradesh, as well as almost 150 priests. Over the next few months, the dawdling increase in the number of cases, contrasted with the mayhem caused by the pandemic in Western countries, lulled India into delusional hope. Its young population was a sturdy defence against a disease that picked off the aged, some believed. The impressive rates of childhood immunisation would protect them from death, if they were at all infected, others opined. According to another view, it was the turmeric in the diet. Many trusted that the pollution or Indian 'proximity to nature' were natural disinfectants. By the beginning of 2021, Indian leadership seemed to genuinely believe that they had conquered COVID-19.

As usual, the prime minister paved the way. Addressing world leaders at the World Economic Forum on 28 January

2021, he sought accolades for saving masses of humanity from catastrophe by containing the virus. Within a few weeks, the BJP followed suit and began to lavish praise on its leader 'for introducing India to the world as a proud and victorious nation in the fight against COVID-19'—his leadership was praised as 'able, sensitive, committed and visionary'.[22] India was in the endgame of the pandemic, Health Minister Harsh Vardhan announced in March. Through the first three months of 2021, the National Scientific Task Force did not meet even once. The august Kumbh Mela, a devotional gathering of millions aspiring to cleanse their sins, was brought forward to April 2021 for the first time since Independence as if in celebration of his leadership. Buoyed, Modi strove for even greater heights.

One such lofty aspiration was to crush the political opposition that had persisted in West Bengal and annex the state to the cause of Hindu Rashtra. West Bengal's paradoxes purportedly baffled the Hindu right. On the one hand, it had produced some of the most iconic thinkers of Hindutva: the poet-philosopher Bankim Chandra Chattopadhyay, the historian Jadunath Sarkar, the physicist Meghnad Saha, the polemicist U.N. Dey and, of course, Shyama Prasad Mookerji who founded the Bharatiya Jana Sangh, the forerunner of the BJP. On the other hand, it stubbornly refused to hand over a full majority to the BJP despite the ravages of the Partition and the influx of Hindu refugees fleeing persecution from Islamic revanchism, and despite the betrayal of the Dalits (comprising 25 per cent of the state's population) by the Muslim League, which hounded Jogendra Nath Mandal out of Pakistan, as well as the Congress Party, which refused to address acute landlessness among them, and then by the CPI(M), which ruled the state for thirty-four years but refused to allow them access to the levers of power. If anything, the CPI(M) had actively fomented division between Muslims and Dalits by setting Muslim thugs on Dalit refugees when the latter settled in Marichjhapi, an island set in the picturesque Sundarbans, on land that had been promised to them by the party leaders (but later revoked when it became clear that the refugees took party promises seriously). Despite a history of mutual antipathy and violence between Muslims and Hindus, the state seemed quite inoculated against actually electing the BJP to power. Modi was determined to change that.

In an eight-phase election over March and April 2021, the prime minister of the world's largest democracy held twenty-three rallies in West Bengal. Home Minister Amit Shah addressed seventy-nine rallies. Over fifty luminaries of the BJP—cabinet ministers, members of Parliament, chief ministers—descended on the state to support the prime minister's bid. He delighted in the numbers of people who turned up at his rallies without sanitary masks. He taunted Chief Minister Mamata Banerjee by drawling out that now-infamous turn of phrase 'Didi, o Didi'. As COVID cases rapidly increased, so did the length of the Modi's beard in an attempt to present himself to the people of West Bengal as analogous to poet-laureate Rabindranath Tagore. The charade failed. Although the BJP made impressive gains, mostly at the expense of the CPI(M) and the Congress (which, for the first time in the state's history, failed to win a single seat), Mamata Banerjee stayed put as chief minister. The prime minister's machinations had failed.

Death and Despair ...

In the meantime, India burned. As the coronavirus unfolded across the country, crematoriums and funeral ghats struggled to keep pace with the bodies that toppled through the large gaps of India's dysfunctional healthcare infrastructure. The capital city's municipal governments had to seek the forest department's help to arrange firewood.[23] Public parks and parking lots were converted into ghats so Indians could be afforded some dignity in death.[24] From Ranchi[25] to Surat,[26] cremation grounds simply could not keep pace with the number of bodies fed to them. The chimneys and metal structures of the furnaces glowed red as corpse after corpse burned.[27] Pyres blazed non-stop in Varanasi's revered ghats[28] as mass cremations became a normal occurrence during the dark months of April, May and June 2021.[29] Where the ghats failed to keep up, Mother Ganga embraced the bodies that were consigned to her. But even the river could not consume all of death's offerings. Swollen corpses washed up across towns on the Ganga to remind us that they had once led full lives[30] and would have continued to had it not been for political callousness. Hospitals, including posh private ones, ran out of oxygen as patients begged, pleaded and gasped before healthcare professionals. Experts, all of Indian origin, at the Washington DC-based Centre for Global Development, estimated that up to 60 lakh people might have perished in India due to COVID-19.[31]

... Could Not Vanquish Hope

Even as the pandemic snuffed out lives, it could not erase the spirit of the people. Away from the hustle and bustle of electoral politics and corporate newsrooms, an array of people worked steadily to ameliorate the lives of their fellow human beings. Although they were saviours to those they comforted, they did not seek recognition as heroes, nor did they perceive themselves as resisting an uncaring state. That they emerged as reservoirs of hope was less the result of their intentions and more to do with their actions.

At the frontline of the battle against COVID-19 were village-level health workers, the Accredited Social Health Activists (ASHA) workers as well as the Auxiliary Nurse Midwives (ANMs), who laboured to the best of their ability.[32] Despite the incompetent leadership and poor resources that stymied them, these frontline workers went above and beyond to ensure that the communities in which they lived suffered less. They refused to enforce draconian laws curtailing people's movements, ensuring instead that people covered their mouths and nostrils with a clean cloth when they did step out for work.

Bolstering the efforts of health workers at the frontline of protecting people from the pandemic were a plethora of others. Crematorium workers, sanitation workers and postal workers all went well beyond the call of duty to keep things going. School teachers, drafted in to help with panchayat elections in Uttar Pradesh despite the obvious threat to their lives, supported the election of 8,00,000 representatives to those foundational units of Indian democracy. As the ineptitude of the state in addressing the pandemic brought India to its knees, it was the collective labours of ordinary folk that prevented complete collapse.

Gurudwaras in Delhi have long provided free meals called langars to people in need. During the summer of 2021, they realised that people needed oxygen more than food to be able to survive. To meet the rapidly rising demand, they established oxygen langars. Volunteers organised hundreds of cylinders that could supply oxygen to patients even as they waited for hospital-linked beds. For people who were too weak to leave their houses, the gurudwaras arranged to supply and/or refill their cylinders at their homes. When it became clear that beds were just not available given the extent to which demand outstripped supply, they created community-based hospitals equipped with beds, oxygen and trained staff.

Non-government organisations (NGOs) aided these efforts. The Hemkunt Foundation established temporary health centres across north India where they administered oxygen to COVID-19 patients free of charge. Where the patients were unable to make their way to the health centre, the foundation reached their homes. Director Harteerath Singh was soon flooded with cooked food for his volunteers prepared by grateful residents of Uttarakhand. In Telengana, Azam Khan, businessman and philanthropist, convened a team of volunteers who created an application for those searching for oxygen refills so team members could lead them to the nearest source. Harsh Mander's Karwan-e Mohabbat worked with the Archbishop of Delhi and the Green Crescent in Darya Ganj to create two fifty-bed facilities which provided COVID-19 care to the city's homeless residents. These endeavours represented only a drop in the vast oasis of compassion that provided solace to the millions braving the dreary Indian summer of 2021.

Beyond these institutions, countless individuals across the country stepped in to fill the void left by a state whose priorities lay elsewhere. They emerged from all walks of life and belonged to different castes, religions, genders and sexual orientations. They barely knew each other. But they were bound together by a shared hope in humanity and a belief that action was integral to realising the goals they harboured. And so, in their own small ways, they worked with their communities and others through turbulent times.

Patna-based Gaurav Rai had narrowly escaped death towards the end of the first wave. Upon his recovery, he decided that he would make it his life's mission to supply oxygen to those in need. He and his wife pooled in their savings and started an oxygen bank. Friends and strangers contributed to his endeavours: from ten cylinders, Rai's bank grew to 200. When the second wave engulfed India, the Rais worked tirelessly through the parched summer of 2021 to provide succour to patients needing oxygen supplies in Patna and eighteen neighbouring districts in Bihar. Rai came to be affectionately known as the Oxygen Man for his efforts.

Mumbai's Malad suburb had its own Oxygen Man in Shahnawaz Sheikh. Sheikh sold his SUV in the wake of the first wave in the summer of 2020 to start an oxygen supply scheme. This proved to be hopelessly inadequate when the second wave erupted. But there were others in Malad and elsewhere in Mumbai who were similarly trying to meet the growing demand for oxygen cylinders. So, Sheikh and his friends set up a control room from where they could coordinate efforts across the city and deliver oxygen to those who needed it. On some days, he was responding to as many as 600 calls, each more desperate than the other in their quest for air.

Vidhit Singh Bhaduria lost his father to COVID-19 on 24 April 2021 in Kanpur. Devastated, he too resolved to help others in dire need of oxygen. Over the next few weeks, he coordinated between people in need of oxygen and those supplying it, often fielding over 500 calls a day. Each call reminded him of his own sorrow. But Bhaduria embraced his grief. Conversations were punctuated with sniffles as he let his tears lubricate his conviction to help people struggling to survive.

Many people transformed their livelihoods into charitable activities. Prayagraj's Faizul had operated a hearse carriage for fifteen years but during the pandemic, he ferried dead bodies to crematoriums without charging a single rupee. Mumbai-based Dattatreya Sawant converted his autorickshaw into a mobile ambulance and transported COVID-19 patients to hospitals free of charge. Javed Khan, from Bhopal, similarly altered the autorickshaw he had been driving for eighteen years into an oxygen-fitted ambulance to take patients to health centres and clinics without charging his passengers for his service.

In Lucknow, e-rickshaw driver Gopi and bicycle-sellers Raja and Shakeel helped quarantined people with daily supplies as well as medicines and medical reports. In Bhopal, Saddam and Danish, trained firemen who were requisitioned as ambulance drivers, took it upon themselves to ensure that the dead received a dignified send-off. Janardhan, a hearing-impaired beedi worker in Kerala's Kunnur, donated his life's savings of ₹2 lakh to the Chief Minister's Vaccine Challenge Fund. We only know the first names of these valiant people.

Others helped shore up services whose delivery fell by the wayside as the nation struggled for breath. Sandhya (who only uses her first name) had just finished her graduate degree in commerce when the pandemic struck and schools were locked down. In the Adivasi hamlet of Chinnampathy in Tamil Nadu's Coimbatore district where she lived, there was no question of online classes. But Sandhya was determined not to let children in the hamlet go without education, and stepped in to offer classes to children across all age groups and subjects. As the only graduate in the hamlet, Sandhya recognised her responsibility towards fellow Adivasi students and worked hard to minimise the disruption caused to them by the closure of schools.

The death, devastation and despair wrought by the COVID-19 pandemic could not vanquish hope. Faced with an incompetent government, a megalomaniac prime minister and a ruling party obsessed only with achieving total domination from Parliament to panchayats, Indians turned to one another for help and encouragement. Hope alone could not supply oxygen to in dire straits. But it brought together strangers willing to help one another despite having little or nothing in common. By spurring action, the human spirit stepped in where the world's largest democracy failed to tread.

Farmers on the March

Three New Laws

The misguided confidence of the Indian government encouraged a brashness in law-making that proved to be based on hubris. In September 2020, within weeks of the consecration of the Ram temple in Ayodhya, the Lok Sabha passed three laws that promised to liberalise agriculture, thereby diluting state oversight over farming. This move, the government claimed, would benefit farmers.

The farmers disagreed. As far as they could see, the laws were designed to favour corporate interests and enable their takeover of Indian agriculture. Together, they sought to dismantle the elaborate protections that had been established to safeguard the interests of Indian farmers since Independence. Such protections guaranteed farmers a minimum support price to guard against fluctuations in the market. Prices of such essential items as cereals, pulses, oilseeds, edible oils, onions and potatoes were regulated to prevent the possible exploitation of farmers by traders. These safeguards also prevented the takeover of agricultural land by corporate entities, thus preventing distress sales in the countryside. By promising to liberalise agriculture, the new laws were a direct threat to the livelihood of farmers.

To be sure, the new laws were not entirely unexpected. Agriculture in India has been in the throes of crisis for a few decades. Farm sizes average a meagre 1.08 hectares,[1] among the lowest in the world. Farming continues to entail hard manual work, as small farm sizes make mechanisation unfeasible. Agricultural incomes remain stagnant as farmers find themselves enmeshed in debt they are unable to repay. A spate of suicides by farmers over the last two decades bears testimony to the crisis that bedevils agriculture as a viable occupation in India. The new legislation was touted as an antidote to such a crisis.

Their stated aims, as introduced in the Lok Sabha in September 2020, were impressive indeed. The Farmers' Produce Trade and Commerce (Promotion and Facilitation) Bill aimed to dismantle the trade and distribution monopoly enjoyed by the state-run Food Corporation of India (FCI) and the Agricultural Product Market Committees (APMCs), thus allowing farmers to deal directly with the markets. The Farmers' (Empowerment and Protection) Agreement of Price Assurance and Farm Services Bill allowed farmers to engage in contract farming and opened up agriculture to domestic and global corporates for investment. Finally, the amendment to the Essential Commodities Act of 1955 deregulated items such as cereals, pulses, oilseeds, edible oils, onions and potatoes. Together, they promised to make agriculture in India more efficient, more productive and more market-oriented.

Given the purported advantages of the farm laws, it was intriguing that the government rushed them through without either consulting the farmers and their representative organisations or encouraging debate on the issue within Parliament. The government easily rammed the laws through the Lok Sabha where it enjoyed a crushing majority but faced dissent from within its own ranks. Harsimrat Kaur, the minister for Food Processing and member of the Punjab-based Shiromani Akali Dal, BJP's oldest coalition partner, quit the government once it made clear its intentions of passing the law. As a 'daughter and a sister' of the farmers, she tweeted, Kaur would rather side with them than with the government. Of course, Kaur's resignation and the loss of its longest-standing alliance partner did little to dent the government's strength in Parliament. But it foreshadowed the extent of the opposition it was to face in the coming months.

In the Rajya Sabha, the upper house of Parliament whose assent is essential for bills to become laws, the reception was even colder. Here, the BJP did not enjoy a majority. A nervousness was palpable when the presiding officer called for a voice vote rather than a full vote to determine the opinion of the House. A voice vote entails the presiding officer asking members if they agree or disagree with a piece of legislation. If in support, members are asked to say 'aye', and if against, 'nay'. The decision on whether the motion is passed or not then rests on the presiding officer's discretion based on *their assessment* of which side was louder! The result was a shouting match rather than reasoned debate. When the presiding officer (a member of the BJP) eventually declared in favour of the ayes, suspicions of the legislations began to fester, denting the government's credibility. If the laws were as beneficial to India's farmers as the government claimed, why was it shying away from debate?

Besieging Delhi

And so, on a pleasant November morning, leaders of over 400 farmers' organisations gathered[2] in Chandigarh, the joint capital of the north-western states of Punjab and Haryana, to plan a response. They announced the formation of a Samyukta Kisan Morcha (United Farmers' Front). The movement called upon fellow farmers to march to Delhi to convince the union government to repeal the laws. 'Dilli Chalo!' the leaders urged, instructing protestors to reach the country's capital by 26 November.

The response was overwhelming. Thousands of farmers from Punjab began streaming towards Delhi. Without a clear plan, they stocked up their tractors and trolleys with essential items such as food grains, blankets and mattresses and headed towards the capital. However, they soon encountered a problem. To reach Delhi from Punjab, you have to cross Haryana, which was ruled by the BJP. The state government ordered police to erect barricades that, it hoped, would prevent the Punjabi farmers from entering. Roads were dug up and water cannons were deployed to slow down, if not completely halt, the march.

And then, Haryana's farmers came out in support of their brethren from Punjab, and both parties joined forces. Together, they pulled down the barricades and marched towards Delhi. The joint contingent of farmers from both states arrived at the Singhu border to the north of Delhi on 26 November, just as planned. A smaller contingent of farmers also set up camp at the Tikri border, to the city's west.

Farmers from other states also made their presence felt on the immediate outskirts of Delhi. Protestors began arriving from Uttar Pradesh and Uttarakhand, both ruled by the BJP. They camped at Ghazipur, at the eastern edge of the city. Farmers arriving from Rajasthan occupied Shahjahanpur, a village on the national highway on the southern edge of the city. By December 2020, Delhi was under siege by farmers from across northern India, surrounded on all sides.

The government appeared to be in no mood to concede to

their demands. The media became increasingly hostile in their depiction of the farmers as agents of opposition parties and, worse, as anti-national actors. Delhi's middle class, typically apolitical, was initially bemused by the farmers' strategies of protest but soon became irritated at the inconvenience; after all, blocked highways interfered with winter vacation plans.

But the farmers refused to give up. They persevered through the cold Delhi winter and the colder attitude of Delhi's media outlets and middle classes. Even as temperatures dipped lower and lower, they stayed put. The protest sites turned into a sea of tiny tents and tractor trolleys covered in tarpaulin within which men, women and children huddled together in blankets to brave the cold. But they couldn't sleep inside them for fear of asphyxiation. So, they had no option but to brave the winter nights under the sky. The bonfires they lit to warm themselves flickered like flames in lanterns desperately trying to hold their own in a storm. Dawn brought some relief from cold nights but low visibility on the highways proved to be hazardous—at least ten farmers were killed in road accidents at or near the protest sites.

A Reuters story from the time aptly depicted the farmers' endurance.[3] Balbir Singh, a farmer from Punjab's Patiala district, admitted that it was difficult to protest in such cold weather. But he was defiant. Over eighty years old, he was clear: 'We won't go back until our demands are met. Even if we have to die here, we will.' Wrapped in a blue blanket, seventy-six-year-old Paagh Singh told his interlocutor: 'We don't want more people to die in this protest and I hope Modi and his government take back the laws soon.' He added, for good measure, 'It's a democracy, and he [Modi] has to listen to us.'

An *India Today* feature showed the protesting farmers braving

Delhi's winter.[4] While some of them did spend the night inside open tents, most others had no option but to lay their mattresses on the highway to sleep on. It was not uncommon for farmers to sleep underneath their tractors, and a few reported using fodder instead of mattresses since it regulated body heat. Blankets became treasures and every inch was coveted real estate.

As someone who has spent three decades in gated Delhi neighbourhoods, I have always been enchanted by its winter. There is something joyous about the lukewarm glow of the lazy afternoon sun peering weakly through the dense fog. Colourful cardigans, mufflers with playful prints and pretty shawls jostle for attention. The evening lights are almost magical, interspersed with the crowds of people in shopping areas and public parks. As the nights bear down, you add as many layers as you possibly can to keep your body warm. When dawn breaks, the enigmas of the morning are veiled by fog. Silhouettes of people, animals and buildings add to the mysteries, making the familiar appear strange. Outside the gated neighbourhoods in which I have lived, however, the winters are harsher. As the night wears on, the fog gains strength, adding to the dread. If you are homeless and live on the city's pavements, it can swallow you whole, much like a whale devours krill. Year after year, winter mornings present a neglected ledger of those who made it through the night on the city's streets, and those who did not.

Similarly for the protesting farmers, the harshness of the Delhi winter made their lives miserable. The unwillingness of the powerful bureaucrats and politicians to meet their demands, or even talk to them, added to their disenchantment with the capital. The cruelty of the winter was matched only by the hostility of the media which persisted systematically with painting the farmers as disruptive agents of anti-national forces.

But the farmers did not give up.

Harbouring hope is not easy. It demands a stubborn determination to press on. The odds stack up against you: you face up to them. You resist the temptation to quit. Uncertainty about success might engulf you, like Delhi's fog devours its pavement dwellers. You find forces more powerful than you trying to dictate your present and command your future. You see your world collapsing. But you don't let that deter you. That is hope.

Hope challenges you to stretch the boundaries of your imagination. It lets you stretch the limits of what you think is conceivable. You are told that your way of life is at an end. Every reasonable commentator—even those who are sympathetic to you—would have you accept that your beliefs and practices are doomed. They will have you believe the government is too powerful for you and will overwhelm you in no time. But you insist on imagining the impossible. You insist on visualising an alternative future where the allegedly powerful state is compelled to listen to you. You insist that they respect your perspective. You do not yield.

Reclaiming Republic Day

India's Republic Day is tinged with mixed emotions. Broadcasts from Delhi's central vista might renew your patriotism and instil a sense of national pride, especially when you see the military parade and the fly-pasts. The colourful tableaus from different states might fill you with wonder at the way in which India's diversity has moulded its national unity. Alternatively, you might take a moment to reflect on the missed opportunities in the collective life of the nation; the difficulties faced by people who occupy an existence far removed from the glamour and glory on display. Whatever you do or wherever you are, it is highly unlikely you were ready for the spectacle that unfolded in India's national capital on Republic Day 2021.

As the city readied for the celebrations, farmers' groups at the Ghazipur, Tikri and Singhu borders commenced parallel rallies on tractors. Earlier in the month, they had declared their intention to ramp up their protests to coincide with the official commemoration of the Indian republic and had agreed with the city police to follow a predetermined route that circumvented the city's borders. The official celebrations would continue uninterrupted in the central vista while the farmers' protest rallies would occur in the periphery. In their enthusiasm, the tractors began to assemble at 8.00 a.m., several hours before their rally was to begin. There are broadly two versions of what happened next.[5]

According to the police, the farmers began their rally several hours before their allotted time and refused to follow the allocated route. Instead, they broke through the barricades and entered the city. Once in, they splintered into several smaller processions that unleashed violence and mayhem. Some groups clashed with the police near the Income Tax Office (ITO), a major landmark near the Yamuna River. Others laid siege to the historic Red Fort, the most potent symbol of Indian sovereignty, from whose ramparts the country's prime ministers have delivered their Independence Day speeches year after year since August 1947. At the Red Fort, they unfurled the Nishan Sahib, a religious flag associated with Sikhism, on an empty flag post next to the Indian Tricolour. For a few moments, the Nishan Sahib fluttered higher than the national flag, an intentional insult to the country and a threat to its sovereignty. The farmers' movement had been infiltrated by anti-national elements who were trying not only to topple the government but also undermine India's sovereign existence, according to this version of events.

The farmers themselves offered a contrasting version. Admittedly, they assembled hours before their allotted time. But that was due to their love of the country, not a premediated ploy to humiliate it. They did start their procession along the routes designated by the police. But they soon found that the police had barricaded the routes that they themselves had proposed. As the number of farmers swelled, so did their agitation at being betrayed by the police who were refusing to let the rallies proceed along the assigned routes. It was then that some of the younger, more agitated farmers separated from the mainstream rally and broke through the police barricades to enter the city.

However, they may well have also been aided by the police because it would have been impossible to enter the city without some official support that day. Further, the Red Fort is a national monument and would have been well protected on a day of such national importance as the Republic Day, so it would be impossible to be anywhere near it without police help. And finally, an empty flag post in the Red Fort, right next to the national tricolour, slightly taller than it could not be a mere coincidence. The circumstances were suspicious. It is quite possible that the police orchestrated these events to discredit the farmers.

Whatever the facts, a media already hostile to the demonstrators now truly bared its fangs. Ignoring the thousands of farmers who continued to protest peacefully despite receiving little cooperation from the police,[6] media houses competed with one another to paint them as criminals and seditionists.[7] Arnab Goswami outdid his standard vitriol, ranting:

What happened at the Red Fort today was an absolute and utter disgrace. For all the bleeding hearts who seek sympathy in the name of the farmers, these people whom you call farmers, disgraced my tiranga [tricolour] ... today. On a day that the country honoured 455 of its bravest, a group of rioters displayed their cowardice by replacing the tricolour with their own flag ... the same tiranga for which 25,000 soldiers of the INA [Indian National Army] gave up their lives before Independence. Why did we give these anti-nationals such a long rope, why did we become weak, why are we allowing it, you and I? There is an open conspiracy against Bharat Mata today. India is the target.[8]

Not to be outdone, Times Now commentator Padmaja Joshi repeatedly referred to 'rampaging mobs' running amok in the city. On a popular show titled *The Newshour Agenda*, visuals from ITO and Red Fort were recurrently shown to emphasise the lawless nature of the farmers' movement. But it was left to Sudhir Chaudhary of Zee TV to provide the icing on the cake. Anchoring a show provocatively titled *Andolan mein Khalistan*, he argued that the farmers' movement had been infiltrated by Khalistanis, that is, Sikh secessionists who had aimed to establish a sovereign Khalsa nation in Punjab during the 1980s.

The charge that Khalistani sympathisers were puppeteering the farmers' movement was raised early on in the protest.[9] No less a dignitary than K.K. Venugopal, the attorney general for the government of India, made this claim when the Supreme Court stayed the farm laws a fortnight prior to the fateful events on the Republic Day. Senior advocate Harish Salve also said as much: 'Those who organised rallies for Khalistan have put up flags at the protests.'

Of all the charges hurled at the farmers' protest, the accusation that they were being manipulated by, and serving the interests of, Khalistani supporters was perhaps the most damning. Such allegations ignited fears that the Khalistani militancy of the 1980s might be revived.

Playing on Fear and Anger

It was the afternoon of 31 October 1984. I had just returned from school and was about to sit down for lunch with my grandmother, whom we all called Didi-ji. Just then, my cousin burst in breathlessly to tell us that Indira Gandhi had been assassinated. His announcement made Didi-ji extremely agitated. Uncharacteristically for her, she left her lunch half-eaten, washed her hands and tuned in to the Philips radio that had been her companion for almost three decades. The airwaves crackled to life and mournful music confirmed the news. I vividly remember Didi-ji's face darkening in anger.

Later that evening, my father's sister and her husband, who lived in the neighbourhood, came over for a visit. They were both very agitated. 'Can you imagine their gall?' asked Uncle over and over again through the evening. 'They killed the prime minister. How long before they will break the country?' Aunty nodded pensively. 'It's going to be terrible.' Uncle then began to recount the ways in which 'they' needed to be taught a lesson. Didi-ji reminded him that violence had already taken over the city. 'About time,' he muttered. The pall of gloom in the room was so thick you could reach out and feel it. My father's family were avid Congress supporters, almost devoted to Indira Gandhi. Their grief at her cold-blooded murder was understandable. What was difficult to comprehend was the hatred against an entire community that seemed to have suddenly overtaken everyone in the city, from the posh living rooms in south Delhi to the slums in west Delhi, where Hindus and Sikhs had lived together since the shared trauma of Partition.

Over the next few days, Delhi burned. From the rooftop of our house in Kailash Colony, you could see columns of smoke arise from Amar Colony and elsewhere in the city. The nation was avenging the assassination of the prime minister, we were told. By the time the military was called in and a semblance of normalcy restored, Delhi's 8 per cent Sikh minority had been adequately terrorised enough to satisfy the nation's conscience.

The brutality in Delhi was echoed in Punjab, as a result of which the Sikh majority became even more disgruntled and alienated than before. The demand among sections of the population for an independent Khalistan, a sovereign Sikh state independent of India, ironically gathered even more momentum. The anti-Sikh pogrom in Delhi provided fodder for leaders of the movement who highlighted the impossibility of living in the country as a religious minority. For over a decade, the movement terrorised rural Punjab, claiming hundreds of ordinary people as well as high-profile victims, including the state's chief minister, Beant Singh, who was blown apart in a suicide attack in 1995.

Although observers have remained polarised about the antecedents of the Khalistan movement, they broadly agree that its most dreaded proponent was Jarnail Singh Bhindranwale. Born in 1947 amidst the tumult of Independence and the Partition, Bhindranwale was both a farmer and an ascetic affiliated with a religious school. His meteoric rise within the firmament of Punjab's politics illustrated the possibilities through which agriculture and religion could be entwined to challenge the might and sovereignty of the Indian state. Bhindranwale deftly played the Congress Party—the pole around which Indian politics revolved through much of the 1970s and 1980s—off against the Akali Dal, the most important challenger to the Congress dominance of the Punjab. His cunning knack for politicking enabled him to manipulate the notorious factionalism within both parties to marginalise them as political actors and emerge as a torchbearer of the separatist movement for Khalistan in the early 1980s.

Late in 1982, Bhindranwale and his supporters occupied the precincts of the Golden Temple, Sikhism's holiest shrine. By April 1984, the government, led by Prime Minister Indira Gandhi, worried that a declaration of an independent Khalistan was imminent. In June, she ordered troops into the Golden Temple to flush out Bhindranwale and his associates. Operation Blue Star followed, leading to a twenty-four-hour gun battle, at the end of which Bhindranwale was killed, but so were several innocent pilgrims who had been used as human shields by the separatists. The Akal Takht, venerated as the 'Throne of the Timeless One', was desecrated, causing widespread anger among Sikhs across the world. Two such Sikhs were Gandhi's bodyguards who pumped scores of bullets into her on the morning of 31 October 1984.

Almost four decades on, these fateful events continue to cast a long shadow on the country, invoked by a hostile media to both exaggerate the threat posed by protesting farmers as well as to belittle their claims. Thoughtless comments by individuals did not help either. In a much-publicised interview with the journalist Barkha Dutt, actor Deep Singh Sidhu, who claimed to be part of the farmers' agitation, declared his support for Bhindranwale. The farmer-ascetic was merely a proponent of federalism, neither a secessionist nor a terrorist, insisted Sidhu. In doing so, he downplayed the terror unleashed by Khalistani militants across north-west India through the 1980s and 1990s. Such comments fed into a convenient narrative that connected the protesting farmers to the Khalistani movement.

To be sure, political figures are complex characters. They are people of many parts. By fixating on whether or not Bhindranwale was a terrorist, both Dutt and Sidhu missed an opportunity to build bridges. Despite proclaiming support for the protesting farmers, both, in fact, undermined the solidarity being practised by the farmers' protest movement which brought together Sikhs and Hindus (alongside others) once divided by the prospects of secessionism. Sikh farmers marched shoulder to shoulder with Hindu farmers, received with enthusiasm by residents of different faiths wherever they went. It was precisely this harmony across religious divides that the media narrative sought to shatter.

Despondency

The morning after the drama in Delhi, the city's police filed FIRs against nearly twenty farmers' leaders. Eviction notices were slapped on the protestors, asking them to vacate the protest sites or face arrest for unlawful occupation. Even though the disturbances in Delhi were caused by a handful of miscreants and the farmers' rallies had been largely peaceful, the police held all farmers responsible and ordered them to wind up their protests and return to their villages. Police in Uttar Pradesh and Haryana, where some of the protest sites were located, did the same.

The protests lay in tatters. Despondency was rife. Despair descended on the sites where the farmers has camped. While the farmers were given three days to vacate the sites, their leaders would most likely face arrest for having incited trouble. It had always been known that the government would not repeal the three controversial laws without a fight. Although Delhi's residents were largely sympathetic to the protests, the farmers had never expected their struggle to be a walkover. Indeed, the protestors had been infused with anticipation since the movement began in November 2020. Spirits had been high even through the beastly winter, riding on a wave of hope that the government would at least listen to the farmers' demands and be willing to compromise. Instead, the farmers were now being labelled anti-national. To be vilified as terrorists, as people whose actions had threatened the sovereignty of their beloved country, was humiliating. The dominant atmosphere in the campsites was that of defeat and abject shame.

The backlash faced by farmers illustrates the perils of acting on hope. Even as they refused to cave in, the protestors were subjected to rhetorical attacks by the media and physical assaults by the police. Actions motivated by conviction can invite visceral retribution, especially when directed against those in power. If done right, tactical retributive actions can demonise protestors, which is often far more effective than physical violence. In fact, physical violence might generate sympathy for protestors. But branding them as terrorists delegitimises their actions. Not only that, it makes people fear the objectives of the dissenters. A vilification of hope is the surest way to kill it.

On its part, harbouring hope entails being attentive to the realities of the world and its politics. It recognises the retribution that follows resistance. As it happens, the greater chance of success a movement might have, the higher the possibility of retaliation. The farmers marching to Delhi did not delude themselves into believing that the might of the Indian state would crumble before their slogans and the poetry of well-meaning allies. They recognised that their ranks could include individuals whose thoughtlessness could be manipulated by the government and its stooges. This recognition led not to the abandonment of hope but a conviction that something could be done about it.

Leading a section of the farmers from Uttar Pradesh, Rakesh Tikait had so far been a peripheral player in the farmers' protests. In fact, he was an unlikely ally, having admitted to voting for the BJP as late as 2019. Having once been a constable in the Delhi Police, Tikait was not instinctively against authority. In the present agitation, he had largely been overshadowed by the more belligerent leadership of farmers from Punjab. That was about to change.

Muzaffarnagar, 2013

Kaval is a nondescript village on the outskirts of Muzaffarnagar town in western Uttar Pradesh, a little over 125 kilometres from Delhi. On 27 August 2013, it became the site of three murders that ignited the flames of violence between the region's Muslims and Hindus. Rioting across the villages of the district ripped apart their shared identity as farmers. Over the next few weeks, speeches were made by aspiring politicians to large gatherings, further fanning the flames.[10]

In neighbouring Sisauli, the Tikait household was worried. Naresh Tikait, the head of the household, was also the chief of the Baliyan Khap, a cluster of eighty-four clans covering several of villages in the area. Some of the Khap's members had been accused by the state government of instigating the violence. News reports suggested that his younger brother Rakesh had also been indicted, and a warrant for his arrest had been issued.

Naresh Tikait had inherited the chieftaincy of the Balyan Khap from his father, Mahendra Singh Tikait, the legendary leader of northern India's farmers. In 1988, the elder Tikait had famously led 5,00,000 farmers into the heart of New Delhi, and laid siege on the Boat Club, adjacent to the iconic India Gate. That movement had brought the then Congress government, led by Rajiv Gandhi, to its knees and paved the way for the party's coming collapse across north India. Mahendra Singh Tikait had built the farmers' movement based on unity between Hindus and Muslims who shared the joys and sorrows of tilling the land. He happily split the leadership of the Bharatiya Kisan Union (BKU), a trade union of agriculturists, with farmers of both communities so they could present a united front while demanding protections for agriculture. His activism also extended to issues beyond agriculture—in 1987, when state police kidnapped, raped and killed a young Muslim girl, Tikait's BKU responded. Against police efforts at painting the incident as a Hindu–Muslim conflict, BKU activists swung into action: they blocked the highways, barricaded the police station and took policemen hostage till the administration promised an official enquiry and paid the family a compensation.[11] After his death in 2008, Naresh inherited the mantle of both the Khap as well as the union. But in 2013, the violence that was rapidly engulfing Muzaffarnagar threatened to undo the decades of Hindu–Muslim solidarity that his father had achieved with comrades.

It also presented opportunities. As an aspiring politician, Rakesh Tikait had contested elections in the past but failed miserably. The unfolding situation offered new prospects for his political ambitions. So, when a mahapanchayat (a grand assembly) was called on 7 September, both brothers willingly participated.[12] Incendiary speeches were made, as community leaders as well as local politicians sought to outdo one another to holler for revenge against the Muslims who, it was alleged, had violated the honour of Jat women. The Tikaits did little to calm nerves and merely looked on as their clansmen demanded retribution. If anything, their position in the community and presence in the assembly may well have encouraged the baying for blood. Both brothers were accused by the state government of sparking violence.

Although the violence subsided within months, the scars remained. Around sixty people had been killed and over 5,000 displaced. The Tikaits called for peace. They urged fleeing

Muslims to return to their villages and promised to do their best to restore confidence among them. But Rakesh also claimed that members of Hindu Jats were being wrongly accused of rape and murder, thereby undermining his brother's efforts at promoting peace.

Muzaffarnagar disrupted the hard-earned communal peace in Uttar Pradesh. The region had regularly witnessed religious conflict since the 1920s—the most recent of these occurred in the aftermath of 6 December 1992 when rampaging mobs had pulled down the Babri Masjid in Ayodhya. Since then, however, successive governments had managed to contain passions. Chief ministers across party lines—Mulayam Singh Yadav of the Samajwadi Party, BSP's supremo Mayawati and even the BJP's Rajnath Singh—paid careful attention to the upholding of communal harmony to prevent the recurrence of communal unrest. Social mistrust may well have remained, but an administrative consensus in favour of peace did not allow matters to spill over into violence.

The Turning of the Tables

Two days after the dramatic events of Republic Day 2021, the police began to move into Ghazipur where Rakesh Tikait had camped with a modest contingent of farmers. Their brief was to disperse the farmers and arrest Tikait who had been named as one of the instigators of the violence. It was 5.00 p.m. A vicious attack by the police on the farmers appeared imminent.

The mainstream media had arrived to cover the events as they went down. The suppression of the farmers and their eventual humiliation had to be etched into collective memory. Media persons harangued Tikait and taunted him repeatedly: was he going to be arrested or would he prefer to surrender?

They were raring for the kill. Even as the police numbers swelled at the site, Rakesh Tikait found himself mobbed by impatient reporters. Dressed in a white kurta pyjama, wearing a green cap and a green waistcoat, he had just emerged from a meeting with his colleagues. They were in the tent that had served as the movement's makeshift office and doubled as the main stage from where leaders addressed the farmers. The words 'Kisan Ekta Manch' (or Farmers' Unity Forum) blazed in the backdrop. Posters of revolutionaries such as Chandrashekhar Azad, Bhagat Singh, Rajguru and Sukhdev—all of whom had been martyred by the British colonial administrators while still in their twenties—adorned the sides. A life-size cut-out of Chaudhary Charan Singh, the legendary farmer of the Jat community who had briefly served as India's prime minister, looked on. What was Tikait's plan, a reporter asked, shoving his microphone into the harassed leader's face. When was he going to vacate Ghazipur, another screamed. Was he going to surrender, a third wanted to know.

Tikait tried to answer amidst the din.[13]

> They want to destroy the farmers in this country. We will not let that happen. They are coming to get us. But we will stay put. We are not going anywhere. It is my responsibility to speak up to defend the farmers. And nothing will happen to them under my watch, I tell you that. They will have to withdraw the bills, they will have to listen to us. The BJP is hell-bent on ruining the farmers. We will not let that happen. If the laws are not repealed, let me repeat, if the laws are not repealed, then this Rakesh Tikait will commit suicide.

Tears welled up in Tikait's eyes. Flummoxed, someone asked him why he was crying. Why didn't he just listen to the administration and vacate Ghazipur?

'There is no question of vacating,' he said, shaking his head vigorously. The broadcast warbled as the reporters crowded in. Rakesh Tikait choked on his tears. Unable to speak further, he broke down completely and began sobbing in earnest.

Tikait's emotional breakdown was broadcast live not only into the living rooms of an apathetic middle class but also to homes and communities across rural India and abroad. For farmers across northern India, his tears struck a chord. Within minutes, farmers across religious divides, who had hitherto been unresponsive to the movement, gathered outside the Tikait home in Muzaffarnagar's Sisauli village. They urged Rakesh's elder brother Naresh to convene a mahapanchayat as soon as possible. In the meantime, hundreds of Jat farmers left Sisauli for Delhi to join their clansman. By 11.00 p.m., the campsite, which had worn a desolate look just a few hours ago, was abuzz with activity.

Over the next few hours, you could see thousands of tractors on the highways converging towards Delhi.[14] 'The government has overplayed its hand. By humiliating one of us, they have provoked us all,' one farmer on his way to the capital told a news channel. 'I have nothing to do with the union. But seeing the tears in Chaudhry's [honorific for Tikaits] eyes has moved me. I want to be with him in this hour of need.'

'We had just sat down for a meal,' said another farmer, who had just arrived at Ghazipur, when asked why they were here. It was well past midnight. 'The news showed Chaudhry in tears. We said we had to be there for him. The government should understand if they harm him, they alone will be responsible for the consequences.'

Hundreds of tractors containing thousands of farmers poured into Ghazipur overnight. Short video clips were circulated by contingents that were already on their way, or planning to be. Tiny temples across Haryana and Uttar Pradesh called for devotees to support the protests, urging them to leave as soon as they could. If the national media had been hell-bent on humiliating Tikait, social media users on Twitter, Instagram and Facebook were galvanised to support him. The roads from little-known districts such as Jind, Bhivani, Kaithal, Hissar and others were soon choc-a-bloc with people and their vehicles heading to the capital. The movement had been revived. By the time dawn broke, the protest sites had been bolstered with both numbers and fresh morale.

The following morning, on 29 January, back in Sisauli, Naresh Tikait convened the mahapanchayat that he had been urged to. Thousands of people gathered from across the religious cracks that had spread a few years ago. Among the attendees was Ghulam Muhammad Jaula, an octogenarian farmer who had been a close associate of the older Tikait. Following the riots of 2013 and the Tikaits' unwillingness to intervene in favour of restoring peace, he had split from the BKU to set up a separate union representing mostly Muslims. But now, Naresh beseeched him, the Tikaits needed him. All the farmers in the region needed him.

On Naresh's request, Ghulam Muhammad Jaula addressed the mahapanchayat. His short speech was to the point and minced no words. The Tikaits and the mahapanchayat had made a mistake in 2013. They had killed Muslims or had looked the other way when Muslims had been violated. The audience listened. There was pin-drop silence. No booing. No disagreement. No muttering. The Muslims had always stood by the Jats, but the Jats let them down. The Jats would have to acknowledge this mistake. The Tikaits would have to acknowledge this mistake. Only then would bhaichara, the bonds of brotherhood, that had been forged between the two communities through decades of struggle, be revived in the region. Would Naresh Tikait acknowledge his fault?

As chief of the Balyan Khap, as the son of the legendary Mahendra Singh Tikait and as a leader of the Jat community, Naresh Tikait recognised the error of their ways.[15] They had blundered. They had been angry with specific incidents and made the mistake of allowing the BJP to hijack their anger, which got carried too far. It could not happen again. The Jats in the mahapanchayat cheered. They vouched to boycott the BJP.

When the contingent from Muzaffarnagar left for Ghazipur later that day, both Hindus and Muslims were in it. Over the next few months, Tikait would insist that meetings commenced with '*Har Har Madev*' interspersed with '*Allahu Akbar*' and '*Bole So Nihal, Sat Sri Akal*' to emphasise the inter-religious solidarity among the farmers. The alliances demanded by the political practice of hope broadens people's horizons. Writing in the shadows of Nazism, the historian Ernst Bloch makes exactly this point in his epic three-volume study *The Principle of Hope*. 'The emotion ... goes out of itself,' he writes, '[and] makes people broad instead of confining them.' Rakesh Tikait had grasped this lesson well.

Over the next few months, the protests went from strength to strength. Early in September 2021, over 5 lakh farmers converged at Tikait's home ground in Muzaffarnagar to renew their demands for repealing the laws. Later that month, on 27 September, the farmers' organisations called for a Bharat Bandh, an all-India strike. The strike paralysed Punjab and parts of western Uttar Pradesh, and received extensive support in the southern states of Andhra Pradesh, Tamil Nadu and Kerala. Sensing the ever-increasing support for the farmers' cause, Prime Minister Modi publicly announced on 19 November 2021 that the unpopular farm laws would be repealed at the earliest. Within a fortnight, their withdrawal was approved by both houses of Parliament. The

President signed the Repeal Act on 2 December, almost a year after the protestors had begun their march to Delhi. The farmers had achieved a decisive victory.

The farmers' protest, and their triumph, taught the world an important lesson about the audacity of hope. The protestors faced harsh weather and harsher clampdowns by the state and its allies in the media. But they refused to give up. They had been well-organised and their leaders made strategic choices to reach across social cleavages rather than be confined by them. They had remained focused on their demands and leveraged the popular perception of farmers being annadatas (food providers) in their favour. Not all social groups enjoy such a status. Nor are they able to exercise the leverage the farmers could. But that has not, as we have seen, diminished the importance of hope among them.

The Art of Hope

Narendra Modi is celebrated as the most popular prime minister in the world. His approval ratings regularly outstrip that of his contemporaries. The two massive electoral victories achieved by the BJP under his leadership further evidence his popularity. His victory was eagerly awaited by many Indians tired of the repeated allegations of corruption against the Congress-led UPA government. They hoped for an honest government led by a capable leader. And after Modi's advent, Indians anticipated the prospect of genuine socio-economic progress following a spell of stagnation. Instead, they found themselves consumed by a scorching blaze of hate and anger.

Old scars have been wrenched open and new wounds inflicted upon India's body politic. Fear, suspicion and distrust have exacerbated the country's deeply-rooted gulfs and ruptured its delicate social balance. As crisis after crisis has visited the Indian population, the state has either turned a blind eye or actively fuelled the troubles that are eroding the country's democracy. The previous pages offered a glimpse into how Indians are trying their best to preserve democracy. In their efforts, they have often turned to art for succour, for inspiration and for expression. This concluding chapter presents a slice of the arts that have reinforced Indians as they resist the erosion of their democracy.

Art has long been deployed to express dissent. The arts allow us to reach deep into our emotions. Images, sounds and textures enable people to relate to each other without the need for words or text. Advocates of human rights, environmental justice, transparency and accountability take recourse to art or amplify artistic expressions to advance their claims. Leaders of social movements often appeal to their communities through creative presentations and representations that spark a range of emotions which can shape public sentiment. Artists have often been outspoken critics of regimes as their art has the power to question, disturb and disrupt the status quo. The rise of digital technology has been instrumental in inspiring protest art in social movements across different geographies. It is now possible, more than ever before, to propagate analogue art to diverse audiences: people can click photos of graffiti on a wall somewhere with their mobile phones and share with their followers. It is also possible now, unlike ever before, to digitally produce art, such as memes and digital insignia for social media that can be appropriated and deployed for greater visibility and reach. The scale and speed of digital dissemination has in turn further accelerated the process of inspiring protest art globally. It shows how digital and analogue art can complement each other and inspire people to take to the streets or spark online dissent.

The use of art to protest autocratic tendencies among Indian rulers goes back decades, if not centuries. Roving bands of bards sang songs and wrote couplets that defied the authority of Mughal emperors and Brahmanical elites alike. Colonial rule spawned generations of poets, painters and others who advanced the cause of Indian independence from British rule. Almost immediately after the transfer of power to the Congress Party under Nehru, artists turned their attention to the new Indian government.

From the Indian People's Theatre Association to the Kabir Kala Manch, the repertoire of artworks that have protested draconian tendencies and expressed a desire for a better future has included paintings, posters, songs, poems and theatre.

The Poetics of Politics

Poets are particularly incorrigible. In India, you might even call them equal opportunity offenders since they rile up governments led by the BJP and the Congress alike. Varavara Rao, arrested in the aftermath of the Bhima Koregaon events of 2018, first came into prominence for the agitations he led against Indira Gandhi's regime back in 1973. His poetry and activism earned him the ire of the Congress-led state government in Andhra Pradesh, which rewarded him with a jail term of several years. He was repeatedly harassed and jailed by subsequent governments in his state, irrespective of who was heading it. But Rao remained undaunted. At the end of his very first incarceration, he wrote defiantly:

> This is jail for the voice and the feet
> But the hand hasn't stopped writing
> The heart hasn't stopped throbbing
> Dream still reaches to the horizon of light
> Travelling from this solitary darkness ...[1]

Poetry's indomitable spirit was once again on display during the protests against the CAA. Inspired by the Miya poets in Assam, writers in the Gangetic belt too began to speak up in verse. Within two weeks of the passage of the amendment, comedian Varun Grover performed a piece titled *Hum Kagaz Nahin Dikhayenge* (We will not show our documents). The piece defied the premise of the NRC and the CAA by proclaiming the artist's refusal to show their documents as proof of citizenship. 'We', the people of India, were 'here to stay', Grover insisted, no matter what.

Hum Kagaz Nahin Dikhayenge became an instant classic across the Hindi-speaking world. In the video, wearing a plain white shirt, sitting in front of a wooden panel, Grover conveys powerful simplicity. Born in the small town of Sundarnagar in Himachal Pradesh and brought up in Uttarakhand's Dehradun, Grover had spent his teenage years in Lucknow and studied engineering in Varanasi. His mother was a schoolteacher and his father in the army. Grover was the quintessential small-town north Indian Hindi-speaking man with a privileged caste Hindu name belonging to the demographic most likely to support the BJP's ideological and political agenda. Yet, here he was, defying the political party which many from his social milieu were loyal to. Grover had given up his career in engineering to become a writer, lyricist and comedian in 2015. His performance offered a powerful pushback to the otherwise widespread acceptance of the CAA and the NRC by others in his class. But it was not the only one.

Born in Patna and educated in Delhi, Amir Aziz gave up his corporate job to embrace his passions, theatre and songwriting, in 2019. In March that year, he released *Acche Din Blues*, a song that played on Modi's promise of 'good days' for fellow Indians. The following month saw the release of the darker *Ballad of Pehlu Khan*, in which he wrote about the gruesome lynching of the dairy farmer Pehlu Khan by cow vigilantes in Rajasthan. Around the same time that Grover released *Hum Kaagaz Nahin Dikhayenge*, Aziz reminded his audience about the poetics of nation-building. '*Hindustan ek khwab hai*,' he said to an interviewer. India is a dream and there was place in it for everyone. Two months after the passage of the CAA in Parliament, Aziz mesmerised audiences in Mumbai with his fourth political piece, *Sab Yaad Rakha Jaayega*. Everything will be remembered. The jokes cracked by the oppressors would be met with the justice sought by the oppressed, the poet assured his audience. Injustice on earth would be countered by revolutions in the skies.

Sab Yaad Rakha Jaayega immortalised the struggles against the CAA, including the state's brutal crackdown on dissent. Aziz dedicated the poem to the memory of myriad victims of state violence, from Kashmir to Uttar Pradesh, including students at Jamia, JNU and AMU. The poem, quite literally, drove home the adage that to remember is to resist. The memory of grief, pain and trauma that Aziz's poem brought to life was not intended to paralyse audiences with dejection. On the contrary, Aziz invigorated his listeners by warning those in authority that nothing would be forgotten.

While Grover and Aziz provoked their audiences to reflect on the nation and its dissenting imaginations across north India, the poet Sukirtharani (who only uses one name) was urging her audiences to think about something even more fundamental: the role of their own bodies in dissenting from societal expectations. Born in a village near Tamil Nadu's Vellore district, she was the first in her village to complete her graduation. The gruesome rape and murder of Dalit women in Maharasthra's Khairlanji district back in 2006 shocked her into reflecting on her own identity as a Dalit woman: poetry offered her a means of expressing her thoughts. Her poem *Yen Udal* (My Body) expresses Dalit women's refusal to be confined by a caste-supremacist patriarchal society.[2]

The poet cautions men against harbouring ambitions of controlling women's agency. They are welcome to try but the poem warned such men of the consequences of their actions: such attempts invite women's wrath. 'The more you confine me,' the poet addresses such men, 'The more I will spill over.' If women's bodies were patriarchal sites of class and communal strife, the poem reminds readers that these very same bodies could be reclaimed against such strife.

Yen Udal epitomises Dalit women's intersectional struggle against patriarchy, casteism and classism. It does this by appropriating precisely those features men attribute to women which then form the basis for their marginalisation and infantilisation. Through it, Sukirtharani offers a vision of social equality that is not derived from behaviours deemed appropriate but instead stems from a basic recognition of, and respect for, human personhood. While reminding us of the limits imposed upon women by society, *Yen Udal* harbours hopes for liberation from these constraints.

The poems by Grover, Aziz and Sukirtharani offer stirring thoughts for renewing Indian democracy. As poets, they recognise the political and social assaults on democracy but refuse to cave in. Instead, like the generations of poets before them, they offer stirring compositions that provoke you to ruminate and, perhaps most importantly, to hope.

Comedy as Commentary

Complementing the work of poets in stimulating reflection among Indians are comedians. By tickling the funny bones of their largely privileged audiences in the metropolitan cities of Delhi, Mumbai and Bengaluru, comedians across the country compel their audiences to confront the stark political and social realities. Stand-up comedy offers particularly punchy opportunities for artistes to discuss social and political hierarchy. The humour they generate offers hope that the fortress of political authoritarianism and social inequality is not entirely impenetrable and may well be—eventually—breached.

A week after the Indian government stripped Jammu and Kashmir of statehood in 2019, Sanjay Rajoura of the comedy collective Aisi Taisi Democracy appeared on stage to offer his commentary on the events. Basing his account on his own upbringing as a Jat boy in western Uttar Pradesh, he went where few people in north India dared to tread: to reflect on the normalisation of violence achieved by the Indian government in Kashmir. His act opened on the beats of the azadi slogan that have become the anthem of Kashmiri resistance to state-sponsored violence.

In the act,* Rajoura invokes his background as a member of the Jat community from western Uttar Pradesh. Amid riotous laughter, he jokes about parents beating their children as a form of strengthening family bonds. 'Basically, we are brought up like Kashmiris,' he says matter-of-factly, as the audience claps loudly and roars its approval. His father would hit him whenever he felt like it, he tells his audience, while his mother assured him it was his own benefit: 'Just like the home minister.'[3]

Sometimes, comedy is about appropriating stereotypes and prevailing perspectives in ways that is careful not to invite legal censure or social challenge. Gurugram-based Amar Singh's *Indian Stereotypes and Unmarried Indians* leverages the prevailing stereotypes about Indians from across the country to deliver

---

*Descriptions of certain performances discussed in this chapter have been linked to YouTube via QR codes to encourage readers to engage with the works of these artists directly.

hard-hitting yet poignant criticism of the violence embraced by Hindutva ideologues and politicians. His act approaches the topic from the fairly quotidian observation that Indians are often defined by stereotypes before exposing their darker underpinnings. Singh's act begins innocuously, with a rather banal discussion on the stereotypes attached to Indians which hinder their efforts at matchmaking, a fairly well-known aspect of social life that invites little controversy.

He then goes on confess to his audience that he hides his Gujarati identity. His real name is Amar Patel. But he desists from revealing his identity because of the stereotypes attached to it. People begin to probe Gujaratis' predilections. What stereotypes are attached to Gujaratis? Punjabis are stereotyped as loud, uncouth, rustic. Bengalis are fish-loving, dessert-devouring people. What defines Gujarat? Here, Singh pauses. 'Well, Gujaratis are famous for their love of Muslims.' He pauses again, for effect. 'Like, Gujaratis love Muslims to pieces.'[4] 

Meanwhile, some Gujarati Muslims, who were targeted during the 2002 carnage, have lost neither their hope nor their humour. Munawar Faruqui was barely ten years old when violence exploded in his home state. His family in Junagadh lost their possessions (including their documentation) that summer and his mother died soon after. Faruqui's family moved to Mumbai, where he combined his studies with working at a utensil store. He began his professional career as a graphic designer and moved to stand-up comedy in 2017.

On New Year's Day in 2021, Faruqui's show in Indore's Munro Park Cafe was interrupted by local BJP leaders. They accused him of insulting Ram, Sita and Home Minister Amit Shah. Charges were filed against him and his friends Nalin Yadav and Edwin Anthony as well as Prakash and Priyam Vyas for hurting religious sentiments and for violating COVID-19 protocols. Faruqui and Yadav were imprisoned for thirty-five and fifty-eight days, respectively, before being released on bail. While their arrest reignited the debate about freedom of expression, it exposed the very real dangers of being a comedian in contemporary India. For Faruqui and Yadav, the arrest only strengthened their resolve not to cave in.

Upon his release, Faruqui returned to performing comedy shows which have attracted audiences thirsty for political content that is both funny and satirical. Initially, venues were sceptical of allowing him a platform. Sometimes, shows were scheduled and then cancelled. But that did not deter him. Eventually, Faruqui delivered a show titled *Gujarati, Muslims and Global Warming* in which he drew on his personal life and social milieu as political commentary that was dark and hilarious at the same time. The show garnered almost 150 lakh views on YouTube alone. One viewer commended him for exemplifying the axiom that art should comfort the disturbed and disturb the comfortable.

Faruqui delves into a conversation he has with his co-worker about global warming. His co-worker alleges global warming to be the result of overpopulation among Muslims. The causality offered in his account of her diatribe is outlandish but commonly heard. Muslims bear more children, the children need to be housed, apartment complexes are built for them by clearing out forests and deforestation, of course, leads to global warming. 'We are not even allowed into those properties,' Faruqui protests to his co-worker.

Faruqui now dips out of the conversation with his co-worker and addresses his audience directly. He cites research that suggests 38 per cent modern properties in India refuse housing to Muslims. Builders are rarely enthusiastic about renting or selling properties to a Muslim. 'Go west,' a broker told Faruqui during a house hunt. 'Where?' asks a baffled Faruqui. 'There. Over there. Go to Pakistan,' responded the broker.[5]

The audience is in splits, but Faruqui is not done yet. He now turns to another demographic that faces genuine difficulties finding accommodation: bachelors. The difficulties are well-known, at least anecdotally. Landlords prefer families rather than single people, as families are considered to be safe and stable tenants. Bachelors are stereotyped as troublemakers and unreliable. And male Muslim bachelors, thus, face multiple difficulties finding accommodation. As the audience considers this well-regarded facet of communal discrimination, Faruqui interjects, 'But if you are a Gujarati bachelor, you get to run the whole country.' He is, of course, referring to Prime Minister Modi's celebrated bachelorhood.

Faruqui's friend Nalin Yadav refused to give up as well. Like Faruqui, he faced hostility from venues that had previously been eager to host him. Indeed, to make ends meet, he had to take up odd jobs, including as a daily wage labourer, before finally getting a chance to reintroduce his humour to audiences. *Humour Khatre Mein* gathered over 1,00,000 views on YouTube, relatively modest vis-à-vis Faruqui's show but no less commendable. *Humour Khatre Mein* (Humour is in danger) is a creative play on the Hindu nationalist canard that 'Hindus are in danger'. Yadav used the show to reflect on his time in prison and to offer broader political commentary that was both witty and chilling. Yadav's explicit embrace of Cornel West's suggestion that justice is what love looks like in public helps contextualise much of his humour.

Yadav's act includes reminding his audience that he and Munawar Faruqui both went to jail. But while Faruqui was in jail for thirty-five days, he was imprisoned for fifty-eight. 'And people

are refusing to believe that Hindus are in danger,' he quips, amid loud laughter and cheering.[6]

If political satire has been winning hearts and minds across India, social satire is not far behind. A new generation of comedians who explicitly and unreservedly take on casteist hierarchies has exploded onto the artistic firmament in the country. They leverage their own Dalit identities to drive home the brutality of continuing caste injustice. Manaal Patil, Ankur Tangade, Manjeet Sarkar, Neha Thombre and Ravi Gaikwad are among several emerging comedians who entertain audiences with their stand-up acts that blend social protest with witty humour.

Manaal Patil began performing in 2015 when he was seventeen. The Hyderabad-based comic's early acts tended to punch down by attacking affirmative actions before he realised the political import of these constitutional provisions. His recent acts illustrate the transformation in his thinking. In a show titled *Dating and Reservation*, Patil leveraged the stereotypes associated with affirmative actions to hilarious effect.[7] He narrates an exchange with his father when he fared poorly in his high school exams and was worried about getting admission in a good college and securing a good job thereafter. His father calmed his nerves and assured him that he would benefit from 'a superpower'. When Patil enquired about the nature of the superpower, his father simply said, 'We are scheduled castes,' at which point the audience erupts in laughter. Being in a scheduled caste is associated with poverty, deprivation and suffering. But in this act, Patil suggests the contrary, appearing to affirm the stereotype that scheduled castes were benefiting disproportionately from the system. At that point, many in the audience might have genuinely cheered him for giving voice to their own biases against affirmative actions.

'You'll get admission in a college of your choice quicker than you get a pizza delivery, he said,' Patil continues, drawing further on the hackneyed association of affirmative actions with an easy life. 'You go to a job interview and say "Jai Bhim"—they will make you their CEO.' Patil then says he questions his father. 'Isn't this all a little unfair?' His father chastens him for showing off his English-speaking skills: 'I benefitted from reservation, that is why you know how to speak it.' At this point, it is clear that Patil is not punching down on affirmative actions but recognising its emancipatory capacity. To leave no one in any doubt about the satirical intent of his act, he invites his audience to touch him and gauge if he is real, playing on the 'untouchable' identity that is attached to his community. And then, continuing in his deadpan expression, Patil delivers his punchline: 'That is why I am sitting and doing stand-up, I just wanted a seat.'

Patil's English-language acts are aimed at audiences belonging to privileged castes who are often deprecatory in their attitudes towards affirmative actions. But he has found audiences welcoming and receptive, which illustrates the possibility of humour in shifting social attitudes. This reception has allowed him to focus on establishing the Blue Material Collective which enables the new generation of artistes to carve their niche in a space that tends to be dominated by privileged social classes. The 'blue' in the name of their collective relates to the colour associated with the Ambedkarite movement, suggesting a self-conscious alignment with its anti-caste politics. Patil hopes that the establishment of the Blue Material Collective will inaugurate a new era of Dalit comedy. As he explained in an interview[8] to *Times of India*:

> The whole thing might seem like it's all fun and jokes, but these things matter. I still remember how a security staff member at a venue said he felt good seeing my performance even though he didn't understand a word of English. The only thing he picked

up was 'Jai Ambedkar' which was the first time he had heard such words been said in such a space.

Dalit comedians are often actively involved in social movements. Ankur Tangade combines stand-up comedy with activism in Mahila Kisan Adhikar Manch, a nationwide forum dedicated to securing the rights and recognition of women farmers. Tangade is from Beed, a small town in Maharashtra. As a queer woman, Tangade has faced discrimination on grounds of her sexuality and gender in addition to caste. But her resolve remains as strong as ever. In an interview with *Article 14*, she reveals the source of her inspiration: the stories her parents would tell of anti-caste resistance in her home state.[9] One account is particularly inspiring, that of the nineteenth-century social reformer Savitribai Phule refusing to cower before conservatives who opposed her plans for extending education to women. While walking to the school where she used to teach women, Phule would carry a spare sari. People would throw stones and mud at her, which spoilt the sari she was wearing, so she would change into the spare one after she reached her destination. Phule's determination offers hope for Tangade, just as Tangade's determination offers hope for millions facing overlapping discrimination.

Nagpur-based Neha Thombre is yet another comedian who has taken on caste-based hierarchies with her wit and humour. Her YouTube channel *Nehagiri* presents audience with wide-ranging content that addresses the continued omniscience of caste. In an interview[10] with *The Print*, she recalled one of her performances: 'A few days ago, when I was abroad, I was surprised that nobody there asked me my caste. I'm not used to this. So much equality? It was too much to handle, I felt like I was going to become unconscious.' Thombre insists on using Varhadi—the dialect spoken in the Vidarbha region where Nagpur is located—rather than English, Hindi or Marathi to communicate with her audience. Her rationale for preferring Varhadi is straightforward:

> Savarna bhasha or refined Hindi is considered to be a clean language. Regional languages like Bhojpuri are considered unclean. But using my own dialect has helped me strengthen my community. I just got a call from a Dalit family from Qatar telling me about how much they love my videos for that very reason.

The proliferation of stand-up comedy in India has enabled its appropriation by a variety of artistes to offer critical commentary on the country's political and social affairs. Such criticism punctures elites' projection of power. It allows audiences to imagine other possibilities to prevailing political and social dominance. Their alternative imaginations intimate the many ways in which the ongoing erosion of democracy in India is being tenaciously resisted.

Rhythms of Resistance

Gurkanwal Bharti, better known as Ginni Maahi, was born in the town of Jalandhar in Punjab, on 26 November 1998. By the age of seven, she was singing odes to the sixteenth-century Bhakti ascetic Guru Ravidas, patron saint of her Raidassiya sect. While still in school, one of her friends asked her about the caste to which she belonged. When she replied she was Chamar, a community associated with leather tanning (some of whom, like Maahi's family, are affiliated with the Raidassiya sect), her friend playfully remarked that they were a dangerous community of which others had to be careful.[11] That exchange spurred Maahi to

produce the album *Danger Chamar* in 2015, followed by *Danger 2* the next year, which garnered over 50 lakh views on YouTube. Later in 2016, Maahi topped her own record with *Fan Baba Sahib Di*, a tribute to folk, rap and electronic dance music to Ambedkar as the architect of the Indian Constitution. *Fan Baba Sahib Di* has been viewed over 50 lakh times on YouTube.[12]

Maahi's songs established her as the 'Queen of Chamar Pop', a genre of protest music that popular among Punjab's Dalits for almost four decades. First popularised by the music of Roop Lal Dhir in 1986, Chamar pop continues the search for Begampura, a world without sorrows, that was initiated by Sant Ravidas way back in the sixteenth century. Dhir's compositions illustrate the contemporary hope for such a world.[13]

Invoking Begampura, the allegorical city without sorrow in which the sixteenth-century Bhakti saint Ravidas sought refuge, the verse declares: 'The oppressor has reached the limits of oppression. It's time for us to realise the land without sorrow. If you don't come and stand for the land without sorrow now, when will you? Arise, friends. Arise now.' More recent artistes performing in the Chamar pop genre refuse to entertain the notion of Chamars as untouchables or oppressed. Instead, they celebrate their Chamar identity as a matter of pride, as Babbu Chander does with his composition, which has been translated loosely thus: 'We, the sons of Chamars are so gutsy that it needs courage to confront us. We keep our arms always loaded and are always eager to embrace death.' Maahi's corpus of work builds on this even as she steers clear of singing anything that can be accused of provoking violence or offending others. *Danger Chamar* appropriates the unsafe connotations associated with the community to define Chamar as '*Kurbani deno darrde nahin, rehnde hai tayyar, haige asle toh wadd Danger Chamar*' or 'The one who does not shy away from sacrifice, the one who is always ready [to face adversity], the one who is the real thing is the dangerous Chamar.'[14] Unequivocal about her commitment to equality, Maahi presents her songs as invitations to humanity, decency and dignity. *Fan Baba Sahib Di* exemplifies these commitments and her ability to draw inspiration from Ambedkar's thoughts and writings on equality. Calling herself the daughter of 'Baba Sahib who wrote the constitution', Maahi celebrates the way he fought for rights and truth to change the destiny of millions who had been historically oppressed as 'untouchables':

> I am the daughter of Baba Sahib who wrote the constitution. We are earning our bread by what he wrote. I am such a fan of such thinking. He was a lion who made his pen an arrow. He fought for rights and truth and changed our destiny. He became an angel for the community. The whole world knows this.[15]

Maahi appreciates the heritage of resistance bequeathed upon her and is committed to taking it forward. In an interview with *Mint*, she cites Sant Ravidas's own imagination of equality:

> *Aisa chahu raaj main, jaha mile sabhan ko ann, chot bade sab sam, waise rahe Ravidas pasand* [The government should be such that everyone has food to eat and no one is small or big, this is Ravidas' vision]. So many years ago, he had said that he wants the kind of smart city where people will live with equality, humanity and without caste divisions. *Main sirf apna farz nibha rahi hoon* [I'm just doing my duty]. It is our responsibility to ensure that discrimination is ended and we live with oneness.[16]

Rap music has been creatively blended with hip hop to address caste by Sumeet Samos (Turuk). Born in Tentulipadar village near Koraput, Odisha, Samos went on to pursue postgraduate studies in Latin American literature at JNU. Despite JNU's broadly progressive politics, Samos faced what he eloquently describes as 'polite oppression' from his more privileged peers. An increasingly nuanced understanding of the ubiquitous nature of caste-based discrimination, even in allegedly progressive circles,  led Samos to use hip hop as a means of vocalising his angst. His first album *Ladai Seekh Le* (Learn to Fight) was thus born. The raw anger against the oppressor castes for perpetrating violence is illustrated through lyrics in English and Hindi tones and visuals. Looking squarely into the camera, Samos's rage is illustrated with the skilful use of colour schemes that profoundly disturb the viewer, as the artist intends. He moves forward towards the camera throughout the clips, which are interspersed with images of towers under construction, toiling children and statues of Ambedkar: 'Your midnight freedom burns and destroys our slums.'[17]

Ladai Seekh Le forces audiences to confront the litany of caste violence perpetrated not only against individuals such as Rohith Vemula or other Dalit students but also against entire communities of Dalits such as in Bihar's Laxman Bathe and Baithani Tola, West Bengal's Marichjhapi, Andhra Pradesh's Karamchhedu and Gujarat's Una. The themes explored in *Ladai Seekh Le* were explored further in the Odia–English bilingual album titled *Desia Pila* (Country Boy) in which Samos dips into his personal narratives. Set against the backdrop of his home district of Koraput, he tells us of the discrimination to which he has been subjected, but makes it clear that he has no intention of giving up.

Samos's albums are careful not to limit themselves to evoking sympathy or pity for Dalits, Adivasis and other Bahujans subjected to violence. They imagine a future where they would not remain victims of violence, one where they would be able to assert their presence in the public sphere. Even when highlighting the multiple sources of violence perpetrated upon Bahujans in Koraput, Samos nevertheless manages to convey their yearnings for a brighter future.

In 2021, Samos applied to study for a master's degree in Modern South Asian Studies at the University of Oxford. Although he secured admission, the lack of funding threatened to be an insurmountable obstacle. Undeterred, Samos turned to online crowdfunding and was overwhelmed by the response. Within five hours of his request appearing on the crowdfunding platform Milaap, nearly 1,500 people from across the world helped him raise £36,000.[18] The support Samos received helped him become the first person from his Dalit Christian community in Koraput to pursue postgraduate studies overseas.

Music reaches deep into our feelings and expresses what mere text cannot. Citizens United, a Kolkata-based platform of artistes, assembled a music video celebrating India's political and social diversity. Titled *Nijeder Mowte Nijeder Gaan* (Our Songs About Our Views), the composition interspersed images of people and places from across Kolkata with humanistic messages. The video was a result of collaboration between at least twenty-four artistes that included actors, songwriters, musicians and others. Since its release in April 2021, it has been viewed almost 20 lakh times on YouTube and comprises heavily critical lyrics such as:

> *I looked at Goebbels' mirror*
> *I spotted your reflection there*
> *I've seen your evil teeth*
> *I've seen how venomous they are*

> *You have no love for the poor*
> *You've left no stone unturned to flaunt that*
> *You worship falsehoods*[19]

Combining audio and visuals enables music videos to tap into our deepest emotions and move us in ways that few other mediums can. Not for nothing did music videos become the key means for artistes to protest such unpopular legislation as the CAA. Assam-based singers such as Zubin Garg, who had supported the BJP's electoral campaign in 2016, now compose songs to oppose its policies. Days after the CAA was passed in the Rajya Sabha, a collaborative music video titled *Odhikaar* premiered on YouTube. Challenging the Hindutva-based argument that urged the Assamese people to choose their enemy, *Odhikaar* suggests that they have been fooled by the BJP. The artistes invoke slogans from the Assamese nationalist agitation of the 1980s, urging fellow Assamese to register their opposition to CAA. In a similar vein, the rapper Van M produced the Hindi-language music video *Ache Din??*, in which he lashed out against the CAA with lines such as:

> *Assam aaj jal raha, khoon mera khaul raha* [Assam is burning, my blood is boiling]
> *Democracy is dead, Hitler sashan chal raha hai* [Democracy is dead, Hitler's reign prevails][20]

Almost a year before the CAA was passed, vocalist Rahul Rajkhowa warned about its socio-political and environmental implications. He belted out his angst in an English-language music video simply titled *Rap Against Citizenship Amendment Bill* released in January 2019, in which the singer raps:

> *Now let's talk about citizenship amendment*
> *The constitution kinda feels redundant*

Kinda feels like you made secularism redundant
Cause now you back to dividing religions[21]

Because music transcends linguistic silos, its appeal reaches across diverse geographies and cultures. Composer Poojan Saahil discovered this potential when he rendered the iconic Italian song *Bella Ciao* into Hindi during the protests against the CAA in December 2019 and in Punjabi when the farmers protested the three agricultural bills the following year in December 2020. *Bella Ciao* translates into 'goodbye, beautiful'. It most likely originated as a protest folk song during the nineteenth century among women paddy workers (locally called mondine) toiling on the rice fields in Italy's Po Valley. Its earliest written version dates to 1906. While the lyrics have changed over time, its haunting melody continues to remind listeners of the hardships faced by the mondine and their hope that a day would dawn when they would be free of their hardships.

Since then, *Bella Ciao* has assumed iconic status as an anthem of resistance. From Brazil to Myanmar, and from Kurdistan to Kashmir, its music has appealed to people striving for freedom. Saahil's rendition (not a translation) in Hindi titled *Wapas Jao* (Go Back) beautifully encapsulated this spirit of resistance when it premiered on YouTube within two weeks of the CAA's introduction in Parliament.

Jab tak hai baaki seene me dum, gayenge [Till I have some life in me, I shall sing]
Aye zalim, wapas jao jao jao [O Merciless, go back, go back, go back]
Phir lehrayegi laal gagan me [So the sun can shine again in the sky]
Tere iraadon ki rakh wapas jao [And the ashes of your ploys go back with you]

*Kab tak jhelenge ye kaali raatein? [Till when do you expect us to
endure these dark nights?]*
*Bhor dhakele tumhe wapas jao jao jao [The dawn will push you,
go back, go back, go back]*[22]

A year later, Saahil collaborated with Harsh Mander and film-maker Natasha Badhwar at Karwan-e Mohabbat to produce a Punjabi rendition of *Bella Ciao* in solidarity with the farmers' movement. Also titled *Wapas Jao*, it too memorialised the indomitable spirit of those protesting laws that the government sought to bulldoze over an unwilling population.

Loud determined voices
Have declared
We reject you
Go back, go back, go back
Take your merciless black laws with you[23]

Visualising Democratic Renewal

Among the BJP's major achievements, of course, entirely unintended, is India's transformation over the last ten years into a cornucopia of protest art. Graffiti has flourished across Indian cities, mischievously inviting the state to clamp down. Through much of January 2020 in the wake of the protests against the CAA, for example, Bengaluru's Church Street was awash with playfully provocative graffiti. The usually suspicious slogans were of course present: 'BJP is cancer. Kill it before it kills you', 'Modi fascist' and 'Free Kashmir' were among the many slogans written on its walls. But one stood out for its impishness. 'Sab changa si', it went. Literally, the slogan conveyed by this graffiti translates into 'Everything is fine' or 'All is well', echoing Modi's own words at the Howdy Modi event hosted by his US counterpart Donald Trump the previous year. On the face of it, the graffiti was supportive of the government. In fact, it was satire at its finest.[24]

Political cartoons add to the mosaic of protest art that has taken India by storm. Where mainstream newspapers and news portals have shunned political cartoonists out of fear of official retribution, digital networks on social media have provided such cartoonists a somewhat fragile haven. Here, they have relatively more freedom to offer subversive positions against authority. One particularly apt image by the veteran cartoonist Manjul on his column *Politickle* shows a man with a long, flowing beard wearing a saffron-coloured waistcoat (that is, Modi) chasing after both a blue bird and the letter 'f' (that is, the former logo of Twitter and the logo of Facebook) with a net while hordes of red-coloured pointy-toothed beings (that is, the coronavirus) follow behind, looking very pleased with his antics.[25] The cartoon laid bare the skewed priorities of the Indian state which spent its energies trying to curb criticism on Twitter and Facebook regarding the government's actions around the pandemic even as the second wave of the virus brought the country to its knees.

Another political cartoonist whose work has invited the ire of the Indian state is Richa Taneja, who founded the webcomic *Sanitary Panels*. Currently facing legal proceedings for one of her cartoons involving the influential news anchor Arnab Goswami, Taneja's stick figures evoke a thoughtful smile among her audiences for the simple, yet powerful messages they convey.

Then there is Ayesha Renna, the Jamia student who stood up to police brutality during the protests against the CAA in Delhi, and inspired a Tamilian painter to create an illustration that came to define the bravery of students across the country. 'A young, unarmed girl is seen bravely fending off a group of policemen in full riot gear from hitting a student, and it made me sad and emotional. The way she tells the policemen who are armed with helmets, shields and sticks, to back off, while wagging her finger—it's very powerful,' the painter told *Mumbai Mirror* in an interview.[26] The illustration was aptly titled *One Finger Revolution*.

As influential sections of the mainstream media have been crawling when asked to bend, the importance of alternative media in imagining possibilities of democratic renewal can hardly be exaggerated. For instance, *Khabar Lahariya*, a news channel run under the leadership of Editor-in-Chief Kavita Devi in Bundeli, Awadhi and Bajjika languages of north India, publishes local news that is written, edited, produced, distributed and marketed entirely by a collective of forty rural women journalists. News portals such as these do not shy away from challenging those in authority. By painstakingly piecing together news and views that are wilfully neglected by the mainstream media, and hosting artistic representations that are otherwise ignored, these alternative media portals offer hope that democracy in India may yet be saved.

Audacious Hope:
How to Save a Democracy?

Hope for Democratic Renewal

Hope is crucial to democratic renewal. Far from being a wasted emotion that hinders action, hope is what motivates people to act collectively against democratic backsliding. It entails that we identify the challenges we face. We must recognise the nature of the political crisis that engulfs us. Such an evaluation is crucial if we are to recognise actions that resist the ongoing erosion of democracy.

That said, we must avoid the pitfalls of perfectionism. Politics is far from perfect. A search for utopia that postpones any sort of action until all investigations have been concluded is as far away as it gets from the practice of realistic hope that will help save democracy.

Realistic hope is attentive to the possibility that our lives will be marked by uncertainty and chaos. It enables us to recognise that any certitudes that might have once ordered social life are crumbling. However, even as the collapse of such certitudes might augment anxieties about anarchy, it also offers opportunities for reimagining order. Realistic hope allows us to salvage what we can from the remains of the past and join them with new ideas and materials to build an alternate world.

What Is Hope?

Hope is, first and foremost, about not giving up. It involves denouncing abuse and acting against injustice. It means believing that there's a way out of desperate situations, not by giving up or caving in but by fighting on. Hope does not obsess with the present, but casts an eye on the future, based on an understanding of the past.

It also entails the pursuit of an objective without quitting. It is about facing up to the odds stacked up against you, based on a realistic assessment of those odds. As the Wangan-Jagalingou activist Murrawah Johnson put it recently: 'We've seen the end of the world ... and we've decided not to accept it.'[1] This way of thinking about hope is refreshingly different from the position taken by several influential intellectuals of the twentieth century. The philosopher Albert Camus declared that 'hope equals resignation'—for him, living in hope was equivalent to surrendering to inertia, fatalism and defeat. However, pessimism of this type is not a luxury that activists like Johnson or those resisting the erosion of India's democracy can afford. Caving to such pessimism would entail giving up the values that they hold dear. Instead, their actions remind us that, as the theologian Mary Grey suggests in *The Outrageous Pursuit of Hope: Prophetic Dreams for the Twentieth Century*, 'hope stretches the limits of what is possible'.

Harbouring hope is no easy task. As the educator Paulo Freire reminds us, 'the struggle for hope means the denunciation, in no uncertain terms, of all abuses ... '[2] The continuous condemnation of abuse, he suggests, could result in a virtuous cycle that awakens hope in others, enlivening them to the need to act against abuse and injustice in this world. Such an approach, grounded in action, contrasts with perspectives that hope is merely an illusion that people hold onto when they are distressed. 'Hope is a rope', the sociologist Henri Desroche[3] wrote, alluding to the shaman or fakir who throws a rope into the air and makes it stay mid-air through magic. But as we have seen, hope is not a sorcerer's trick. Far from it, hope arises out of attentiveness to the realities of this world, its injustices and inequalities, and a conviction that something can be done about it.

For that reason, living in hope means taking the next step. In her much-acclaimed *Teaching Community: A Pedagogy of Hope*, the feminist bell hooks suggests that hope is linked with a basic trust in life that motivates the 'next step'. It is about believing that our families, cultures and societies are important, and for whom it is worth living and dying. Far from being a hindrance to action, as the philosopher Hannah Arendt feared, hope is about confronting oppression. The 'next step' could, therefore, involve individual acts of sabotage, collective action or other, quieter, forms of resistance.

The geographer Les Back made a case for 'worldly hope' in a 2019 lecture delivered to the Royal Geographical Society. This emphasis is important because it helps to be wary of hollow promises that are so divorced from reality that they end up fuelling what the cultural theorist Lauren Berlant famously called 'cruel optimism'. Instead, people cultivate a worldly hope in the here and now, based on their evaluations of the difficulties of the present.

While taking the present seriously, worldly hope is not, however, limited by it. The anthropologist Hirokazu Miyazaki reminds us about this 'temporal incongruity' in his 2004 book *The Method of Hope: Anthropology, Philosophy and Fijian Knowledge*. Such a view takes seriously not only the enormity of the troubles of the present world but also how we landed up here in the first place and what we could do about it. Worldly hope is not beholden to a naïve sense of linear progress. Neither, however, is it hostage to a blind nihilism. In his marvellous 2009 book *Cruising Utopia*, the sociologist José Esteban Muñoz describes this strategy as a 'backwards glance that enacts a future vision'.

Living in hope, therefore, accepts the reality of grief, loss and uncertainty in the present moment. It recognises that the past is gone, and the assumptions—political, economic and social—that once shaped our world no longer hold. But it, at the same time, also demands that we carefully and sensitively craft novel alliances that could open up new possibilities. Such radical hope, as the philosopher Jonathan Lear writes, 'is directed towards a future goodness that transcends the current ability to understand what it is'.[4] Radical hope is not only a psychological practice. It is also a political position that refuses to accept that defeat is inevitable. Radical hope avoids what the author and critic James Bradley calls 'fixating on collapse'.[5] It calls instead for a granular appreciation of the ways in which people navigate and negotiate crises.

Sadly, it is a fixation on collapse that beguiles much of Modi's opponents in India. In March 2023, Rahul Gandhi, one of India's foremost opposition leaders and fourth-generation Congress dynast, made a much-publicised trip to Britain. He was hauled over the coals for allegedly badmouthing India before foreign audiences. Many were annoyed because they believe he called for Western intervention to achieve regime change. The BJP government and its spokespersons were so rattled you would be forgiven for believing that Gandhi delivered fiery speeches that galvanised the Indian diaspora in Britain against Modi. The truth, sadly for those who believed he would emerge as an icon of resistance to ongoing erosion of democracy in India, was rather sobering.

Rahul Gandhi spoke to audiences in Cambridge and London, holding at least three public interactions in the British capital. I attended the meeting organised with parliamentarians, academics and community leaders in London, at which we hoped he would outline his vision for India in the event that he won the 2024 elections. The meeting room was packed, the air thick with anticipation. He made some excellent points about Indian democracy being a global public good and the ways in which it was being undermined. Democracy was in danger, minorities were facing persecution and the economy was in a shambles. Apart these pronouncements, however, he offered no clear way out.

Hope is, like I mentioned earlier, about not giving up. It requires believing that there's an alternative. Rahul Gandhi waxed eloquent about the ways in which his hundred-day long walking march across India, the Bharat Jodo Yatra, allowed him to understand the problems faced by ordinary Indians under Modi. But he failed to outline his roadmap to address those problems. How exactly would he repair democracy? How would he reverse the series of persecutions to which Muslims and other minorities were subjected? How would he fix the economy? Not a word was said about governance, although welfare made an appearance in the context of addressing poverty. Fair enough, except even here it was difficult to see what he would do differently from what the present dispensation is doing (and the previous UPA governments had done). In failing to outline a roadmap, Gandhi shied away from offering hope to an audience starving for it.

To further probing from his brilliant discussants in London, Gandhi suggested enhancing production as a means of fixing not only the national economy but also the global polity. The world's democracies had stopped producing, with the result that manufacturing had relocated to authoritarian regimes such as China. Revitalising production would revitalise democracy. But we were offered no clues as to how and why it would do so. Would revitalising production create more jobs? What sorts of jobs would these be and what kind of training and skills would be required? Who would provision these? How was his vision different from, and superior to, the numerous initiatives bandied by the BJP government?

Hope is attentive to the difficulties of the present moment. But it does not hanker for a return to an idealised past. Rather, hope appreciates the possibility that something new and unanticipated could arise from the ruins of the present. Gandhi's assumption that manufacturing would automatically create jobs reveals an outdated mindset that ignores the technological advancements that are making labour redundant to production. The world of work in the twenty-first century is very different from what it used to be in previous decades. His harping on production suggested a wishful return to the past rather than embracing the possibilities of the present and the uncertainties of the future. Moreover, by constantly invoking the role of the Congress Party in India's freedom struggle and the legacy he has inherited, Gandhi squandered an opportunity to present himself and his party as the face of India's future rather than a relic of its past.

Gandhi was right to note that India's democracy was being severely eroded. But in neglecting to note the resistance to such erosion, he failed to link his struggles with those of others. Gandhi's failure to even refer to the farmers' protests that forced

Modi to withdraw the contentious farming bills, the mass dissent that had brought Hindus and Muslims together in unprecedented shows of solidarity against the CAA and the vibrant protests against discriminations based on caste, gender and sexuality that reinvent democracy in myriad everyday ways suggests he has a great deal to learn about building a movement against the spectre of authoritarianism that haunts India. Living in hope demands that we carefully and sensitively craft novel alliances that could open new possibilities. Unfortunately for his expectant audience, Gandhi's interventions in London offered no glimpse into his thinking about new possibilities.

Gandhi's audience craved hope to help them navigate the ambiguous possibilities of a new India. All he presented them was a futile lament on the passing of the old India. Such an approach is simply not fit for purpose if he seriously intends to lead the battle to save India's democracy.

The alliances demanded by the political practice of hope broadens people's horizons. Writing in the shadows of Nazism, the historian Ernst Bloch makes exactly this point in his epic three-volume study *The Principle of Hope*. 'The emotion of hope goes out of itself, makes people broad instead of confining them,' he writes. In a similar vein, the geographer David Harvey urges people to reflect on the 'spaces of hope', which is also the title of his 2009 book on the same subject. In it, he urges his readers to develop shared solidarities with those exploited and marginalised by the dominant political economy. The title of Harvey's book mirrors the work of Raymond Williams, the cultural theorist who wrote a collection of essays titled *Resources of Hope*. In this collection, Williams emphasises the importance of community and culture as repertoires of optimism on which people draw from in despairing times.

It is tempting to conflate hope with utopia, the imagination of a flawless world in which the human condition is perfected. The last two centuries have seen the rise and fall of utopian visions that aimed to radically improve human life through social engineering, economic redistribution and civilising people deemed to be savage. Despite their differences, fascism, socialism and liberalism all shared this obsession with perfecting humanity. With the collapse of such utopias by the end of the twentieth century, reflecting on hope has never been more urgent. The incremental changes envisioned by hope are fundamentally different from the revolutionary transformations heralded by utopias. After all, hope is what remains when utopias die.

Saving Democracy in India

India's democratic achievements since Independence have been eroded after 2014. Yet, as the preceding pages have illustrated, Indians are not letting their democracy quietly slip away without putting up a good fight. The actions of countless Indians—ranging from farmers to students, politicians to artists, social activists to daily wage labourers—show the many ways in which they are resisting the onslaughts on their democratic freedoms. Their immense courage and fortitude warn observers that fixating on democracy's collapse in India (or anywhere else for that matter) is not only counter-productive but also extremely unfair to their increasingly desperate attempts at salvaging their democracy. To say that there is no hope for democracy to survive in India is to mirror the actions of those who seek to strangle it. Hopelessness is a luxury no Indian who cares about their democracy can afford.

It is impossible to forecast the outcome of these struggles. While the farmers' movement seems to have won a clear immediate victory, the same cannot be said of the myriad struggles by students or those challenging caste hierarchies. The pandemic stalled the protests against the CAA as well as the state's efforts at creating the NRC, even as it visited death and destruction across the land. Although artists find themselves increasingly under siege, there can be little doubt that there has, in fact, been a proliferation of different artistic mediums of conveying dissent.

Such uncertainty is integral to hope since it is, after all, prone to disappointment. But then: 'Not all battles are fought for victory. Some are fought simply to tell the world that someone was there on the battlefield,' the intrepid journalist Ravish Kumar reminded his audience when he was conferred the Ramon Magsaysay Award in 2019.[6] You might recognise the essence of this message to be similar to the one Krishna gives Arjuna on the eve of the battle in the Mahabharata:

> You have the right to act, but no right over the fruits of your actions
>
> Let not the fruit of action be your motive, nor let not your attachment be to inaction.

In this tale as old as time, Arjuna falters when he sees the array of adversaries opposed to him. They are greater in number and better organised. Is there any chance of victory, he wonders? And he is ready to lay down his arms and concede defeat even before the war had begun. It is at that point that Krishna—his charioteer, friend and spiritual mentor—steps in to guide him out of his confusion. Whether Arjuna wins the war or loses it is immaterial, Krishna tells him firmly. What matters is that he fights in it, that he does not let injustice go unchallenged. It is a similar commitment to action that underpins the spirit of audacious hope and motivates millions of Indians to preserve democracy.

Notes

Hope for Democracy

1. 'Francis Fukuyama, 'The End of History?', *The National Interest*, 1989.
2. Thomas Carothers, 'The End of the Transition Paradigm', *Journal of Democracy*, 2002.
3. PTI, 'I am a Hindu nationalist as I am a born Hindu: Narendra Modi', *The Indian Express*, 12 July 2013, https://indianexpress.com/article/india/latest-news/i-am-a-hindu-nationalist-as-i-am-a-born-hindu-narendra-modi/.
4. Freedom House, 'Freedom in the World 2021: India', https://freedomhouse.org/country/india/freedom-world/2021.
5. V-Dem Institute, 'Autocratization Turns Viral: Democracy Report 2021', https://www.v-dem.net/documents/12/dr_2021.pdf.
6. A well-established literature on the coup that overthrew President Allende exists. For examples, see Oscar Guardiola-Rivera's *Story of a Death Foretold: The Coup Against Salvador Allende*, Kevin John McEnvoy's *Before the Rubble: Britain's Secret Propaganda Offensive in Chile (1960-1973)* and Jack Devine's *What Really Happened in Chile: The CIA, The Coup Against Allende, and the Rise of Pinochet*.
7. Much has been written about Bhutto's hanging and Zia's rise to power. See, for example, Shahid Javid Burki's 'Pakistan under Zia, 1977-88', Sameel Ahmed Qureshi's 'An Analysis of Contemporary Pakistani Politics: Bhutto versus the Military' and W.L. Richter's 'Pakistan'.
8. Hitler's acquisition of dictatorial powers has been scrutinised by several generations of scholars. A sample of this scholarship is available in Gilbert Fergusson's 'A Blueprint for Dictatorship: Hitler's Enabling Law of March

1933', Richard Evans's 'Hitler's Dictatorship' and Sven Kellerhoff's *The Reichstag Fire: The Case Against the Nazi Conspiracy*.

9.   India's Emergency spawned a vast literature on its underlying politics. See, for example, Sudipta Kaviraj's 'Indira Gandhi and Indian Politics', Vijay Prashad's 'Emergency Assessments' and Christophe Jaffrelot and Anil Pratinav's *India's First Dictatorship: The Emergency, 1975-77*.

10. See Archana Parashar and Jobair Alam's 'The National Laws of Myanmar: Making of Statelessness for the Rohingya'.

11. The emergence and establishment of Apartheid in South Africa has been widely studied. See Harold Wolpe's 'Capitalism and Cheap Labour in South Africa: From Segregation to Apartheid', Paul Maylam's *South Africa's Racial Past* and contributions in William Beinart and Saul Dubow's (eds.) *Segregation and Apartheid in Twentieth-Century South Africa* for illustrative examples.

12. An enormous literature on the origins, implementation and legacy of Jim Crow laws exists. See, for example, David Fremon's *The Jim Crows Laws and Racism in United States History*, Gary Andersson and Dennis Halcoussis's 'The Political Economy of Legal Segregation: Jim Crow and Racial Employment Patterns' and Ruth Thompson-Miller, Joe Feagin and Leslie Picca's *Jim Crow's Legacy: The Lasting Impact of Segregation*.

13. A fascinating discussion of these arpilleras is available here: https://slate.com/human-interest/2014/09/history-of-quilting-arpilleras-made-by-chilean-women-to-protest-pinochet.hml.

14. This translation of Faiz's iconic poem is by Mustansir Dalvi and is publicly available at: https://faizahmedafaiznewtranslations.blogspot.com/2012/10/faiz-hum-dekhenge.html.

15. See contributions in Alexander Lloyd's (ed.) *The White Rose: Reading, Writing, Resistance*.

16. Gyan Prakash, *Emergency Chronicles: Indira Gandhi and Democracy's Turning Point*, Penguin Viking, 2018, pp. 271-2.

17. See https://time.com/4365138/soweto-anniversary-photograph/?amp=true for a fuller discussion of those events.

18. Martin Luther King Jr., (eds) James M. Washington, *A Testament of Hope: The Essential Writings and Speeches of Martin Luther King Jr.*, New York: Harper Collins, 1991, pp. 313–330.

19. Ibid.

The Erosion of India's Democracy

1. Milan Vaishnav, Devesh Kapur, Neelanjan Sircar, 'Growth Is No. 1 Poll Issue for Voters, Survey Shows', *Carnegie Endowment for International Peace*, 16 March 2016, https://carnegieendowment.org/2014/03/16/growth-is-no.-1-poll-issue-for-voters-survey-shows-pub-54999.

2. The full interview is available here: https://www.youtube.com/watch?v=JIjMGNwStt0. Its reportage in *The Economic Times* is available here: https://economictimes.indiatimes.com/news/politics-and-nation/narendra-modi-governments-should-cater-to-needs-of-poor-ensure-job-creation/articleshow/34842937.cms.

3. I Support Narendra Modi, 'I Am a Hindu Nationalist: Narendra Modi's Explosive Reuters Complete Interview', YouTube, 13 July 2013, https://www.youtube.com/watch?v=rSp2WVorCM4.

4. Pratap Bhanu Mehta, 'Modi's moment alone', *The Indian Express*, 17 May 2014. https://indianexpress.com/article/opinion/editorials/modis-moment-alone/.

5. Sunil Khilnani, 'A democratic asteroid that wiped out many old habits', *The Economic Times*, 18 May 2014, https://economictimes.indiatimes.com/opinion/et-commentary/a-democratic-asteroid-that-wiped-out-many-old-habits-sunil-khilnani/articleshow/35294334.cms.

6. Chetan Bhagat, 'BJP could attain an all-time high of Hindu power, but it must use this wisely', *The Times of India*, 17 May 2014, https://timesofindia.indiatimes.com/blogs/The-underage-optimist/bjp-could-attain-an-all-time-high-of-hindu-power-but-it-must-use-this-wisely/?source=app&frmapp=yes.

7. Ramachandra Guha, 'Modi: The cult of the great leader', *Prospect*, 18 June 2014, https://www.prospectmagazine.co.uk/essays/46416/modi-the-cult-of-the-great-leader.

8. Ramachandra Guha, 'The Fear of Fascism - India's democratic institutions are too strong to let fascists win', *The Telegraph*, 22 March 2014, https://www.telegraphindia.com/opinion/the-fear-of-fascism-india-s-democratic-institutions-are-too-strong-to-let-fascists-win/cid/206914.

9. James Manor, 'A New, Fundamentally Different Political Order: The Emergence and Future Prospects of "Competitive Authoritarianism" in India', *Economic and Political Weekly*, 6 March 2021, Vol. 56, Issue No. 10.

10. Indrajit Roy, 'Passionate Politics: Democracy, Development and India's 2019 General Elections', Manchester University Press, pp. 1–21.

11. Srinivasan Ramani, 'Analysis: Highest-ever national vote share for the BJP', *The Hindu*, 24 May 2014.

12. Bharti Jain, 'Lok Sabha elections: At 67.1%, 2019 turnout's a record, Election Commission says', *The Times of India*, 21 May 2019, https://www.thehindu.com/elections/lok-sabha-2019/analysis-highest-ever-national-vote-share-for-the-bjp/article27218550.ece.

13. Alex Finnis, 'How many people voted in 2016 US election: Turnout for last presidential vote, and what we know about 2020', *inews.co.uk*, 3 November 2020, https://inews.co.uk/us-election-2020/how-many-people-voted-2016-us-election-turnout-2020-presidential-vote-latest-voters-740680/.

14. Milan Vaishnav, 'The battle for India's soul', *Carnegie Endowment for International Peace*, Foreign Affairs, 6 May 2019, https://carnegieendowment.org/2019/05/06/battle-for-india-s-soul-pub-79071.

15. For full details of the survey methodology, see: https://www.lokniti.org/media/PDF-upload/1565073104_34386100_method_pdf_file.pdf.

16. Shreyas Sardesai, Vibha Attri, 'Post-poll survey: the 2019 verdict is a manifestation of the deepening religious divide in India', *The Hindu*, 30 May 2019, https://www.thehindu.com/elections/lok-sabha-2019/the-verdict-is-a-manifestation-of-the-deepening-religious-divide-in-india/article27297239.ece.

17. Patralekha Chatterjee, 'Hashtags, hysteria, and hope', *The Asian Age*, 30 December 2016, https://www.asianage.com/opinion/oped/301216/2016-hashtags-hysteria-hope.html.

18. During polls conducted in January, Modi enjoyed an approval rating of 45 per cent against 30 per cent garnered by opposition leader Rahul Gandhi. Polls conducted in February after the attack suggest Modi's approval ratings increased to 52 per cent. See data here: https://timesofindia.indiatimes.com/india/post-pulwama-pm-narendra-modis-ratings-rise-by-7-to-52-poll/articleshow/68350217.cms

19. Commentator Milan Vaishnav went on to assert that nationalism would be the biggest theme in the Indian elections. See the full interview here: https://carnegieendowment.org/2019/02/11/nationalism-not-hindutva-will-be-big-theme-for-2019-pub-78344.

20. 'Dadri: Outrage after mob lynches man for allegedly consuming beef', *The Indian Express*, 25 December 2015, https://indianexpress.com/article/india/india-others/outrage-after-man-lynched-over-rumour-of-storing-beef-in-house/.

21. Andrew Marzsal, 'Protests rock Gujarat after Hindu vigilantes brutally beat low-caste youths accused of killing cow', *The Telegraph*, 20 July 2016, https://www.telegraph.co.uk/news/2016/07/20/protests-rock-gujarat-after-hindu-vigilantes-brutally-beat-low-c/.

22. See more details about them here: https://www.abvp.org/#secondPage

23. Read about their vision and mission in their own words: https://www.rss.org/Encyc/2015/3/13/Vision-and-Mission.html

24. Ayesha Ray, 'India's colossal blunder in Kashmir', *The Conversation*, 8 August 2019, https://theconversation.com/indias-colossal-blunder-in-kashmir-121657.

25. Ibid.

26. PTI, 'Abrogation of Article 370 unconstitutional, people of J&K bypassed: Petitioners to SC', *The Economic Times*, 10 December 2019, https://economictimes.indiatimes.com/news/politics-and-nation/sc-commences-hearing-on-pleas-challenging-abrogation-of-article-370/articleshow/72454345.cms.

27. Rahul Singh, 'We are now one nation with one Constitution, says PM Modi', *Hindustan Times*, 15 June 2020, https://www.hindustantimes.com/india-news/we-are-now-onenation-with-one-constitution-says-pm-modi/story-O0UyBDxra42he8iXqWCG7I.html.

28. Kumar Anshuman, 'Many opposition leaders defied party line on Article 370', *The Economic Times*, 12 August 2020, https://economictimes.indiatimes.com/news/politics-and-nation/many-opposition-leaders-defied-party-line-on-article-370/articleshow/70649502.cms.

29. J.P. Yadav, Umanand Jaiswal, 'Detention centres: Is PM Modi saying the truth, the whole truth and nothing but the truth?', *The Telegraph*, 22 December 2019, https://www.telegraphindia.com/india/detention-centers-is-pm-modi-saying-the-truth-the-whole-truth-and-nothing-but-the-truth/cid/1729496.

30. Vikas Pandey, 'Coronavirus lockdown: The Indian migrants dying to get home', *BBC*, 20 May 2020, https://www.bbc.com/news/world-asia-india-52672764.

31. Harsh Mander, Amitanshu Verma, 'Following authoritarian regimes around the world, India is using Covid-19 pandemic to crush dissent', *Scroll.in*, 15 May 2020, https://scroll.in/article/961431/delhi-police-is-making-arbitrary-arrests-and-crushing-dissent-under-the-cloak-of-lockdown.

32. Vasudha Venugopal, 'Delhi lockdown: Anti-CAA protesters removed from Shaheen Bagh, other places', *The Economic Times*, 25 March 2020, https://economictimes.indiatimes.com/news/politics-and-nation/coronavirus-lockdown-delhi-police-vacate-protesters-at-shaheen-bagh/articleshow/74785253.cms?from=mdr.

33. G. Sampath, 'Who is Anand Teltumbde, and why was he arrested recently?', *The Hindu*, 16 February 2019, https://www.thehindu.com/news/national/who-is-anand-teltumbde-and-why-was-he-arrested-recently/article26292219.ece.

34. Ibid.

35. The Farmers Produce Trade and Commerce (Promotion and Facilitation) Bill aims to dismantle the trade and distribution monopoly enjoyed by the state-run Food Corporation of India (FCI) and the Agricultural Product Market Committees (APMCs), thus allowing farmers to deal directly with the markets. The Farmers (Empowerment and Protection) Agreement of Price Assurance and Farm Services Bill allows farmers to engage in contract farming and opens up agriculture to domestic and global corporates for investment. Finally, the amendment to the Essential Commodities Act of 1955 deregulates items such as cereals, pulses, oilseeds, edible oils, onions and potatoes. For further details, see https://www.downtoearth.org.in/blog/agriculture/farm-laws-2020-who-are-they-meant-to-serve--74540.

36. Navyug Gill, 'A popular upsurge against neoliberal arithmetic in India', *Aljazeera*, 11 December 2020, https://www.aljazeera.com/opinions/2020/12/11/a-popular-upsurge-against-neoliberal-arithmetic-in-india.

37. 'How Pakistanis are using current Punjab farmer protests to fuel pro-Khalistan sentiments', OpIndia, 23 December 2020, https://www.opindia.com/2020/12/how-pakistanis-are-using-current-punjab-farmer-protests-to-fuel-pro-khalistan-sentiments/.

38. Mojo Story, 'Deep Sidhu was the Viral Voice of The Farmers Protest Until He Said This | Barkha Dutt', YouTube, 28 November 2020, https://www.youtube.com/watch?v=yBIH_R5jMO4.

39. https://www.facebook.com/KarwaneMohabbat/videos/960796757783603

40. Pranav Dixit, 'Violent Protests Erupted In India. Then Calls For Police To Shoot The Protesters Went Viral On Twitter', *BuzzFeed News India*,

26 January 2021, https://www.buzzfeednews.com/article/pranavdixit/india-protests-viral-tweets-police-brutality.

41. 'India farmer protests: "War-like fortification" to protect Delhi', *BBC*, 3 February 2021, https://www.bbc.com/news/world-asia-india-55899754.

42. 'India: Journalists Covering Farmer Protests Charged', *Human Rights Watch*, 2 February 2021, https://www.hrw.org/news/2021/02/02/india-journalists-covering-farmer-protests-charged.

43. Apurva Vishvanath, 'Explained: The Krishna Janmabhoomi case in Mathura, and the challenge to the 1968 "compromise" between the Hindus and Muslims', *The Indian Express*, 21 May 2021, https://indianexpress.com/article/explained/explained-krishna-janmabhoomi-case-mathura-mosque-1968-compromise-hindus-muslims-7927363/.

44. Soutik Biswas, 'Gyanvapi masjid: India dispute could become a religious flashpoint', *BBC*, 18 May 2022, https://www.bbc.com/news/world-asia-india-61476741.

45. For a detailed expansion of his speech in the Rajya Sabha, see here: https://www.youtube.com/watch?v=Wh8oTygecEI.

46. Neelam Pandey, Shanker Arnimesh, 'RSS in Modi govt in numbers—3 of 4 ministers are rooted in the Sangh', *The Print*, 27 January 2020, https://theprint.in/politics/rss-in-modi-govt-in-numbers-3-of-4-ministers-are-rooted-in-the-sangh/353942/.

47. Archis Mohan, 'RSS chief disputes Modi, says countless good people involved in cow protection', *Business Standard*, 11 October 2016, https://www.business-standard.com/article/politics/rss-chief-disputes-modi-says-countless-good-people-involved-in-cow-protection-116101100163_1.html.

48. Christophe Jaffrelot, 'A *De Facto* Ethnic Democracy?: Obliterating and Targeting the Other, Hindu Vigilantes, and the Ethno-State', *Majoritarian State: How Hindu Nationalism is Changing India,* (eds.) A. Chatterji, T. Hansen, C. Jaffrelot, C Hurst & Co Publishers Ltd, pp. 41–67.

Mobilising Against Caste

1. BI India Bureau, 'Full text of Modi's first speech after historic election victory', *Business Insider India*, 26 May 2019, https://www.businessinsider.in/full-text-of-modi-speech-lok-sabha-election-2019/articleshow/69467611.cms.

2. M.S. Golwalkar, *Bunch of Thoughts*, https://www.thehinducentre.com/multimedia/archive/02486/Bunch_of_Thoughts_2486072a.pdf.

3. Jaya Menon, 'In Meenakshipuram, conversions continue in hope of social dignity', *The Times of India*, 17 May 2019, https://timesofindia.indiatimes.com/city/chennai/in-meenakshipuram-conversions-continue-in-hope-of-social-dignity/articleshow/68913456.cms.

4. Prabhu Chawla, 'Sudden spurt in conversions of Harijans to Islam forces govt to study the "issue"', *India Today*, 15 September 1981, https://www.indiatoday.in/magazine/indiascope/story/19810915-sudden-spurt-in-conversions-of-harijans-to-islam-forces-govt-to-study-the-issue-773219-2013-11-11.

5. https://www.news18.com/news/immersive/25-years-of-babri-demolition/such-a-long-journey.html

6. Sumit Mitra, 'Virat Hindu Samaj holds massive rally to protest against conversion of Harijans to Islam', *India Today*, 15 November 1981, https://www.indiatoday.in/magazine/religion/story/19811115-virat-hindu-samaj-holds-massive-rally-to-protest-against-conversion-of-harijans-to-islam-773435-2013-10-28.

7. Ibid.

8. Badri Narayan, *Kanshiram: Leader of the Dalits*, Penguin, New Delhi, 2014.

9. Ibid.

10. Javed M Ansari, Dilip Awasthi, 'In India, 50 per cent of the media is pro-BJP: Kanshi Ram', *India Today*, 31 December 1993, https://www.indiatoday.in/magazine/interview/story/19931231-in-india-50-per-cent-of-the-media-is-pro-bjp-says-kanshi-ram-811980-1993-12-30.

11. John R. Wood, 'Reservations in Doubt: The Backlash Against Affirmative Action in Gujarat, India', *Pacific Review*, 1987, Vol. 60, No. 3, pp. 408–430.

12. Ibid.

13. Ibid.

14. Ibid.

15. Ibid.

16. Ornit Shani, 'The Rise of Hindu Nationalism in India: The Case Study of Ahmedabad in the 1980s', *Modern Asian Studies*, Vol. 39, No. 4, October 2005, pp. 870.

17. Government of India, 'Report of the Backward Classes Commission First Part: Volume I and II', Backward Classes Commission, New Delhi, 1980, p. 58.

18. 'Raja's caste war', *Organiser*, 26 August 1990, p. 1.

19. Yogendra Yadav, 'Electoral Politics in the Time of Change: India's Third Electoral System, 1989-99', *Economic and Political Weekly*, Vol. 34, No. 34/35, 1999, p. 2394.

20. The data in this table draws from secondary analysis of National Election Surveys conducted by the Delhi-based Centre for Study of Developing Societies and Lokniti. Data for 1991, 1996 and 1998 is drawn from Oliver Heath's 'Anatomy of BJP's Rise to Power: Social, Regional and Political Expansion in 1990s'. Data for 1999 and 2004 taken from Yogendra Yadav, 'The Elusive Mandate of 2004'. Data for 2009, 2014 and 2019 taken from Christophe Jaffrelot, 'Class and Caste in the 2019 Indian Election–Why Have So Many Poor Started Voting for Modi?'. Data for lower and higher OBC only available for 1999 and 2004. For all other years, only data for OBCs as a consolidated category is available.

21. Manish Kumar, '"Our Intention Clear": Nitish Kumar Explains Purpose of Bihar Caste Census', *NDTV*, 7 January 2023, https://www.ndtv.com/ india-news/bihar-caste-census-2023-our-intention-clear-nitish-kumar-explains-purpose-of-bihar-caste-headcount-3671649.

22. G. Sampath, 'Explained: Why is the government against caste census?', *The Hindu*, 3 October 2021, https://www.thehindu.com/news/national/ explained-what-are-the-governments-objections-to-a-caste-census/ article36713236.ece.

23. ANI, 'Caste-based census in Bihar will enable govt to scientifically carry out development work, says Tejashwi Yadav', *The Economic Times*, 7 January 2023, https://economictimes.indiatimes.com/news/politics-and-nation/caste-based-census-in-bihar-will-enable-govt-to-scientifically-carry-out-development-work-says-tejashwi-yadav/videoshow/96809751. cms.

24. PTI, 'Bihar govt should hold caste-based census on its own: Tejashwi Yadav', *The Indian Express*, 29 July 2021, https://indianexpress.com/ article/india/bihar-govt-should-hold-caste-based-census-on-its-own-tejashwi-yadav-7429070/.

25. Ipsita Chakravarty, 'The forgotten riot: How Bhagalpur 1989 left a memory trace in Bihar politics', *Scroll.in*, 12 August 2015, https:// scroll.in/article/747650/the-forgotten-riot-how-bhagalpur-1989-left-a-memory-trace-in-bihar-politics.

26. Giridhar Jha, '23 years after Bhagalpur riots, Bihar govt to give pension

to victim', *India Today*, 12 August 2012, https://www.indiatoday.in/india/east/story/bhagalpur-riots-bihar-govt-to-give-pension-to-victim-114473-2012-08-26.

27. As it happens, the results of the Bihar caste census, released on 2 October 2023 revealed that 'lower castes' made up 63 per cent of the State's population. The Kurmis are less than 3 per cent of the population. Almost 15 per cent of the State's people are Yadav. Please see https://theprint.in/opinion/india-has-gone-into-data-discomfort-explains-silence-on-bihar-caste-inequality/1839572/ for an early analysis of the caste census undertaken by the Bihar government.

28. Purnima S. Tripathi, 'Bihar Caste Census May Restart Mandal Politics', *The Citizen*, 16 January 2023, https://www.thecitizen.in/india/bihar-caste-census-may-restart-mandal-politics-555358.

29. '"Ramcharitmanas" should be burnt as it spreads hatred: Bihar Edu Minister Chandrashekhar', *ETV Bharat National*, 11 January 2023, https://www.etvbharat.com/english/national/state/bihar/ramcharitmanas-should-be-burnt-because-it-spreads-hatred-bihars-education-minister-chandrashekhar/na20230111225508936936483.

30. Rajat Sharma, 'Opinion: Sack Bihar minister for his obnoxious remarks about Ramcharitmanas', *India TV News*, 14 January 2023, https://www.indiatvnews.com/news/india/opinion-sack-bihar-minister-chandrashekhar-for-his-obnoxious-remarks-about-ramcharitmanas-aaj-ki-baat-rajat-sharma-blogpost-2023-01-13-838902.

31. 'Ambedkar Dalit Army Fights Caste Atrocities In Uttar Pradesh', *The Quint*, https://www.thequint.com/quintlab/ambedkar-dalit-army-fights-caste-atrocities-in-uttar-pradesh/.

32. Kabir Agarwal, 'After Violence and NSA Charges, Caste Lines Are Deeper Than Ever in Saharanpur', *The Wire*, 23 November 2017, https://thewire.in/caste/saharanpur-caste-violence-nsa-chandrasekhar.

33. '"Resolve to Fight for Just Society Still Alive": Elgar Accused on Completion of 4 Years of Jail', *The Wire*, 6 June 2022, https://thewire.in/rights/resolve-to-fight-for-just-society-still-alive-elgar-accused-on-completion-of-4-years-of-jail.

34. Shoaib Daniyal, '"Your mother, you take care of it": Meet the Dalits behind Gujarat's stirring cow carcass protests', *Scroll.in*, 23 July 2016, https://scroll.in/article/812329/your-mother-you-take-care-of-it-meet-the-dalits-behind-gujarats-stirring-cow-carcass-protests.

35. Sudipto Mondal, Danish Raza, 'At Una rally attended by Kanhaiya, Dalits warn of fresh protests', *Hindustan Times*, 15 August 2016, https://www.hindustantimes.com/india-news/at-una-rally-attended-by-kanhaiya-dalits-warn-of-fresh-protests/story-TibFTTXAvgHKC3Lod3wZbM.html.

Students on the Streets

1. TNN, 'Full text: Dalit scholar Rohith Vemula's suicide note', *The Times of India*, 19 January 2016, https://timesofindia.indiatimes.com/city/hyderabad/full-text-dalit-scholar-rohith-vemulas-suicide-note/articleshow/50634646.cms.

2. 'Discrimination Rot: 8 Dalit Suicides in HCU, Dozens Across India', *The Citizen*, 20 January 2016, https://www.thecitizen.in/index.php/en/NewsDetail/index/2/6572/Discrimination-Rot:-8-Dalit-Suicides-in-HCU-Dozens-Across-India?infinitescroll=1.

3. 'Rohith Vemula Suicide: Protesters Converge On Hyderabad University', *NDTV*, 25 January 2016, https://www.ndtv.com/india-news/rohith-vemula-suicide-protesters-converge-on-hyderabad-university-1269787.

4. Sudipto Mondal, 'Rohith Vemula: An unfinished portrait', *Hindustan Times*, https://www.hindustantimes.com/static/rohith-vemula-an-unfinished-portrait/.

5. Laxminarayana, 2017.

6. Anusha Puppala, 'Student anger turns into art, HCU campus awash with graffiti, posters, paintings', *The News Minute*, 23 January 2016, https://www.thenewsminute.com/article/student-anger-turns-art-hcu-campus-awash-graffiti-posters-paintings-38066.

7. Balakrishna Ganeshan, '4 years after his death, Rohith Vemula lives on as the face of dissent in universities', *The News Minute*, 17 January 2020, https://www.thenewsminute.com/article/4-years-after-his-death-rohith-vemula-lives-face-dissent-universities-116273.

8. TNN, '"Justice for Rohith" movement gets bigger', *The Times of India*, 25 January 2016, https://timesofindia.indiatimes.com/city/hyderabad/Justice-for-Rohith-movement-gets-bigger/articleshow/50711038.cms.

9. Yogita Rao, 'Thousands from city participate in rally in support of "Justice for Rohith" movement, block traffic in South Mumbai, *The Times of India*, 1 February 2016, https://timesofindia.indiatimes.com/city/mumbai/thousands-from-city-participate-in-rally-in-support-of-justice-for-rohith-

movement-block-traffic-in-south-mumbai/articleshow/50810300.
cms?from=mdr.

10. 'Rohith Vemula Library: The new face of revolution', *Torchlight*, 26 January 2016, https://journal.bookwormgoa.in/rohith-vemula-library-the-new-face-of-revolution/.

11. 'Kolkata students on hunger strike in protest against Rohith's death', *The Hindu*, 25 January 2016, https://www.thehindu.com/news/cities/kolkata/Kolkata-students-on-hunger-strike-in-protest-against-Rohith%E2%80%99s-death/article14019412.ece.

12. 'Rohith Vemula suicide: My birth is my fatal accident!', *Feminists India*, 25 January 2016, https://feministsindia.com/rohith-vemula-suicide-my-birth-is-my-fatal-accident/.

13. Shreya Roy Chowdhury, 'Rohith Vemula suicide: JNU students start hunger strike in solidarity with Hyderabad University protests', *The Times of India*, 26 January 2016, https://timesofindia.indiatimes.com/city/delhi/rohith-vemula-suicide-jnu-students-start-hunger-strike-in-solidarity-with-hyderabad-university-protesters/articleshow/50706338.cms.

14. Leonard, 2020.

15. Harshit Agarwal, 'The students at the JNU meet on Afzal Guru weren't carrying guns - they only carried ideas', *Scroll.in*, 15 February 2016, https://scroll.in/article/803607/the-students-at-the-jnu-meet-on-afzal-guru-werent-carrying-guns-they-only-carried-ideas.

16. Caitlin Huey-Burns, 'Amnesty International Cites Human Rights Abuse in Kashmir', *US News*, 28 March 2011, https://www.usnews.com/news/articles/2011/03/28/amnesty-international-cites-human-rights-abuse-in-kashmir.

17. Harshit Agarwal, 'The students at the JNU meet on Afzal Guru weren't carrying guns - they only carried ideas', *Scroll.in*, 15 February 2016, https://scroll.in/article/803607/the-students-at-the-jnu-meet-on-afzal-guru-werent-carrying-guns-they-only-carried-ideas.

18. Anmol Saxena, 'New Delhi campus row grabs national attention', *Aljazeera*, 14 February 2016, https://www.aljazeera.com/features/2016/2/14/new-delhi-campus-row-grabs-national-attention.

19. Shubhra Dixit, 'From student to anti-national to terrorist – how TV channels constructed Umar Khalid', *Scroll.in*, 19 February 2016, https://scroll.in/video/803841/from-student-to-anti-national-to-terrorist-how-tv-channels-constructed-umar-khalid.

20. Kritika Sharma Sebastian, 'JNU students give shutdown call', *The Hindu*, 14 February 2016, https://www.thehindu.com/news/cities/Delhi/jnu-students-give-shutdown-call/article8236090.ece

21. Soudhriti Bhabani, 'After JNU, slogans of freedom raised at Jadavpur University', *India Today*, 18 February 2016, https://www.indiatoday.in/mail-today/story/after-jnu-slogans-of-freedom-raised-at-jadavpur-university-309267-2016-02-17.

22. JNU students' protests get support from universities across India, *Hindustan Times*, 17 February 2016, https://www.hindustantimes.com/india/jnu-students-protests-get-support-from-universities-across-india/story-ZyAPUXcr3H7wzgMmhyxWsK.html.

23. Kunal Anand, 'Everything You Wanted To Know About The JNU Protest, And Its Aftermath', *India Times*, 24 April 2017, https://www.indiatimes.com/news/india/everything-you-wanted-to-know-about-the-jnu-protest-and-its-aftermath-250686.html.

24. JNU row: Kanhaiya Kumar to lead push for Umar and Anirban's release from custody', *Firstpost*, 14 March 2016, https://www.firstpost.com/india/jnu-row-kanhaiya-kumar-to-lead-push-for-umar-and-anirbans-release-from-custody-2672974.html.

25. 'Full Speech: Kanhaiya Kumar, Out On Bail, Speaks Of "Azadi" On JNU Campus', *NDTV*, 4 March 2016, https://www.ndtv.com/india-news/full-speech-kanhaiya-kumar-out-on-bail-speaks-of-azadi-on-jnu-campus-1283740.

26. Mayank Jain, 'In pictures: Allahabad University students protest to stop Yogi Adityanath from entering the campus', *Scroll.in*, 19 November 2015, https://scroll.in/article/770358/in-pictures-allahabad-university-students-protest-to-stop-yogi-adityanath-from-entering-the-campus.

27. Lalmani Verma, 'AUSU president says won't let Adityanath enter Allahabad University campus', *The Indian Express*, 18 November 2015, https://indianexpress.com/article/india/india-news-india/ausu-president-says-wont-let-adityanath-enter-allahabad-university-campus/.

28. Suhasini Krishnan, 'They Need Protection, Not Independence: How CM Yogi Views Women', *The Quint*, 21 March 2017, https://www.thequint.com/news/politics/yogi-adityanath-views-on-women-uttar-pradesh-chief-minister.

29. Abhimanyu Singh, '"If Modi Govt. Is Being Challenged, It Is By Students': Former AUSU Prez. Richa Singh', *Youth Ki Awaaz*, 6 March

2016, https://www.youthkiawaaz.com/2016/03/richa-singh-allahabad-university-interview/.

30. PTI, 'ABVP targeting AUSU chief Richa Singh for resisting saffronisation: CPI', *The Economic Times*, 7 March 2016, https://economictimes.indiatimes.com/news/politics-and-nation/abvp-targeting-ausu-chief-richa-singh-for-resisting-saffronisation-cpi/articleshow/51297766.cms?from=mdr

31. IFP Bureau, 'Thanks Biren for reminding us', *Imphal Free Press*, 21 October 2022, https://www.ifp.co.in/editorial/thanks-biren-for-reminding-us.

32. Times Now, 'General G D Bakshi Gets Emotional Over Tricolor Issue On The Newshour Debate (18th Feb 2016)', YouTube, 19 February 2016, https://www.youtube.com/watch?v=vWu0rdmfl6o.

33. Express News Service, 'To "instil nationalism", Smriti Irani and VCs agree to national flag on campus', *Indian Express*, 19 February 2016, https://indianexpress.com/article/india/india-news-india/hrd-ministry-national-flag-central-universities/.

34. 'Manipuri boy writes open letter to GD Bakshi: Will you cry for us?', *DailyO*, 11 March 2016, https://www.dailyo.in/politics/open-letter-to-major-general-gd-bakshi-kashmir-manipur-northeast-afspa-manipur-arnab-goswami-smriti-irani-9492.

35. '"These Fellows Must Be Eliminated": Relentless Violence and Impunity in Manipur', https://www.hrw.org/reports/2008/india0908/2.htm#_ftnref13.

36. Ninglun Hanghal, 'Manipur Under AFSPA: Rape, Fake Encounter And Unending Wait For Justice', *Outlook India*, 28 December 2021, https://www.outlookindia.com/magazine/story/india-news-manipur-under-afspa-poignant-stories-of-rape-fake-encounter-and-unending-wait-for-justice/305298.

37. '"These Fellows Must Be Eliminated": Relentless Violence and Impunity in Manipur', https://www.hrw.org/reports/2008/india0908/3.htm.

38. Simran Sirur, '17 years since their naked protest against Army, "Mothers of Manipur" say fight not over yet', *The Print*, 22 July 2021, https://theprint.in/india/17-years-since-their-naked-protest-against-army-mothers-of-manipur-say-fight-not-over-yet/700093/.

39. 'Self-immolation protest against AFSPA by Chittaranjan remembered', *The Morung Express*, 16 August 2016, https://morungexpress.com/self-immolation-protest-against-afspa-chittaranjan-remembered.

40. Vangamla Salle K.S., 'Manipur: AMSU stages protest against Nagaland killings, AFSPA', *EastMojo*, 10 December 2021, https://www.eastmojo.com/northeast-news/2021/12/10/manipur-amsu-stages-protest-against-nagaland-killings-afspa/.

41. Madhu Purnima Kishwar, 'The Azadi Kashmiris Want', *Outlook India*, 3 February 2022, https://www.outlookindia.com/website/story/the-azadi-kashmiris-want/267233.

42. Gauri Lankesh, 'Why Kashmir cries for "Azadi"', *Bangalore Mirror*, 16 August 2016, https://bangaloremirror.indiatimes.com/opinion/views/why-kashmir-cries-for-azadi/articleshow/53714363.cms.

43. Heena Kausar, Shradha Chettri, 'JNU row a year later: Kanhaiya to Khalid, how lives of 5 students changed', *Hindustan Times*, 2 March 2017, https://www.hindustantimes.com/delhi/jnu-protests-a-year-on-how-the-feb-9-anti-national-event-changed-five-lives/story-4jbNO1ByQtC9B8XbOMFFUK.html.

44. Aranya Shankar, 'Arrest of Kanhaiya Kumar: Human chain on JNU campus as teachers demand 'arbitrary charges' be dropped', *Indian Express*, 15 February 2016, https://indianexpress.com/article/cities/delhi/arrest-of-kanhaiya-kumar-human-chain-on-jnu-campus-as-teachers-demand-arbitrary-charges-be-dropped/.

45. TNN, 'Despite warning, JNU kicks off lecture series', *The Times of India*, 19 January 2017, https://timesofindia.indiatimes.com/city/delhi/despite-warning-jnu-kicks-off-lecture-series/articleshow/56654376.cms?from=mdr.

46. Aakash Karkare, 'Watch: "March March March", film about JNU protests that I&B ministry blocked', *Scroll.in*, 19 June 2017, https://scroll.in/reel/841025/watch-march-march-march-film-about-jnu-protests-that-i-b-ministry-blocked.

47. Vijayta Lalwani, 'Meet the brave women of Jamia who rescued a fellow student from the clutches of Delhi Police', *Scroll.in*, 16 December 2019, https://scroll.in/article/947026/meet-the-brave-women-of-jamia-who-rescued-a-fellow-student-from-the-clutches-of-delhi-police

Reimagining Citizenship

1. Angana P. Chatterji, Mihir Desai, Harsh Mander, Abdul Kalam Azad, Detention, 'Criminalisation, Statelessness: The Aftermath of Assam's

NRC, *The Wire*, 9 September 2021, https://thewire.in/rights/detention-criminalisation-statelessness-the-aftermath-of-assams-nrc.

2. Myithili Hazarika, '"Hindus aren't our enemies"—why final NRC is not what BJP promised and envisioned', *The Print*, 22 November 2019, https://theprint.in/theprint-essential/hindus-arent-our-enemies-why-final-nrc-is-not-what-bjp-promised-and-envisioned/324713/.

3. Rohan Venkataramakrishnan, 'Who is linking Citizenship Act to NRC? Here are five times Amit Shah did so', *Scroll.in*, 20 December 2019, https://scroll.in/article/947436/who-is-linking-citizenship-act-to-nrc-here-are-five-times-amit-shah-did-so.

4. The figures for the 1941 population of different communities in West Punjab have been gleaned from data provided for the districts of Lahore, Sialkot, Gujranwala, Sheikhupura, Gujrat, Shahpur, Jhelum, Rawalpindi, Attock, Mianwali, Montgomery, Lyallpur, Jhang, Multan, Muzaffargargh, Dera Ghazi Khan, one tehsil (Shakargarh, which was then part of Gurdaspur District) and one princely state (Bahawalpur) in the 1941 census. The figures for the population of different communities in the Punjab districts that remained in India have been gleaned from the districts of Hisar, Rohtak, Gurgaon, Karnal, Jalandhar, Ludhiana, Firozpur, Amritsar, Simla, Kangra, Ambala, Hoshiarpur and Gurdaspur (without Shakargarh Tehsil), and princely states (Loharu, Dujana, Pataudi, Kalsia, Kapurthala, Malerkotla, Faridkot, Patiala, Jind, Nabha, Sirmoor, Simla Hill, Bilaspur, Mandi, Suket and Chamba). See the Government of India's 1941 *Census of India*, Volume 6 (Punjab), p. 58–63. An accessible table of the same data is also available in Bhimrao Ram Ambedkar's *Pakistan or the Partition of India*; the Appendix IV is available online at https://franpritchett.com/00ambedkar/ambedkar_partition/appendices/04app.html. The figures for the populations of religious communities in West Punjab is taken from Government of Pakistan's 1951 *Population According to Religion*, Table 6, Karachi, Ministry of the Interior, p. 1. For the figures of the population of Muslims in the Punjab districts that remained in India, see the Government of India's *Census of India 1951, Volume 8, Part I-A*.

5. Data on religious composition of West Bengal and East Bengal have been taken from Nahid Kamal's *The Population Trajectories of Bangladesh and West Bengal During the Twentieth Century: A Comparative Study*.

6. Ibid.

7. Ibid.

8. Recent census data from Bangladesh shows that the proportion of Hindus declined to 8.54 per cent of the population in 2011 and further to 7.95 per cent in 2021. See the Government of Bangladesh's 2022 *Population And Housing Census: A Preliminary Report*, Dhaka, Bangladesh Bureau of Statistics.

9. All data in this paragraph has been taken from Ayesha Jalal, *The Sole Spokesman: Jinnah, the Muslim League, and the Demand for Pakistan*, Cambridge University Press, 1994, p. 172.

10. PTI, 'Anti-CAB stir: People defy curfew, police open fire as Assam', *The Economic Times*, 12 December 2019, https://economictimes.indiatimes.com/news/politics-and-nation/anti-cab-protests-in-assam-police-opens-fire-on-protestors/articleshow/72487251.cms.

11. Sushanta Talukdar, 'Census 2011 Language Data: Assam records decline in percentage of Assamese, Bodo, Rabha and Santali speakers', *Nezine*, 28 June 2018, https://www.nezine.com/info/bnhUV3Npcjls UkxwVTVkNkFhdFJKdz09/census-2011-language-data:-assam-records-decline-in-percentage-of-assamese,-bodo,-rabha-and-santali-speakers.html.

12. Suraj Gogoi, Angshuman Choudhury, 'Nellie massacre: a lesson and a forewarning', *Mint*, 18 February 2022, https://lifestyle.livemint.com/news/big-story/nellie-massacre-a-lesson-and-a-forewarning 111645099 526707.html.

13. PTI, 'Assam publishes first draft of NRC with 1.9 crore names', *The Times of India*, 1 January 2018, https://timesofindia.indiatimes.com/india/assam-publishes-first-draft-of-nrc-with-1-9-crore-names/articleshow/62320193.cms

14. Karwan-e Mohabbat, 'I Am "Miya"—Reclaiming Identity Through Protest Poetry', Sabrang, 3 July 2019, https://sabrangindia.in/article/i-am-miya-reclaiming-identity-through-protest-poetry/.

15. Md Shalim Muktdir Hussain, 'In Conversation with Dr Hafiz Ahmed: "The Char Chaporis Cut Their Roots to Fit into 'Greater' Assamese Culture"', Sahapedia, 27 November 2019, https://www.sahapedia.org/conversation-dr-hafiz-ahmed-char-chaporis-cut-their-roots-fit-greater-assamese-culture.

16. Parasher Baruah, 'Witness Us', YouTube, 17 March 2020, https://www.youtube.com/watch?v=yfVrZvdAzJU.

17. Abdul Kalam Azad, 'NRC in Assam: That state of statelessness', Wordpress, 1 June 2023, https://abdulkazad.wordpress.com/.

18. https://raiot.in/in-praise-of-miya-poetry-of-assam/.

19. 'Ex-IAS officer to Amit Shah: Will disobey', *The Telegraph*, 10 December 2019, https://www.telegraphindia.com/india/ex-ias-officer-to-amit-shah-will-disobey/cid/1725808.

20. Jinal Bhatt, 'When India Got Creative With Its Anti-CAA Protests: A Roundup Of Some of The Best Slogans', *Mashable*, 20 December 2019, https://in.mashable.com/social-good/9672/when-india-got-creative-with-its-anti-caa-protests-a-roundup-of-some-of-the-best-slogans.

21. TNN, 'Jantar Mantar: Will continue protest till government listens to us', *The Times of India*, 23 December 2019, https://timesofindia.indiatimes.com/city/delhi/jantar-mantar-will-continue-protest-till-govt-listens-to-us/articleshow/72930383.cms

22. PTI, 'Protest march held in Raipur against CAA, NRC', *Business Standard*, 15 December 2019, https://www.business-standard.com/article/pti-stories/protest-march-held-in-raipur-against-caa-nrc-119121500896_1.html.

23. Mohammad Suffian, 'Odisha: Thousands hit road against CAA, NRC', *India Today*, 17 December 2019, https://www.indiatoday.in/india/story/odisha-thousands-hit-road-against-caa-nrc-1629073-2019-12-17.

24. Prashant Jha, 'Protest against CAA, NRC reaches Uttarakhand', *The Times of India*, 24 December 2019, https://timesofindia.indiatimes.com/city/dehradun/protest-against-caa-nrc-reaches-hills/articleshow/72944969.cms.

25. Robert Sapam, 'Protests rock Manipur hubs', *The Telegraph*, 18 November 2019, https://www.telegraphindia.com/north-east/protests-rock-manipur-hubs/cid/1720220.

26. Dr Ravindra Kumar (ed.), *The Selected Works of Maulana Abul Kalam Azad*, Atlantic Publishers and Distributors, 1991, p. 81.

27. 'Night of horrors, death on other side: Inside Jamia Millia when it was stormed by police', *India Today*, 18 December 2019, https://www.indiatoday.in/india/story/night-of-horrors-death-on-other-side-inside-jamia-millia-when-it-was-stormed-by-police-1629328-2019-12-18.

28. Piyush Srivastava, 'Bared: Police "brutality" on AMU students', *The Telegraph*, 27 December 2023, https://www.telegraphindia.com/india/bared-police-brutality-on-amu-students/cid/1728324.

29. Ibid.

30. Eram Agha, '"Unacceptable in Land of Gandhi, Tagore": After Arrest of Students, BHU Professors Campaign Against CAA', *News18*, 26 December 2019, https://www.news18.com/news/india/not-acceptable-in-land-of-gandhi-tagore-after-students-arrest-bhu-professors-campaign-against-caa-2436661.html.

31. '21,500 booked for violence in Kanpur', *India Today*, 24 December 2019, https://www.indiatoday.in/amp/india/story/21-500-booked-for-violence-in-kanpur-1631048-2019-12-24.

32. '"Go to Pakistan", says India officer as leader praises crackdown', *Aljazeera*, 28 December 2019, https://www.aljazeera.com/amp/news/2019/12/pakistan-india-officer-leader-praises-crackdown-191228080506372.html.

33. Uday Singh Rana, 'Cops Barged Into Our Homes at Night, Smashed Everything, Snatched Cash and Jewellery, Say Muzaffarnagar's Muslim Families', *News18*, 25 December 2019, https://www.news18.com/amp/news/india/cops-barged-into-our-homes-at-night-smashed-everything-snatched-cash-and-jewellery-say-muzaffarnagars-muslim-families-2435565.html.

34. Supriya Sharma, '"Why kill our children?": Blood and tears in an Uttar Pradesh town', *Scroll.in*, 23 December 2019, https://scroll.in/article/947626/why-kill-our-children-blood-and-tears-in-an-uttar-pradesh-town.

35. PTI, 'Explain or pay for damage: UP administration sends notice to 26 people in Sambhal for CAA violence', *India Today*, 26 December 2019, https://www.indiatoday.in/india/story/explain-or-pay-for-damage-up-administration-sends-notice-to-26-people-in-sambhal-for-caa-violence-1631638-2019-12-26.

36. Utpal Parashar, 'University, college students in northeast boycott classes in protest against citizenship act', *Hindustan Times*, 22 January 2020, https://www.hindustantimes.com/india-news/university-college-students-in-northeast-boycott-classes-in-protest-against-citizenship-act/story-jLecduuOiUC1DnvgXK54TL.html.

37. Prejomon Sunny, 'What Meghalaya wants: How CAA protests assume a different meaning in the state', *The Week*, 4 January 2020, https://www.theweek.in/news/india/2020/01/04/what-meghalaya-wants-how-caa-protests-assume-a-different-meaning-in-the-state.html.

38. Ratnadip Choudhury, '"No Space To Accommodate Any More": Tripura

Royal Scion On Citizenship', *NDTV*, 12 January 2020, https://www.ndtv.com/india-news/no-space-to-accommodate-any-more-tripuras-pradyot-manikya-debbarma-on-citizenship-act-2162788.

39. Manoj Kumar Ojha, 'Marches, slogans in Arunachal Pradesh', *The Telegraph*, 4 January 2020, https://www.telegraphindia.com/north-east/marches-slogans-in-arunachal-pradesh/cid/1732961.

40. Saurav Kumar, 'Bihar's Tribals Face Disenfranchisement Threat in Wake of CAA', *NewsClick*, 12 February 2020, https://www.newsclick.in/Bihar-Tribals-Face-Disenfranchisement-Threat-Wake-CAA.

41. Santoshi Markam, 'Why Adivasis Are Demanding Recognition for Their Religions', *The Wire*, 2 April 2019, https://thewire.in/rights/adivasi-religion-recognition-census.

42. Vinod Babu, Manoj Kumar, 'Tens of thousands march in southern India to protest citizenship law', *Reuters*, 4 January 2020, https://www.reuters.com/article/us-india-citizenship-protests/tens-of-thousands-march-in-southern-india-to-protest-citizenship-law-idUSKBN1Z30DK.

43. Maya Sharma, 'Watch: Hundreds Travel By Sea To Protest Citizenship Law In Mangaluru', *NDTV*, 15 January 2020, https://www.ndtv.com/karnataka-news/caa-protests-in-mangaluru-karnataka-hundreds-travel-by-sea-to-protest-caa-citizenship-amendment-act-2164622.

44. PTI, 'Battle over CAA reaches skies: Kites with messages for and against amended citizenship law flown in Gujarat on Makar Sankranti', *Firstpost*, 14 January 2020, https://www.firstpost.com/india/battle-over-caa-reaches-skies-kites-with-messages-for-and-against-amended-citizenship-law-flown-in-gujarat-on-makar-sankranti-7906331.html.

45. 'Punjab: Nearly 20,000 Farmers, Women Take to Malerkotla Streets Against CAA', *The Wire*, 2 February 2020, https://thewire.in/rights/malerkotla-punjab-caa-rally.

46. TNN, '12k women protest against CAA, NRC in Malegaon', *The Times of India*, 7 January 2020, https://timesofindia.indiatimes.com/city/nashik/12k-women-protest-against-caa-nrc-in-malegaon/articleshow/73129281.cms.

Pandemic Communities

1. 'Bharat Bandh today: Bhim Army's Chandrashekhar Azad to lead protest against SC quota order', *The Indian Express*, 23 February 2020,

238 NOTES

    https://indianexpress.com/article/india/bharat-bandh-bhim-army-chandrashekhar-azad-sc-reservation-jobs-promotion-6281464/.

2.   Rakhi Bose, '"My Husband Was Burnt In Front Of My Child": Delhi Riot Victims Await Justice and Closure', *Outlook*, 3 March 2022, https://www.outlookindia.com/national/-my-husband-was-killed-burnt-in-front-of-my-daughter-two-years-on-delhi-riot-victims-await-justice-and-closure-news-184981.

3.   'Delhi violence: Four video clips that court made cops watch', *India Today*, 26 February 2020, https://www.indiatoday.in/india/story/delhi-violence-four-videos-clips-that-court-made-cops-watch-1650273-2020-02-26.

4.   The full speech is available at: https://www.youtube.com/watch?v=QQA OnUZt9BA. Translation mine.

5.   'Jumping jacks to frog jumps: Indore Police's style of punishing lockdown violators', *Hindustan Times*, 22 April 2020, https://www.hindustantimes.com/india-news/jumping-jacks-to-frog-jumps-indore-police-s-style-of-punishing-covid-19-lockdown-violators/story-TSN6YTwob2oYvPkOhzaHnO.html.

6.   'Migrant workers sprayed with disinfectant in UP', *The Times of India*, 30 March 2020, https://timesofindia.indiatimes.com/india/migrant-workers-sprayed-with-disinfectant-in-up/articleshow/74888075.cms.

7.   '22 Migrant Workers, Kin Have Died Trying to Return Home Since the Lockdown Started', *The Wire*, 30 March 2020, https://thewire.in/rights/coronavirus-national-lockdown-migrant-workers-dead.

8.   David Gilbert, 'People In India Are Dropping Dead After Walking Hundreds of Miles During Coronavirus Lockdown', *Vice*, 30 March 2020, https://www.vice.com/en/article/qjd5z5/people-in-india-are-dropping-dead-after-walking-hundreds-of-miles-during-coronavirus-lockdown.

9.   '22 Migrant Workers, Kin Have Died Trying to Return Home Since the Lockdown Started', *The Wire*, 30 March 2020, https://thewire.in/rights/coronavirus-national-lockdown-migrant-workers-dead.

10.   'Indian migrant deaths: 16 sleeping workers run over by train', *BBC*, 8 May 2020, https://www.bbc.co.uk/news/world-asia-india-52586898.

11.   'Without Food for Days and in Searing Heat, Migrants Die on Shramik Special Trains', *The Wire*, 27 May 2020, https://thewire.in/labour/without-food-for-days-and-in-searing-heat-migrants-die-on-shramik-special-trains.

12.   Samyak Pandey, '"Better to die with families"—no food or money, Delhi migrants prefer the long walk home', *The Print*, 28 March 2020, https://

theprint.in/india/better-to-die-with-families-no-food-or-money-delhi-migrants-prefer-the-long-walk-home/390037/.

13. Maya Sharma, '"They Told Us They Would Take Us Home": Migrants Protest In Karnataka', NDTV, 5 May 2020, https://www.ndtv.com/karnataka-news/coronavirus-india-lockdown-migrants-protest-in-karnataka-they-told-us-they-would-take-us-home-2223604.

14. 'Gujarat lockdown: Protests by migrant workers erupt again in Surat, this time over quality of food being served', *Financial Express*, 16 April 2020, https://www.financialexpress.com/india-news/gujarat-lockdown-protests-by-migrant-workers-erupt-again-in-surat-this-time-over-quality-of-food-being-served/1930651/.

15. Qazi Faraz Ahmed, 'Thousands of Migrants Protest, Block Mathura Highway After Yogi Adityanath's No Movement on Foot Order', *News18*, 17 May 2020, https://www.news18.com/news/india/thousands-of-migrants-protest-block-mathura-highway-after-yogi-adityanaths-no-movement-on-foot-order-2623801.html.

16. Piyush Rai, 'Over 6,000 Bihar migrants protest in Saharanpur', *The Times of India*, 18 May 2020, https://timesofindia.indiatimes.com/city/meerut/over-6000-bihar-migrants-protest-in-saharanpur/articleshow/75799651.cms.

17. Anindita Adhikari, Rajendran Narayanan, Sakina Dhorajiwala, Seema Mundoli, '21 Days and Counting: COVID-19 Lockdown, Migrant Workers, and the Inadequacy of Welfare Measures in India', *The Hindu*, 15 April 2020, https://www.thehindu.com/news/resources/article31442220.ece/binary/Lockdown-and-Distress_Report-by-Stranded-Workers-Action-Network.pdf.

18. Madhusree Ghosh, 'HT Salutes: A student-led network of volunteers solves crises', *Hindustan Times*, 30 June 2020, https://www.hindustantimes.com/india-news/a-student-led-network-of-volunteers-solves-crises/story-iAfZxiMA1FiG7tqtxZfWzH.html.

19. Mukesh Rawat, 'Coronavirus in India: In 13 states, NGOs fed more people than govt did during lockdown', *India Today*, 12 April 2020, https://www.indiatoday.in/india/story/in-13-states-ngos-fed-more-people-than-govt-during-coronavirus-lockdown-1665111-2020-04-09.

20. '"Finding a Scapegoat": 109 Citizens Urge Govt, Media to Stop Communalising COVID-19', *The Wire*, 8 April 2020, https://thewire.in/communalism/coronavirus-tablighi-jamaat-scapegoat-muslims.

21. Susmita Pakrasi, 'End of Covid-19 to begin with start of Ram Temple's construction: BJP's Rameshwar Sharma', *Hindustan Times*, 23 July 2020, https://www.hindustantimes.com/india-news/end-of-covid-19-to-begin-with-start-of-ram-temple-s-construction-bjp-s-rameshwar-sharma/story-7vlddMuTJHI9hkilB8nk3L.html.

22. 'BJP hails PM for "defeating" Covid-19', *The Hindu Business Line*, 21 February 2021, https://www.thehindubusinessline.com/news/national/bjp-hails-pm-for-defeating-covid-19/article33896405.ece.

23. Soumya Pillai, 'Delhi's crematoriums run out of wood, seek forest dept's help', *Hindustan Times*, 28 April 2021, https://www.hindustantimes.com/cities/delhi-news/delhis-crematoriums-run-out-of-wood-seek-forest-dept-s-help-101619559472773.html.

24. Mayank Aggarwal, 'India coronavirus: Delhi builds makeshift funeral pyres in public parks as it runs out of space for dead', *The Independent*, 28 April 2021, https://www.independent.co.uk/asia/india/india-delhi-pyres-public-parks-b1838649.html.

25. Dhritiman Ray, 'Burning Ghats Run Low On Timber As Covid-19 Deaths Rise In Ranchi', *The Times of India*, 17 April 2021, https://timesofindia.indiatimes.com/city/ranchi/burning-ghats-run-low-on-timber-as-covid-19-deaths-rise-in-ranchi/articleshow/82108057.cms.

26. Yagnesh Bharat Mehta, 'State crematoriums overflow with dead amid Covid-19 surge', *The Times of India*, 11 April 2021, https://timesofindia.indiatimes.com/city/surat/state-crematoriums-overflow-with-dead-amid-covid-19-surge/articleshow/82009416.cms.

27. ABP News, 'Corona Crisis: Chimneys in Surat's crematorium melts due to 24 hr cremation', YouTube, 13 April 2021, https://www.youtube.com/watch?v=o9Lsi5DID1U.

28. Mojo Story, 'Varanasi | Bodies Pile Up At Ghats For Cremation | Covid-19', YouTube, 19 April 2021, https://www.youtube.com/watch?v=nHGj50NcKQI.

29. 'Shocking Pictures Show Mass Covid Cremations In India', *Outlook*, 28 April 2021, https://www.outlookindia.com/photos/photoessay/shocking-pictures-show-mass-covid-cremations-in-india/2752?photo-4.

30. Mukesh Ranjan, 'Bodies of suspected COVID-19 victims found floating in Ganges in Bihar', *The Tribune*, 10 May 2021, https://www.tribuneindia.com/news/nation/bodies-of-suspected-covid-19-victims-found-floating-in-ganges-in-bihar-250822.

31. Sneha Mordani, '2nd Covid wave was India's worst tragedy since Partition, saw up to 49 lakh excess deaths: Report', *India Today*, 21 July 2021, https://www.indiatoday.in/coronavirus-outbreak/story/2nd-covid-wave-was-india-worst-tragedy-since-partition-saw-up-to-49-lakh-excess-deaths-1830894-2021-07-21.

32. Arima Mishra, '"Aren't we frontline warriors?" Experiences of grassroots health workers during COVID-19', Azim Premji University, December 2023, https://azimpremjiuniversity.edu.in/faculty-research/arent-we-frontline-warriors-experiences-of-grassroots-health-workers-during-covid-19.

Farmers on the March

1. Vishnu Padmanabhan, 'The land challenge underlying India's farm crisis', *Mint*, 15 October 2018, https://www.livemint.com/Politics/SOG43o5ypqO13j0QflaawM/The-land-challenge-underlying-Indias-farm-crisis.html.

2. 'Delhi Chalo On Nov 26-27: Farmers' protest march call gets support of 472 farm outfits', *The Indian Express*, 20 November 2020, https://indianexpress.com/article/india/delhi-chalo-on-nov-26-27-farmers-protest-march-call-gets-support-of-472-farm-outfits-7057772/.

3. Danish Siddiqui, Sunil Kataria, 'Indian farmers vow to carry on protests despite cold, deaths', *Reuters*, 21 December 2020, https://www.reuters.com/article/us-india-farms-protests-coldwave-idUSKBN28V19U.

4. India Today, 'Protesting Farmers At Delhi Borders Brave Winter | Farmers Protest Over Farm Laws | India Today', YouTube, 16 December 2020, https://www.youtube.com/watch?v=dEFTPKFhlFM.

5. Vivek Gupta, 'Republic Day Violence: A Tale of Two Conspiracies', *The Wire*, 18 September 2021, https://thewire.in/agriculture/republic-day-violence-a-tale-of-two-conspiracies.

6. Rohit Kumar, 'Here's What Really Happened During the Republic Day Tractor Rally', *The Wire*, 27 January 2021, https://thewire.in/agriculture/farmers-republic-day-tractor-march-eyewitness-account.

7. Ziya Us Salam, 'Prejudice on show in the media coverage of farmers' rally on Republic Day', *The Hindu*, 10 February 2021, https://frontline.thehindu.com/cover-story/prejudice-on-show/article33775752.ece.

8. Ibid.

9. A. Vaidyanathan, '"Khalistanis Infiltrated Farmers' Protest," Government Tells Supreme Court', *NDTV*, 12 January 2021, https://www.ndtv.com/india-news/khalistanis-infiltrated-farmers-protest-government-tells-supreme-court-2351310.

10. https://web.archive.org/web/20130921073451/http://www.tehelka.com/everybody-loves-a-good-riot/.

11. Ajay Singh, 'Beyond Google with Ajay Singh: State has forgotten Naeema's tragedy of 1987 that once united Jats and Muslims', *Firstpost*, 10 February 2017, https://www.firstpost.com/politics/up-election-2017-up-election-2017-state-has-forgotten-naeemas-tragedy-of-1987-that-once-united-jats-and-muslims-3270690.html.

12. Prashant Jha, 'Their role under a cloud, Tikaits give call for peace', *The Hindu*, 13 September 2013, https://www.thehindu.com/news/national/other-states/their-role-under-a-cloud-tikaits-give-call-for-peace/article5121633.ece.

13. Satabdi Das, 'When Rakesh Tikait Cried Like A Man: Deconstructing Masculinity', *Feminism In India*, 9 February 2021, https://feminisminindia.com/2021/02/09/rakesh-tikait-crying-farmers-protests-masculinity/.

14. ABP News, 'Rakesh Tikait's Tears Gives A U-Turn To The Farmers' Protest, Gains Momentum | ABP News', YouTube, 29 January 2021, https://www.youtube.com/watch?v=I1lfM-K5TW8.

15. J.P. Yadav, 'Farmers' protest: Revival of brotherhood between Jats and Muslims in western Uttar Pradesh', *The Telegraph*, 23 February 2021, https://www.telegraphindia.com/india/farmer-protest-revival-of-brotherhood-between-jats-and-muslims-in-western-uttar-pradesh/cid/1807503.

The Art of Hope

1. Indradeep Bhattacharyya, 'Writing as Righting: The Politics and Poetics of Varavara Rao', *The Wire*, 22 July 2020, https://thewire.in/rights/varavara-rao-poet-rights-activist-elgar-parishad.

2. A useful overview of the poet's work, drawing on an extensive interview with her, is available here: https://thewire.in/caste/dalit-poet-discrimination-female-body-poetry.

3. Aisi Taisi Democracy, 'Kashmir & Wash-basin Ka Pipe: Aisi Taisi Democracy || Sanjay Rajoura || Rahul Ram || Varun Grover', YouTube, 14 August 2019, https://www.youtube.com/watch?v=0-8K2pP2pZA.

4.   Stand Up Comedian Amar, 'INDIAN STEREOTYPES and UNMARRIED INDIANS-Stand up Comedy by Ama', YouTube, 4 May 2017, https://www.youtube.com/watch?v=zDeEY7Atazo.

5.   Munawar Faruqui, 'Gujarati, Muslims & Global Warming | Standup Comedy by Munawar Faruqui | 2022', YouTube, 1 February 2022, https://www.youtube.com/watch?v=vTrH8mr0C4g.

6.   Nalin Yadav, 'Humour Khatre Mein | Stand Up Comedy | Nalin Saaheb', YouTube, 3 January 2022, https://www.youtube.com/watch?v=tUBcuMSzsd4.

7.   Manaal Patil, 'Dating & Reservation | Stand Up Comedy by Manaal Patil', YouTube, 30 May 2021, https://www.youtube.com/watch?v=r1dHTkdUpJU.

8.   Donita Jose, 'Dalit comic tests boundaries of humour', *The Times of India*, 28 August 2022, https://timesofindia.indiatimes.com/city/hyderabad/dalit-comic-tests-boundaries-of-humour/articleshow/93832671.cms.

9.   Betwa Sharma, 'Young Dalit Comedians Keen To Make It On Their Own Learn To Live With Trolling & Caste Discrimination', *Article 14*, 3 March 2023, https://article-14.com/post/young-dalit-comedians-keen-to-make-it-on-their-own-learn-to-live-with-trolling-caste-discrimination--64015971d0c17.

10. Gaurvi Narang, '"I'm Dalit but identify as a Brahmin"—How Dalit comedians in India are smashing elite nexus', The Print, 21 August 2022, https://theprint.in/feature/im-dalit-but-identify-as-a-brahmin-how-dalit-comedians-in-india-are-smashing-elite-nexus/1092090/.

11. http://www.redelephantfoundation.org/2017/03/the-danger-chamar.html

12. Mad 4 Music, 'New Punjabi Shabad 2016 || FAN BABA SAHIB DI || GINNI MAHI || Guru Ravidas Ji Shabad 2016', YouTube, 6 February 2016, https://www.youtube.com/watch?v=H5XzHJBNyoI.

13. Shubhangi Misra, Urjita Bhardwaj, 'Punjab's Dalits are shifting state politics, flocking churches, singing Chamar pride', The Print, 17 October 2021, https://theprint.in/feature/punjabs-dalits-are-shifting-state-politics-flocking-churches-singing-chamar-pride/751873/.

14. Gayatri Manu, 'How 18-Year-Old Ginni Mahi of Punjab Is Singing to End Social Inequality', The Better India, 30 August 2016, https://www.thebetterindia.com/66560/ginni-mahi-b-r-ambedkar-dalit-assertion/.

15. http://www.redelephantfoundation.org/2017/03/the-danger-chamar.html.

16. Elizabeth Kuruvilla, 'Ginni Mahi: The rise of a brave singer', *Mint*, 30 December 2016, https://www.livemint.com/Leisure/vInFgOP6POSxx OOznQ7qzO/The-rise-of-a-brave-singer.html.

17. Qweed Media, 'Ladai Seekh Le by Sumit Samos', YouTube, 2 August 2018, https://www.youtube.com/watch?v=qsigWJdUl6U.

18. 'Dalit rapper from Odisha's Koraput raises Rs 37 lakh to study in Oxford University', *The New Indian Express*, 6 June 2021, https://www. newindianexpress.com/states/odisha/2021/jun/06/dalit-rapper-from-odishas-koraput-raises-rs-37-lakhto-study-in-oxford-university-2312450. html.

19. Citizens United, 'নিজেদের মতে নিজেদের গান (Nijeder Mawte Nijeder Gaan) || CITIZENS UNITED || FULL SONG', YouTube, 24 March 2021, https://www.youtube.com/watch?v=ey_aCNzis8E.

20. Van M, '"Ache Din??" (Prod. By Memo) || Rap Against CAA || Van M || New Hindi Rap ||', YouTube, 30 December 2019, https://www.youtube. com/watch?v=Z6ClrxCA9ao.

21. Rahul Rajkhowa, 'Rap against Citizenship Amendment Bill', YouTube, 30 January 2019, https://www.youtube.com/watch?v=2PS95QWuHy4.

22. Poojan Sahil, 'BELLA CIAO - Hindi Version | WAPAS JAO | Money Heist | Netflix', YouTube, 21 October 2019, https://www.youtube.com/ watch?v=GntDBSMj1kM.

23. Poojan Sahil, 'Bella Ciao - Punjabi | Wapas Jao', YouTube, 17 December 2020, https://www.youtube.com/watch?v=yOH7BDvOzxY.

24. Pallavi Pundir, 'India Has Become a Gallery of Protest Art, Despite a Crackdown', *Vice*, 17 January 2020, https://www.vice.com/en/article/ epgxkw/india-has-become-a-gallery-of-protest-art-despite-a-crackdown.

25. Nishtha Gautam, '"Shocked and Angry": Political Cartoonist Manjul on Twitter Notice', *The Quint*, 17 June 2021, https://www.thequint.com/ videos/news-videos/in-an-exclusive-conversation-with-the-quint-manjul-explains-how-the-current-government-is-suppressing-dissent#read-more.

26. Chaitanya Marpakwar, 'Victory for citizens, activists: 11-hectare Malad plot set to be Juhu beach's saviour as builder offers land for casting yard', *Mumbai Mirror*, 16 December 2019, https://mumbaimirror.indiatimes. com/mumbai/cover-story/11-hectare-malad-plot-set-to-be-juhu-beachs-saviour/articleshow/72707554.cms.

Audacious Hope: How to Save a Democracy?

1.   Wangan & Jagalingou People, 'Wangan Jagalingou Traditonal Owners -
     We will not surrender', YouTube, 27 January 2017, https://www.youtube.
     com/watch?v=xIN8b1MAwvs.

2.   Paulo Freire, *Pedagogy of Hope: Reliving Pedagogy of the Oppressed*,
     Bloomsbury, 2014.

3.   Henri Desroche, *Sociology of Hope*, Law Book Co of Australasia, 1979.

4.   Jonathan Lear, *Radical Hope: Ethics in the Face of Cultural Devastation*,
     Harvard University Press, 2008.

5.   James Bradley, 'The Library at the End of the World', Sydney Review
     of Books, 2020, https://sydneyreviewofbooks.com/essay/library-end-
     world-bradley.

6.   NDTV, '"Not All Battles Fought For Victory": NDTV's Ravish On
     Magsaysay Award', YouTube, 9 September 2019, https://www.youtube.
     com/watch?v=btGX0bL5XY4.

Acknowledgements

This book began as a series of conversations with family, friends and colleagues about the challenges before Indian democracy. I am grateful to the numerous activists, artists and authors who have contributed to our understanding of these challenges as well as charted pathways forward to deal with them. The book would not have been possible without their commitment to democracy in India and a willingness to publicly confront the creeping authoritarianism in the country. My eternal gratitude to them all.

The grave dangers facing our democracy make it tempting for publishers to regurgitate narratives of despair, hopelessness and fatalism. But, as the cultural theorist Raymond Williams has said, 'To be truly radical is to make hope possible rather than despair convincing.' Westland Publishers deserve special thanks for buckling publisher fads and showing a willingness to support this project. I could not have asked for a better editor than Ajitha, who consistently and constructively challenged me to sharpen my writing. I am especially grateful to her for the idea of seamlessly weaving the text with audio-visual aspects in one of the chapters through the strategic placement of QR codes. Sanjana T. worked tirelessly and patiently to iron out the manuscript and improve its readability.

Colleagues around India and elsewhere in the world have helped me think through the idea of 'hope' that is deployed in the book, for which I am truly grateful. Early conversations with Harsh Mander and Natasha Badhwar at the Jaipur Literature Festival back in 2022 helped lay the foundations for this work. I am grateful to them and to Ghazala Wahab, Suraj Yengde and Yamini Aiyar for offering their comments on the manuscript and for eventually endorsing this work. The wisdom of interlocutors at subsequent lectures in São Paulo, York and Edinburgh (online) as well as the York Festival of Ideas, the York Festival of Social Sciences and the Renewing Democracy Seminar Series co-hosted by the University of York and Jindal Global University helped me refine my thoughts on the subject. Conversations with my co-conspirators on the Economic and Social Research Council-funded 'Citizenship Futures' project, Simon Parker, Carole Gayet and Suryakant Waghmore, as well as the ever-generous Vera Schattan Coelho Pereira, have helped me develop my thoughts considerably. I have also hugely benefited from nourishing debates on hope and its pitfalls with my amazing colleagues at the Department of Politics and International Relations as well as the Interdisciplinary Global Development Centre. Heartfelt thanks to them all.

My family has remained a consistent pillar of support throughout this project, as always. My mother, Rita, my brother, Prithvijit and daughter, Tia, have offered me valuable glimpses into hope across three generations. My thanks to them. And to Uma, my partner-in-crime whose wit, uncommon sense and love has made this journey and everything else so worthwhile—and hopeful.

599
WBF/self
4A6N
BC-

C1173075

344
24JN 178 336

DK-CO 10764
DK-319334 AJ 08/03/2025